LEAD GUITAR WORKSHOP

Lead Guitar: Level 3

Library of Congress Control Number:

Any references to historical events, real people, or real places are used fictitiously. Names, characters, and places are products of the author's imagination.

Front cover image by Suke Cerulo
Book design by Suke Cerulo
Front Cover Photo by Jessica Maceli
About Author Photo by Paul Citone
Inside/Back Cover Photo by Paul Citone
Student Reviewer Linda Ameroso

Printed by Lead Guitar Workshop, Inc., in the United States of America.

First edition 2021.

SCAN FOR MORE

for all backing tracks and videos

www.LeadGuitarWorkshop.com

PREFACE

I always enjoyed music as a kid but my immediate family was not musical. There wasn't a lot of music playing in the house and we were never the type of family to sing. But my Grandfather George Lane was a Big Band musician and bandleader in the 1950's in Boston and New York. I don't have any memories of him playing music but he would have hilarious stories "from the road" traveling with the band. Later in life I really learned to appreciate them as I toured extensively.

It was 1984 and I heard Van Halen for the first time. I knew right then and there that I wanted to play music. I got my first guitar for Christmas in that year and quickly took lessons because I had no idea what to do. At the time I was really into playing football and I was good at it. I realized I was never going to be in the NFL or make a career out of it. But I did realize there was no NFL of music, anybody could play! That was so exciting. I knew I was going to play music for my whole life. I just had to figure out how to make it a career.

I had weekly guitar lessons from the time I was twelve until I graduated High School. For most of this time my teacher was Sandy Prager. He played "third stream jazz" on a nylon string guitar. This was as far away from Van Halen as possible without being a classical guitarist. But I learned so much about music, how to think about it and improvise. He constantly had me creating. Once I finished High School I went to **Berklee College of Music**. It was the only school I wanted to go to. After four years I got my Bachelors Degree in Professional Music.

My one goal upon graduating was to join a band. Fortunately for me I met my future bandmates of 30 plus years. We formed the band **"Schleigho"** in 1993 and toured full time within a year or so. We toured 200 plus dates a year for almost five years straight and still play to this day. We recorded and released 5 albums. We signed a label with the **Allman Brothers Band**, toured with **Derek Trucks**, and played with so very many people all over the country. This was my "real world" music education.

But even though I had lessons in High School and a great experience at Berklee I still felt like I was slow learning and still really didn't get the true nature of music and guitar. I struggled to connect the musical dots.

I had to build confidence to make my own conclusions about music. I heard so many different ideas, terms, explanations and they were confusing. I was perplexed that music had been around for hundreds of years and there was still so much indecision about ideas and terminology.

I had to separate music from the instrument. This was one of my biggest realizations. It came into fruition when I started playing flute. I realized the music was its own language independent of the instrument that plays it. When I started really practicing flute my guitar playing got better! I was stunned, but I realized my musicianship was better and it was now translating to guitar.

Once my band started touring I had guitar players (and flute players) asking me for lessons. I think I gave my first lesson in 1995. It was very casual and it was new to me but I was just trying to help people out. I realized I had a good way of explaining things and I was able to connect with people. Over the years I kept teaching. It was rewarding and I was learning a lot by having to explain music to people in many different ways.

About six months after I moved to NYC in 2003 I got my first real teaching job at a guitar school in NYC. I was touring and teaching full time. I was engulfed in playing and teaching music and it was wonderful. As touring slowed down the teaching picked up. I was teaching ten classes and about thirty private students. Close to eighty folks a week were coming to see me to learn about guitar and music. After years of teaching groups and private students I was able to refine my approach to teaching and to understanding music and how it relates to the guitar. Years ago I estimated that I hit my 10,000 hours as a guitar player. Now I was hitting my 10,000 hours as a teacher.

In 2003 I wrote my first book "Lead Guitar Basics" for me to use at the guitar school. Over the years this grew into five complete books and a number of rewrites. I also became the Director of the Lead Guitar Department. I trained other teachers to teach my material and musically evaluated all incoming teachers to the school.

I was amassing an unprecedented amount of teaching experience and gaining access to hundreds, if not thousands, of guitar players struggling in the same way I had. Over years of refinement I was able to develop this entire pedagogy for learning lead guitar.

These books have three decades of experience behind them and seventeen years of in-classroom development. I believe in these books, and I think they will help you immensely as you become a better guitarist and musician. These are all the things I wish I had when I was starting my journey.

HOW TO USE BOOK

Each book is written as ten lessons continually building on each other. The books all work together and are meant to extend and expand your knowledge as you work and grow with them. Go through them in order and go back later to revisit topics.

These books were initially created as 10 week courses, one chapter per week. You can use it in the same way. Each Chapter is about an hour long. There are enough warm-ups, exercises, new skills and practice to last you for a week. There is overlap and repetition in the books to really help reinforce the core ideas.

Every lesson is structured the same way. It is meant to optimize your learning, efficiency, and time. The repetition creates good habits.

Tune in: First you have to get in the right head space. You must remind yourself that you are a musician and a guitar player. That music is Melody, Harmony, and Rhythm; and that rhythm is the number one factor to sounding good. It's like a mantra.

Warm up: These are exercises to get your musical blood flowing and synchronize your internal clock. There are usually up to three warm-ups; *Muted String Ladders, Shells,* and *Changing Gears.* They are all music based and are like push-ups and jumping jacks to athletes.

Exercises: These are straight up music exercises like scales, arpeggios and more.

Review: This is part of the learning circle. You must review everything you learn. Eventually that will become part of your everyday language.

New Topic: Learn something new. It can be big or small, but it should expand your knowledge, even if it's learning something new about something you already know.

Practice: Play! Get better by playing music. Use your new idea/technique, concept in real time in the music you are playing, even if it is a one chord jam by yourself. Self-Generating music and backing tracks are a focal point.

Summary: A reminder of what has been learned so far. Summaries compound with each chapter.

Going through each word and each note as written in these books is only part of the bigger picture. You have to imagine how music is working and how it relates to your instrument. You have to have a desire to grow and a never ending curiosity about music. If you keep questioning music you will find more answers and go deeper and deeper. You have to "drive" music, start a song yourself, jam on it and make it music all by yourself. When you're playing by yourself and someone walks in they should ask you "What song are you playing?" not "What are you practicing?" Learning music and playing is not about checking off a list of requirements. It's about sounding like a musician playing good music, and not someone noodling at the guitar store.

At a certain point in your musical life, you will learn all the information about music that you will ever use. Then your growth is about becoming closer to that information and growing deeper with it every time you revisit it. There isn't a learning path in music, it's a learning circle. An ever expanding circle is like rings in a tree. It's the growth in the rings, in the trunk of the tree that allows those branches to grow and extend.

Music is just a language and a guitar is just an instrument. Both are silent without you, you are music!

As guitarists Pat Martino and Mike Stern both told me, and I will tell you, "Just keep playing." Enjoy!

Suke Cerulo

Table of Contents

Lead Guitar Level 3

This book is for those who have completed Level one and two and are familiar with playing a Major, minor and Blues pentatonic scale in any key. This book is for those comfortable with the guitar techniques of hammer-ons, pull-offs, slides, and bends but still want to improve and expand as a guitar player and a musician. This book is for those who want to expand on the five patterns, learn the neck and use the whole instrument in a more musical way.

CHAPTER 1

TUNE IN

Whenever you grab your guitar and start to play, two separate worlds are active. One is the instrument you are playing, wood and wire plucked at specific times and making sounds. Then there are the notes, the actual tones created and combined in the air molecules. This is a language of 12 notes that every instrument is built to play, a language older than any instrument that currently plays it except the voice.

You are growing as a musician and a guitar player. As a musician you are learning about notes and scales and how they relate to chords and especially their Relatives. As a guitar player you are a craftsperson learning scale patterns and how to navigate them on the fretboard according to what musical scale you need. As guitar players we learn hammer-ons, pull-off's, bends, slides and so many different ways to make our notes sound cool, lyrical.

Music has three elements: MELODY, HARMONY, and RHYTHM.

"I am a musician and a guitar player. Music is my language and my guitar is my voice. Music is Melody, Harmony and Rhythm. I develop my language skills and my instrument skills. They are two separate worlds working together to complete the circle of music."

Rhythm is the number one factor to sounding great as a musician.

MUTED STRING LADDERS (MSL)

Muted String Ladders are a fantastic warm up that exercise the picking hand and your rhythmic abilities. Mute the strings with your fretboard hand.

- Choose how many strings (1-6). Mute strings with fretboard hand.

- Start with quarter-notes, then change gears (eighth-notes, triplets, sixteenth-notes).

- Start with ALL DOWN picks.

- Change to ALL UP picks.

- Change to ALTERNATE picking. *(can just do alt picking if time limited)*

- Change to NEXT GEAR.

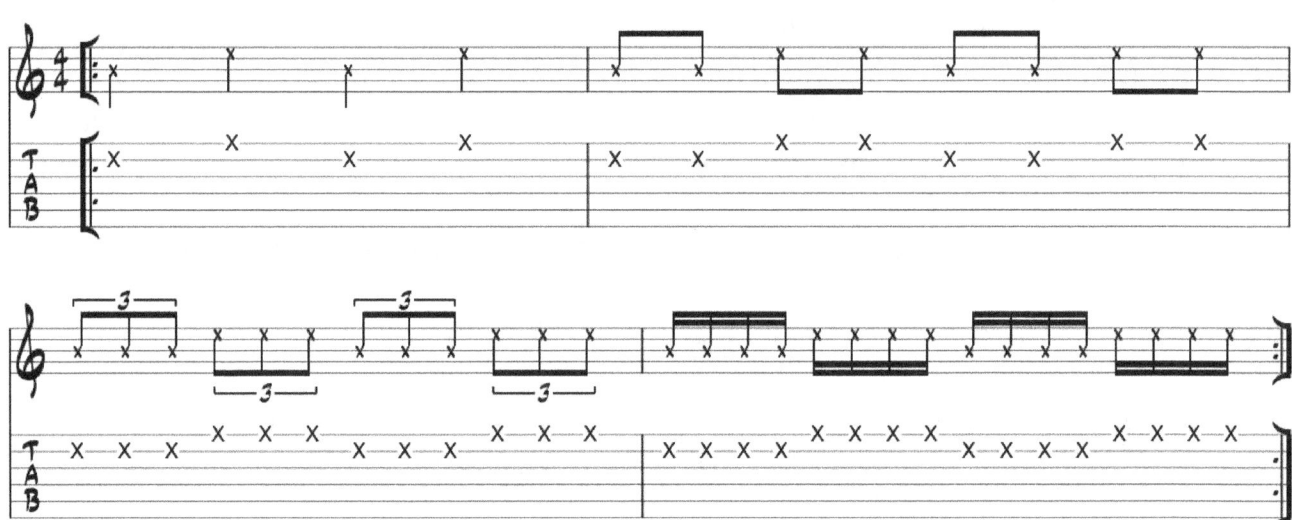

To mute the strings, gently lay your fretboard hand across all of the strings. Do not press down, simply keep enough pressure to mute the strings but not enough to press down and make a note.

SHELLS

Shells are like "wax on, wax offs." They are actions that practice real world moves. They are scale segments. These exercises help you in real musical situations and overcome guitar hindrances. These are *not* scale exercises *but* **dexterity exercises**. Any time you are having a fingering issue make a shell out of it to help you.

Your musicianship should not be dictated by your finger habits.

- Choose any combination of fingers. (example 1 3)
- Pick a RHYTHM and a starting fret. (8th notes and 5th fret).
- Use that fingering (1 3) to ascend and (1 3) to descend.
- <u>Then REVERSE the fingering (3 1) and ascend and descend again.</u>

Shell 1 3 (2 4) as Eighth-notes

Shell 1 3 (2 4) as Triplets

Shell 1 3 (2 4) as Sixteenth-notes

CHANGING GEARS

- Pick a tempo and start metronome (60 BPM).
- Your first finger will ALWAYS match the metronome. It is the note which we line up to make sure we are playing the gear correctly.
- Each NOTE/Finger adds to the GEAR.
- Only Change gears when ready. You must play the current gear multiple times correctly before switching.
- Later, switch GEARS by BAR and eventually by the beat (advanced).

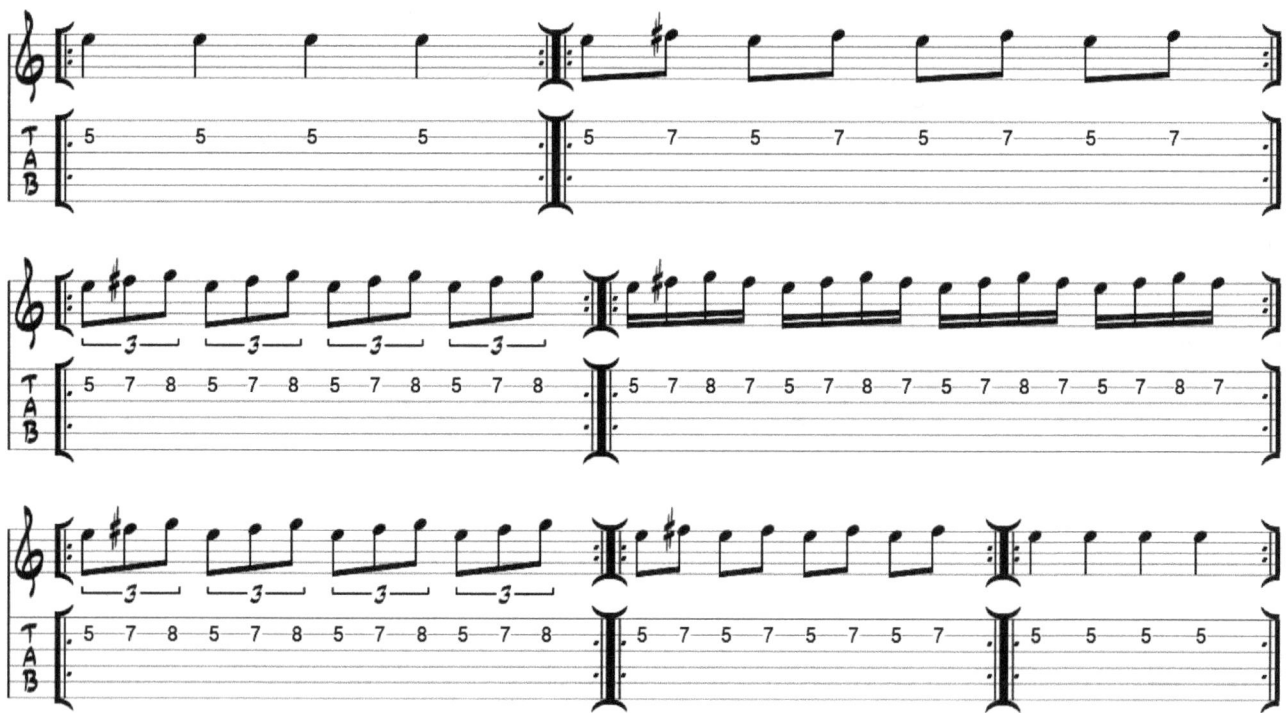

EXERCISE and PATTERN REVIEW

As a musician we learned how a five note pentatonic scale can be used as a Major, minor and Blues scale.

As a guitar player we learned that there are 5 patterns (of the same notes) that encompass the 12 fret fretboard. It is really beneficial to know all five patterns to allow you complete and unrestrained use of your whole instrument.

The five patterns allow you to use the SAME scale over the entire range of your instrument for every key you will ever be in, Major, minor or Blues.

The five patterns are ALWAYS in the same order and are best mapped out relating to pattern #1 (Rock and Roll Rule).

HOW TO PRACTICE THE FIVE PATTERNS

METHOD #1 (Up and Down)

Each of the five patterns is played low note to high note. Repeat the high note and return to the low note again. Since there are 12 total notes in any pentatonic pattern (2 notes per string for six strings) it will always work out cleanly whether they are played as quarter-notes, eighth-notes, triplets, or sixteenth-notes.

Pick a Key (C/Am), a metronome setting (60 BPM) and a rhythm (8th notes). Play each pattern as written above and go directly into the next pattern in time without missing a beat. Ascend and descend the 12 frets including open strings when applicable.

METHOD #2 (Round the Block)

Pick a Key. Pick a metronome setting and a rhythm (always).

Ascend the first pattern that occurs on the neck. After ascending shift up to the next pattern and descend that one. Shift up again and ascend the third pattern. This will create a zig-zag effect on the fretboard.

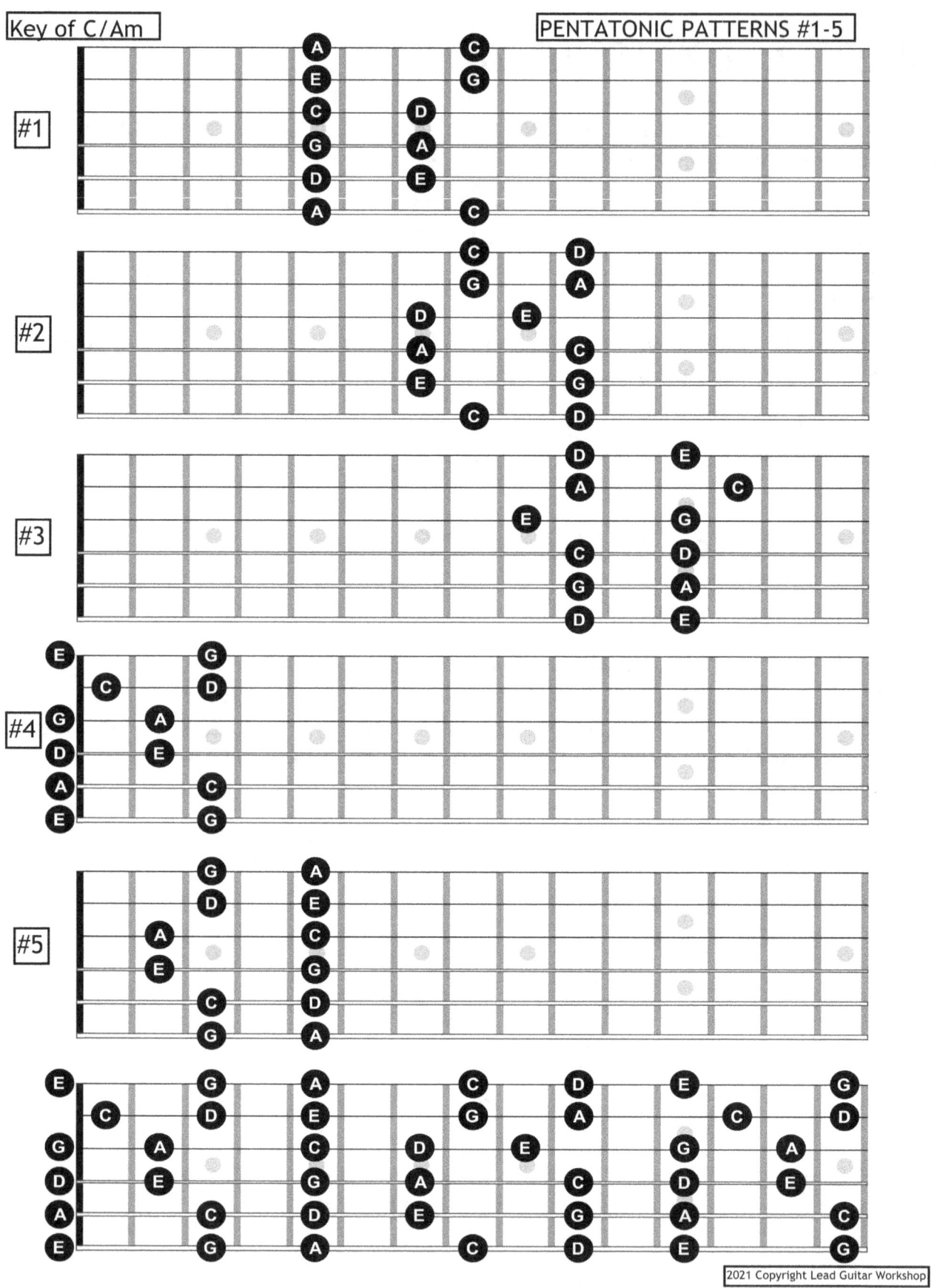

Lead Guitar Level 3   CHAPTER 1

REVIEW

MUSICAL TRUTHS

- **There are only 12 notes**, 7 Natural notes (ABCDEFG) and 5 Accidentals (*#* = sharp = raise ½ step)(*b* = flat = lower ½ step).
- There are 12 Major chords and 12 minor chords (one for each note).
- There are only 12 Keys in music (Key=7 note scale and its 7 chords).
- There are 12 Major pentatonic scales and 12 minor pentatonic scales
- (5 note scale, no half-steps).
- For every *Key*, *Chord*,and *Scale* there is a **RELATIVE** (two-for-one). There are 12 of these relationships.
- Relative minor is ALWAYS 3 half-steps *below* Relative MAJOR and vice-versa.

MUSICAL IDEAS

- Soloing **Globally** we base our scale on the "main chord" of the progression.
- **Major pentatonic** for a Major chord
- **minor pentatonic** for a minor chord
- A **Blues scale** is a *minor* pentatonic over a *Major* chord.
- **Playing the Changes** we base our scale choice on *each* chord.
- The **Blue Note** is an "artificial note" that works great but is not originally part of the key.
- Use **ABAC** as a glorified call and response (call and response x2) to build phrases and develop ideas.
- **Sequences** help us hear, play and develop very natural sounding phrases.
- **Self Generate**: play one bar of chord, one bar of scale/lick/solo. Great way to be musical while playing.

It's really important to think like a musician first and act like a guitar player second. Keep your musical mindset in check. It is so easy on the guitar to go down a rabbit hole for some technique or idea and completely lose sight of what it is your actually trying to accomplish musically.

Once you know the language of music, you know the notes and scales, the chords and the keys, that is it. It doesn't change or grow. It is the same on every instrument. You will be musical and can play any instrument once you physically adapt to it. Focus on the music, the language and the rhythm.

AS A GUITARIST

We have covered a lot of material in the first two books regarding guitar and fretboard information. It's important to keep things in check musically as to what you are really benefiting from when you add more guitar based learning.

- Know the **12 notes on the Low E string** to help navigate scales.

- Once you know the scale you need, use **Pattern #1** to get on the fretboard with the **"Rock and Roll Rule,"** first finger on the relative minor and pinky on the relative Major.

- Pattern #2 is Always above pattern #1 and pattern #5 is always behind pattern #1. They are bookends to our favorite pattern.

- There are **5 total pentatonic patterns** and they are _always_ in the same order, starting over again at the 12th fret.

- **All five patterns have the same 5 notes in any given key**, therefore they all sound _exactly_ the same.

- We use h**ammer-ons**, **pull-offs**, **slides** and **bends** to make our solos sound more natural and voice like.

- **Pick blocking** is a tremendous tool to help you sound tight and clean.

- **Neck Anatomy** is the single greatest way to look at and unlock your whole fretboard. It uses the octaves to navigate the notes instead of black dots in positions. Neck Anatomy unveils the symmetry in music and the ease of seeing it on your fretboard for the full 3 octaves. It can be used for locating notes, arpeggios, and scales.

BSSBS Playing on ONE STRING

You have probably noticed that in the pentatonic scale there are two spacings (intervals) that occur. I call them BIG and SMALL. The BIG space is three frets (minor 3rd interval) and the SMALL is two frets (a whole-step). This is true as a musician and as a guitar player.

It's easy to see this happening on a single string. Start with a minor pentatonic scale and line up the notes on one string. (For E minor it would be E G A B D.) From E to G is a BIG space. From G to A and A to B are a SMALL space, from B to D is a BIG space, and finally from D back to E again is a SMALL space. Together we get the formula:

B S S B S

This is such an easy way to see the minor pentatonic scale on a single string. Think about the idea that EACH string can do this (not always starting with the E note). If you map out BSSBS on every string you would have an E minor pentatonic across your whole fretboard! The is the same exact information you would get if you map out the traditional five patterns, very cool!

Here is BSSBS for E minor pentatonic on the high "E" string.

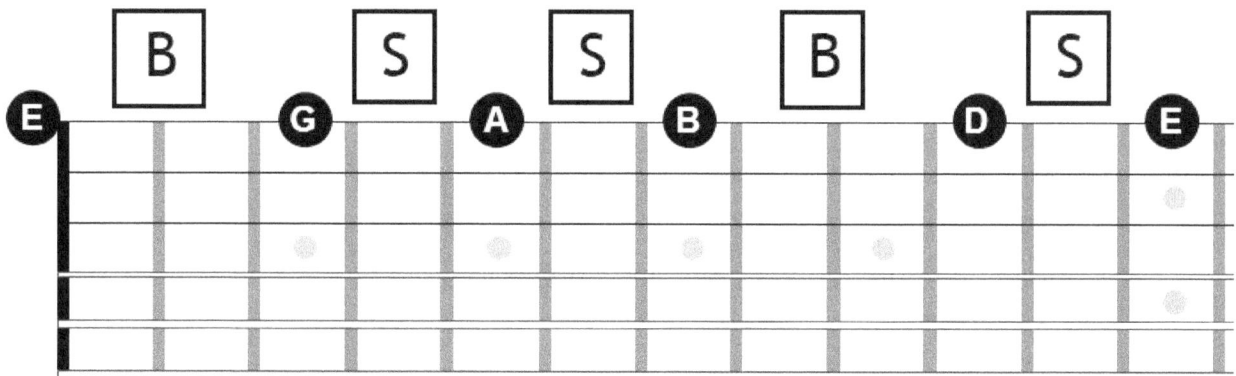

E minor Pentatonic as BSSBS on each string.

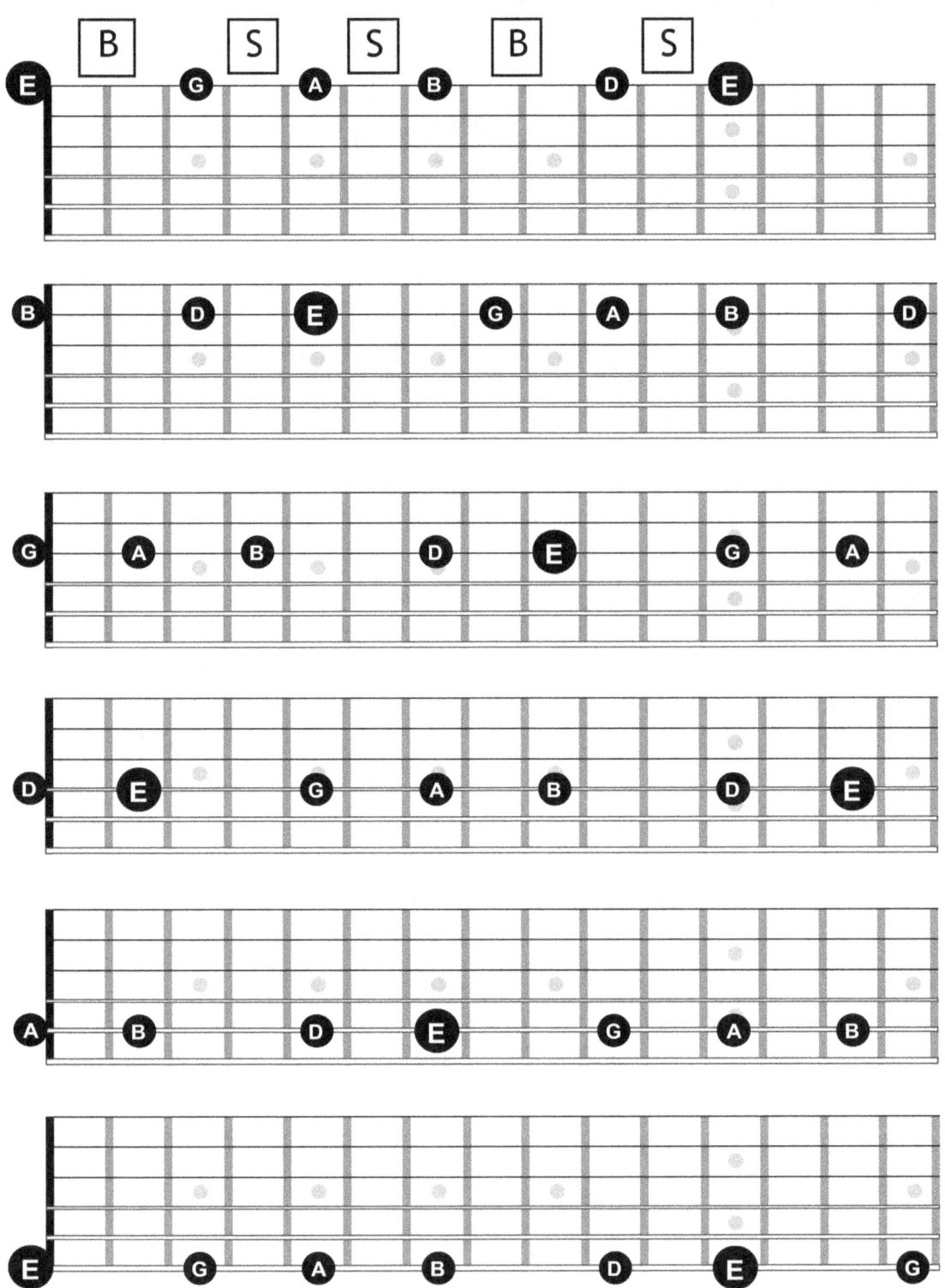

SSBSB The Major pentatonic

As you can imagine it works the same for the Major pentatonic scale. Since our scales are relatives (E minor is the same as G Major), they have the same notes, just a different root note. G Major pentatonic scale is:

G A B D E

The same BSSBS spacing exists and in the same order too. The only difference is the G is the root and not the E. That changes the starting point. A simple way to think of this is to rotate the formula by one letter. Move the first B to the end of the line. Instead of BSSBS it will be:

S S B S B

Almost every Major scale you ever play, pentatonic, Ionian, Lydian, Mixolydian (modes) will start with 2 whole-steps (R to 2nd, then 2nd to 3rd). This is the Do Re Me of the scale. I simply think it of by the intervals, 1 2 3.

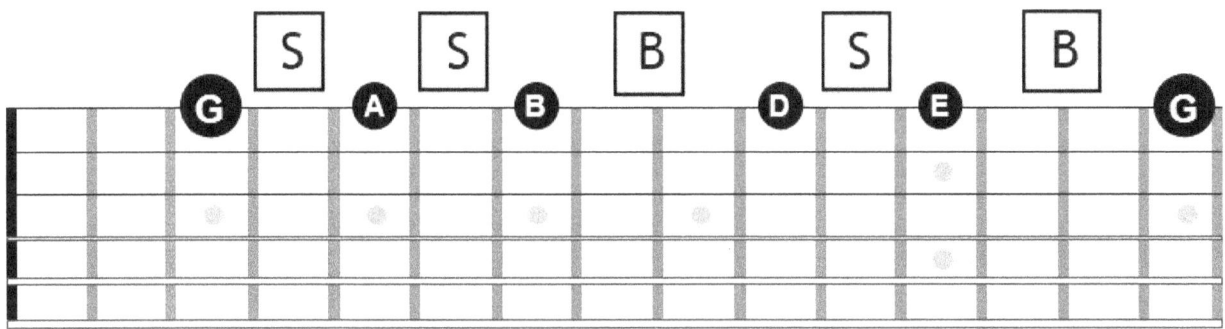

Any scale that starts with 2 whole-steps will sound like Major, because of the Major third interval. You can always lean on the knowledge that everything you ever play in Major will start with SMALL SMALL. The only exception is the Phrygian Dominant scale (Harmonic minor mode) which has a flat 2nd and Major 3rd.

When you play the minor version (BSSBS) compared to the Major version (SSBSB) the BIG space that starts the scale is a minor third interval and our ear immediately hears that as minor.

G Major Pentatonic as SSBSB on each string.

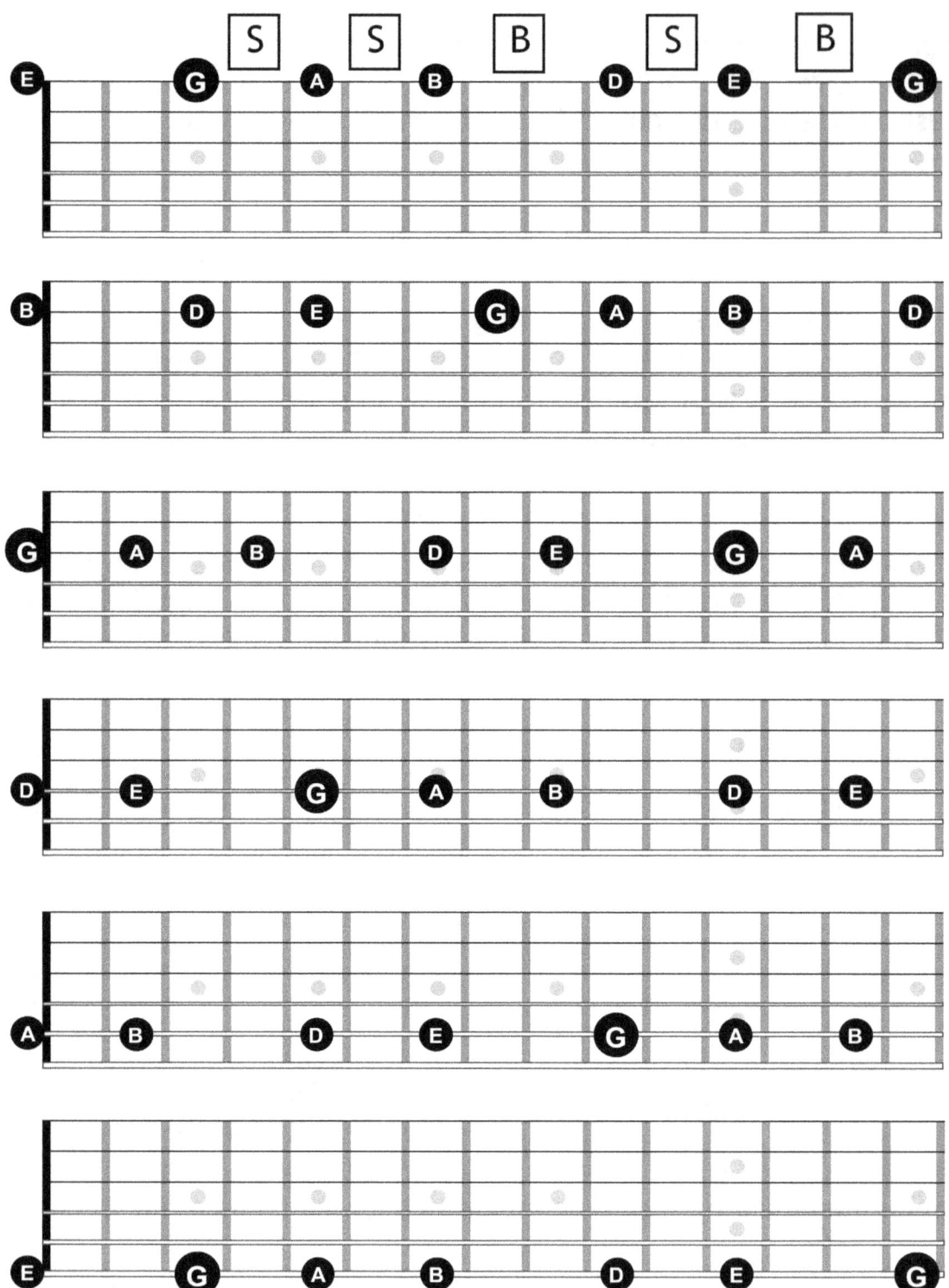

PRACTICE

Start by navigating the top three strings for E minor pentatonic. Find the E on each string (neck anatomy). After a certain point you will just remember where the E notes are. They never move!

Since the guitar is tuned in fourths (5 frets worth) you can choose a note and add 5 frets to the previous string to find the same note. The only difference is from the B to the G string, which adds only 4 frets (Major third). That means your OPEN HIGH E is also on the 5th FRET of the B string, 9th fret of the G string, 14th fret of the D string, 19th fret of the A string and even the 24th fret of the LOW E string (if you have a 24th fret).

Remember that the scale goes up and down from a root on any string. You have to get used to going backwards in the formula too. In the minor pentatonic (BSSBS) there is always a small space behind the root (b7).

The E minor pentatonic scale is a minor scale for an Em chord AND it is an E BLUES SCALE for a E Major chord, especially an E7 chord.

The BLUE NOTE happens in the middle of the second SMALL shape (Major, minor and Blues).

SELF GENERATE E minor pentatonic on E, B and G string
You should ultimately do this on all six strings.

E minor pentatonic on the E STRING

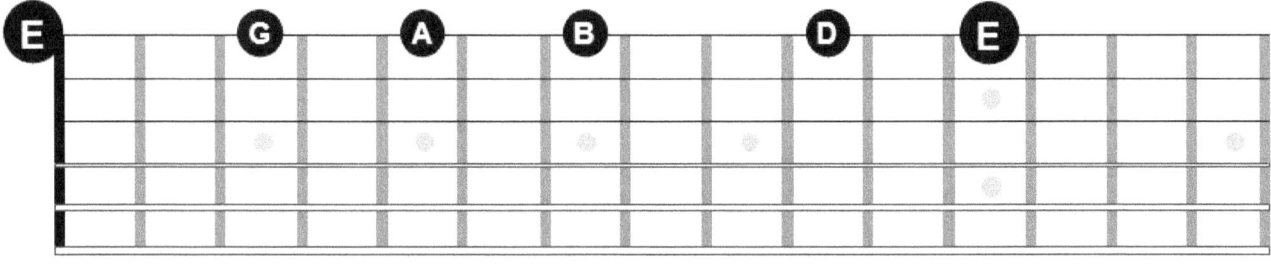

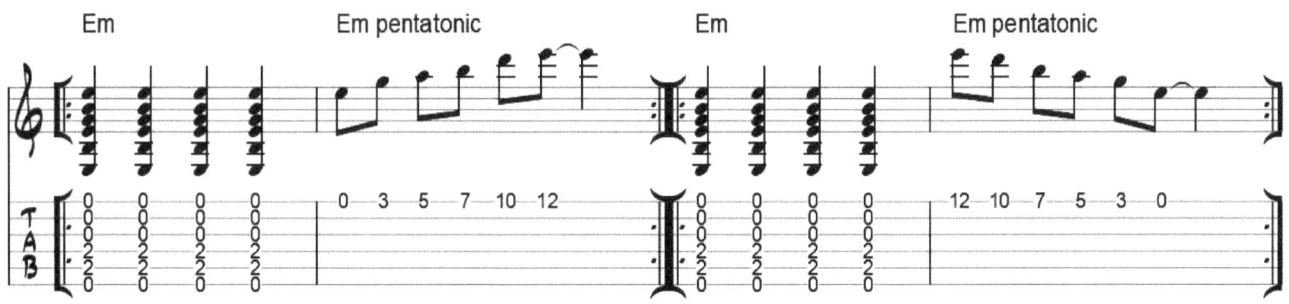

E minor pentatonic on the B STRING

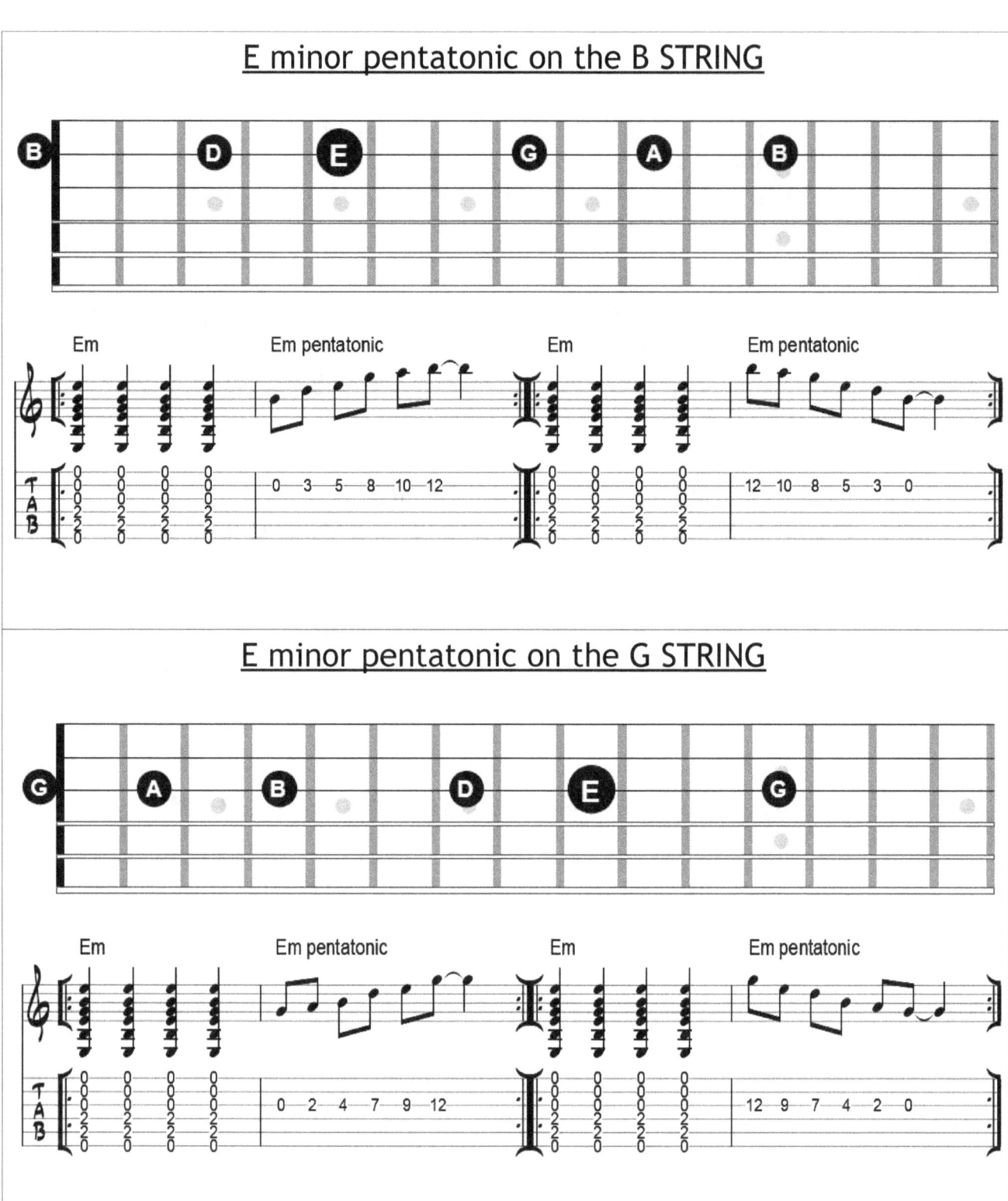

E minor pentatonic on the G STRING

E minor LICKS top 3 strings

Self generating licks is one of the best ways to play music, not practice, but play. It's a way to be musical and get your practice time in.

Here are six licks, two per string using the BSSBS idea. Remember these notes are the same notes that are in the five patterns. You are constantly crossing through the patterns as you ascend and descend the strings.

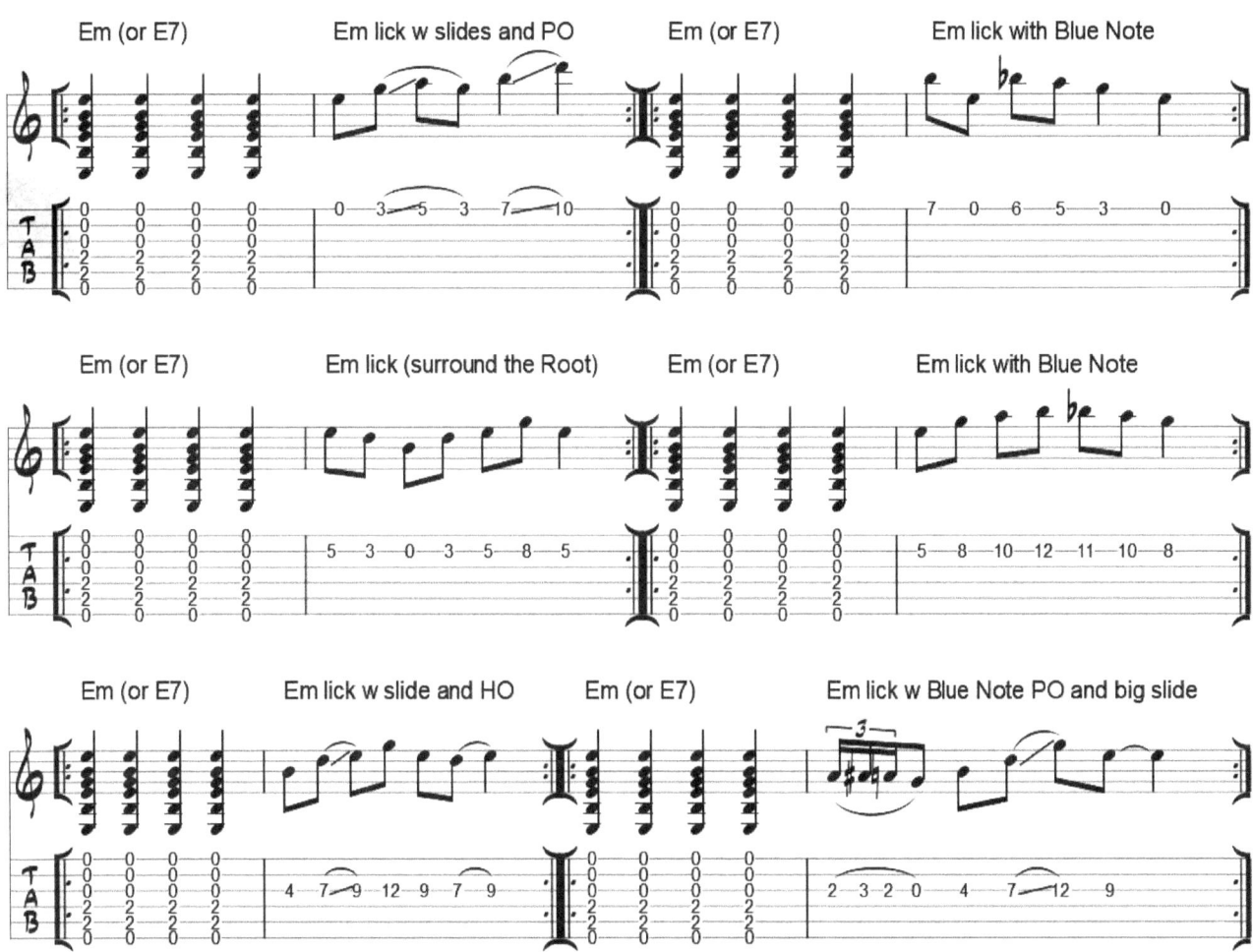

SELF GENERATE G Major pentatonic on E, B and G string

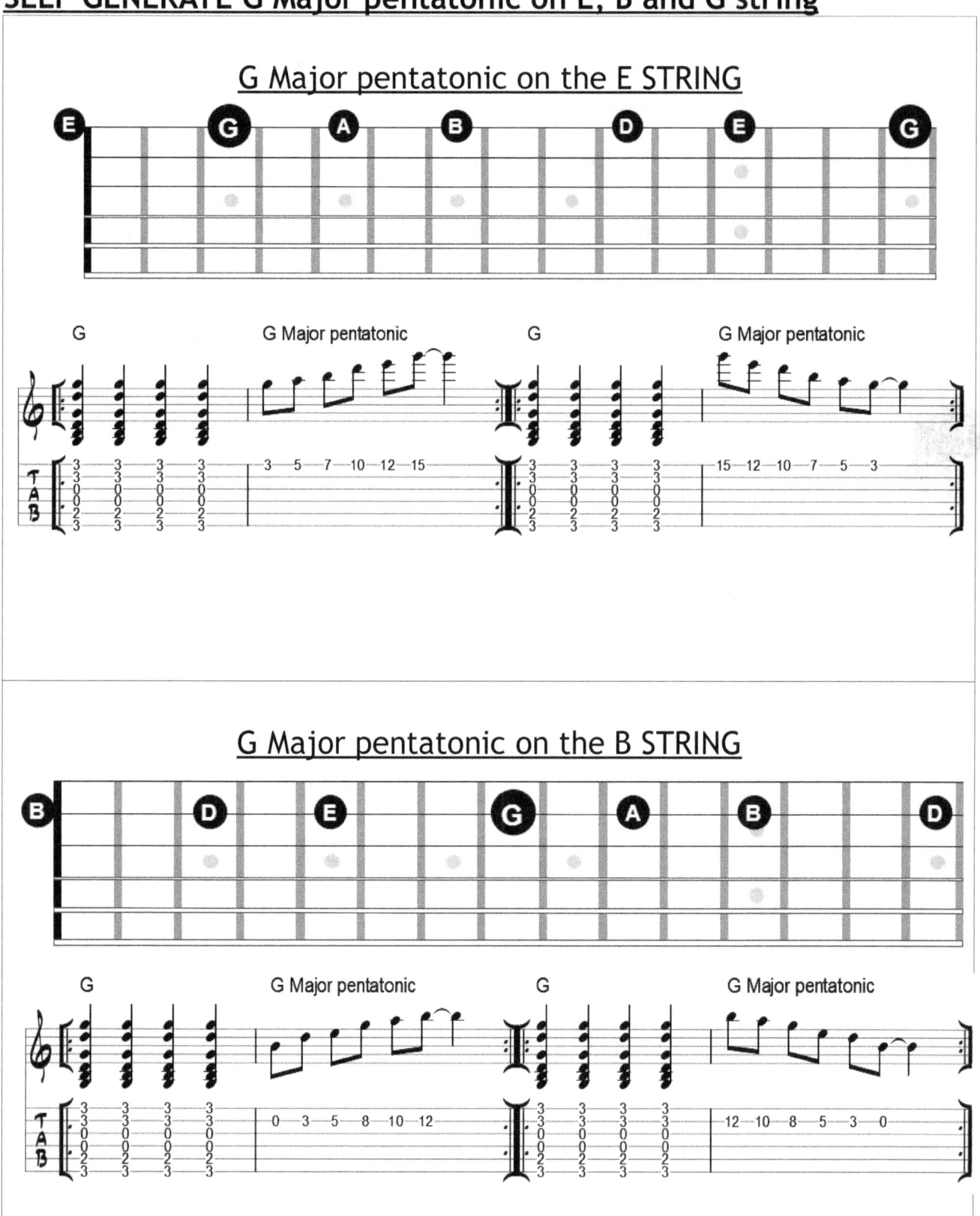

G Major pentatonic on the E STRING

G Major pentatonic on the B STRING

G Major pentatonic on the G STRING

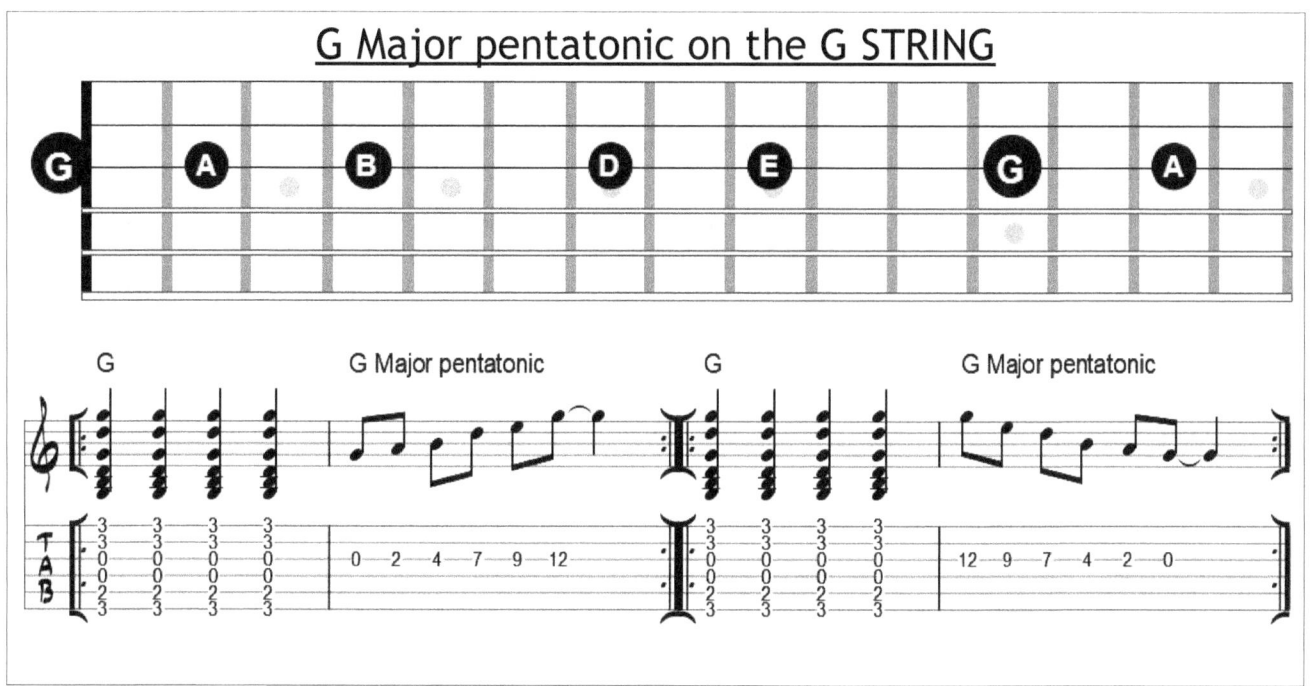

G Major Pentatonic LICKS Top 3 strings

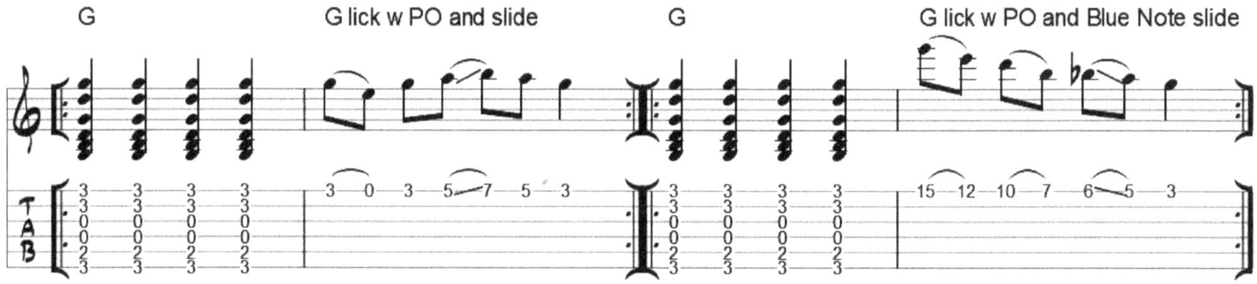

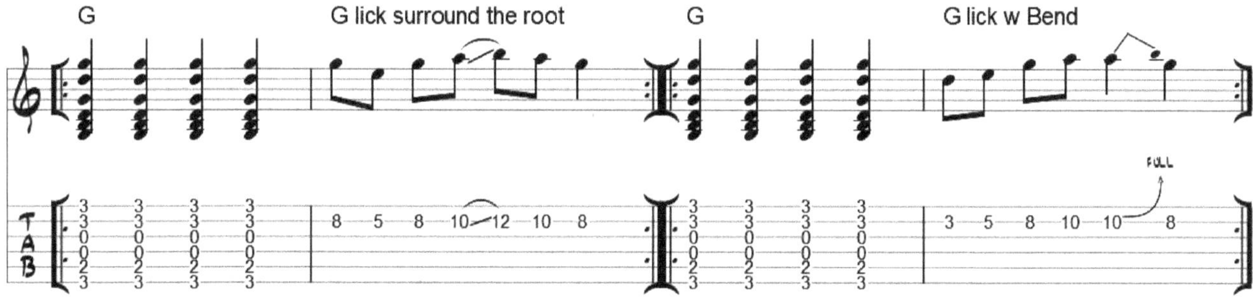

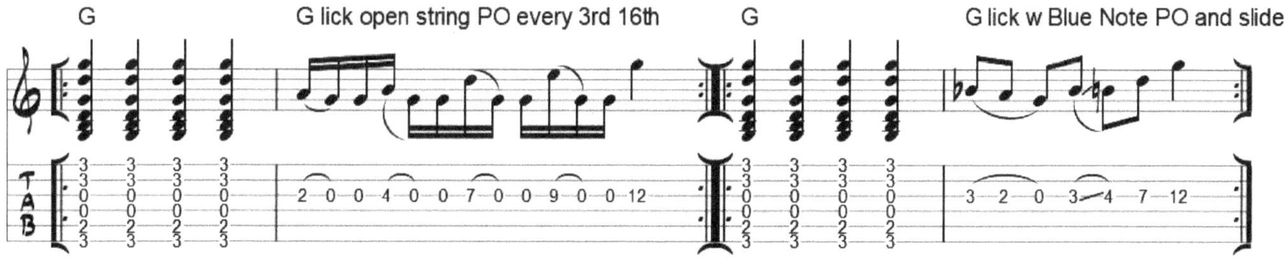

SUMMARY

We are musicians. We are guitar players.
We learn the language of music, Melody, Harmony, and Rhythm.
We learn the craft of playing the guitar as an instrument.

We warm up with Muted String Ladders (MSL), Changing GEARS, and SHELLS.
We Exercise our scales and licks.

AS A MUSICIAN:

- We decide on the "main" chord and base the scale upon that chord to play globally.
- We base a scale on EACH chord when we **"Play the Changes."**
- **MINOR chord gets a MINOR pentatonic scale.**
- **MAJOR chord can get either the MAJOR pentatonic and/or the BLUES pentatonic** (minor pentatonic over a major chord).
- Add the **Blue Note** for extra color.
- **Octaves** are the landings in the staircase. Each octave starts the same and we build scale up and down from them.
- **Rhythm** is the most essential skill to connect to music and sound your best.
- **ABAC** is an ultra simple and extremely powerful tool to help build melodies and nurture ideas.

AS A GUITAR PLAYER:

- Once we know the music scale we need to find the ROOT note on the low E string.
- Then we decide on the the **FIRST FINGER for MINOR or BLUES or we use the PINKY for MAJOR.**
- Once Pattern #1 is on the fretboard everything is relative to it.
- Add Pattern #2, #3, #4, and #5, always connected to each other in the same way to extend the sound further up and down the fretboard.
- **SHORT OCTAVE and LONG OCTAVE** shapes help us see the notes on the fretboard and help us navigate scales and so much more.
- **Sequences** are great for solos and improvising. They help us hear and "build our chops." They are essential on any instrument.
- **Neck Anatomy** is the ultimate tool to unlock your whole fretboard, from Root notes to Blue Notes and SCALES.
- We can build scales with **BSSBS and SSBSB.**

CHAPTER 2

TUNE IN

"I am a musician and a guitar player. Music is my language and my guitar is my voice. Music is Melody, Harmony and Rhythm. I develop my language skills and my instrument skills. They are two separate worlds working together to complete the circle of music."

Rhythm is the number one factor to sounding great as a musician.

WARM UP

Muted String Ladder (MSL) 3 strings all 4 gears

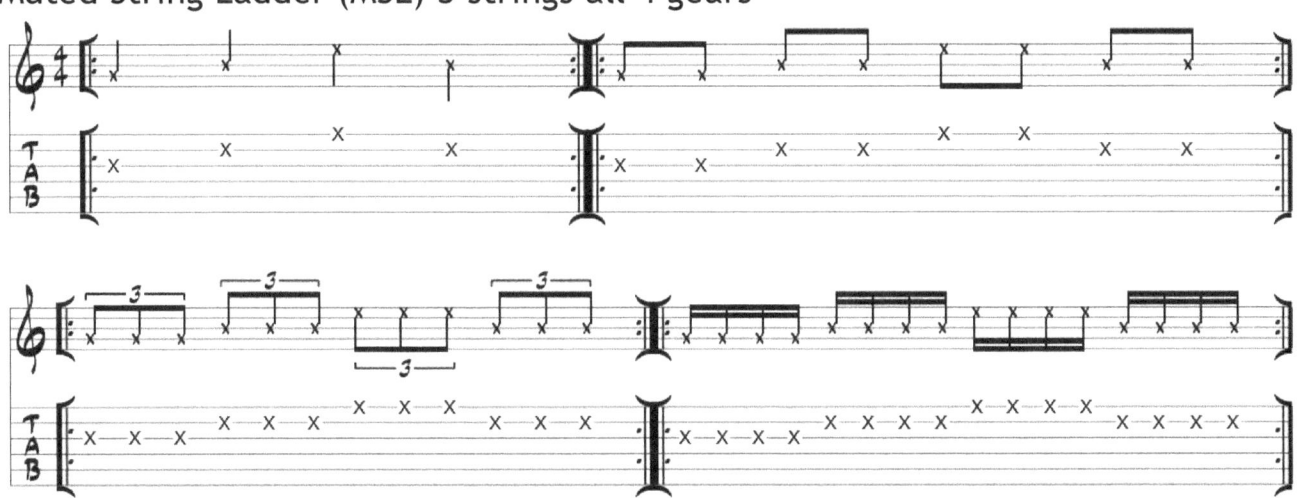

Practice with ALL DOWN PICKS, then ALL UP PICKS, then ALTERNATE PICKS for FIRST Gear (quarter-notes) before moving on to SECOND gear (eighth-notes).

It is especially important to get the feel of ALTERNATE PICKED TRIPLETS.

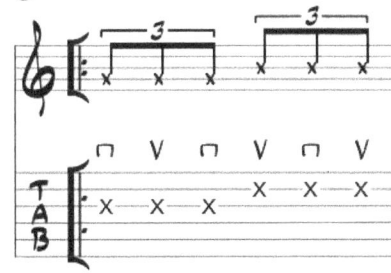

CHANGE GEARS

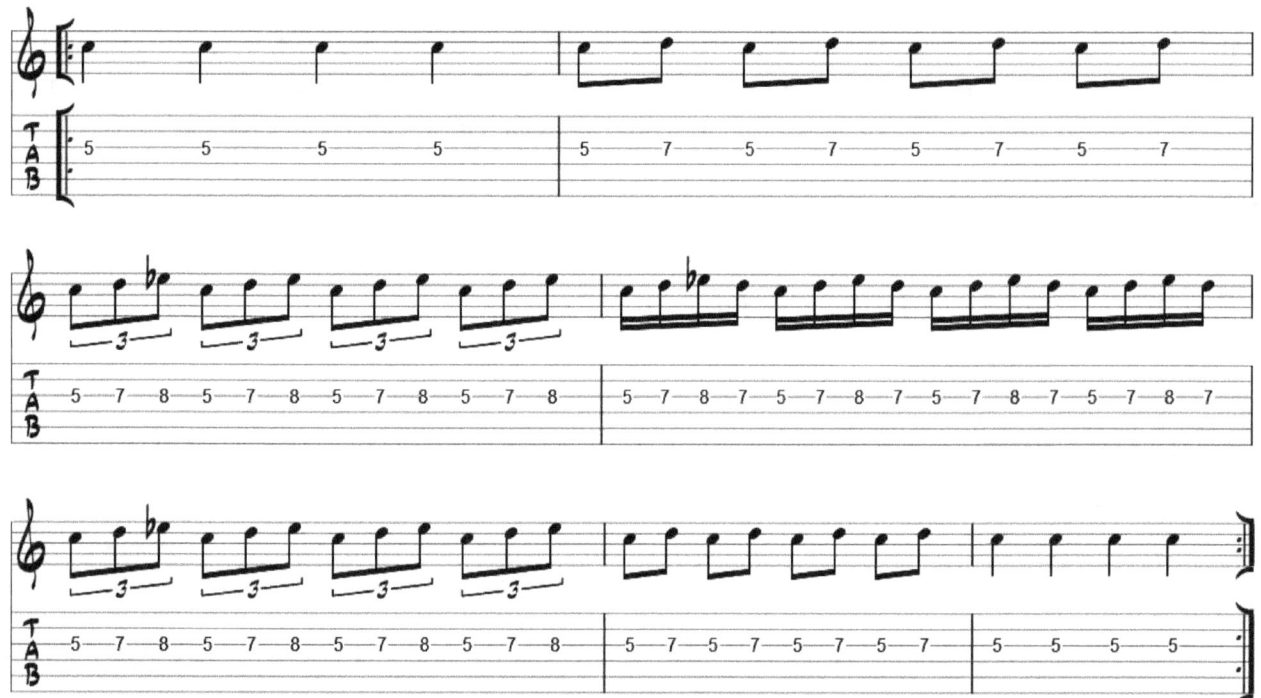

GENERAL TIPS

- Don't change gears until you are ready. Play each gear until you get at least 2 bars perfect (8 beats). Once you are nailing it you can set a limit for each gear. For example play each gear for 2 bars, or as written, once per bar.
- You can do this on any string and any fret.
- You can reverse all of the fingering and start with the PINKY.
- You can make up your own pattern as long as the first note is the same for all the gears.
- Remember this is a rhythm exercise to help you "feel" the gear (rhythm). We matched the number of notes with the gear. THIS IS NOT ALWAYS TRUE IN MUSIC. To me, some of the best sounds are when the number of notes DOESN'T match the rhythm. For example try 3 notes in 16ths, or 2 notes in triplets.

SHELL

Shell 1 4 with Hammer-ons and Pull-offs (HO PO) in quarter-notes

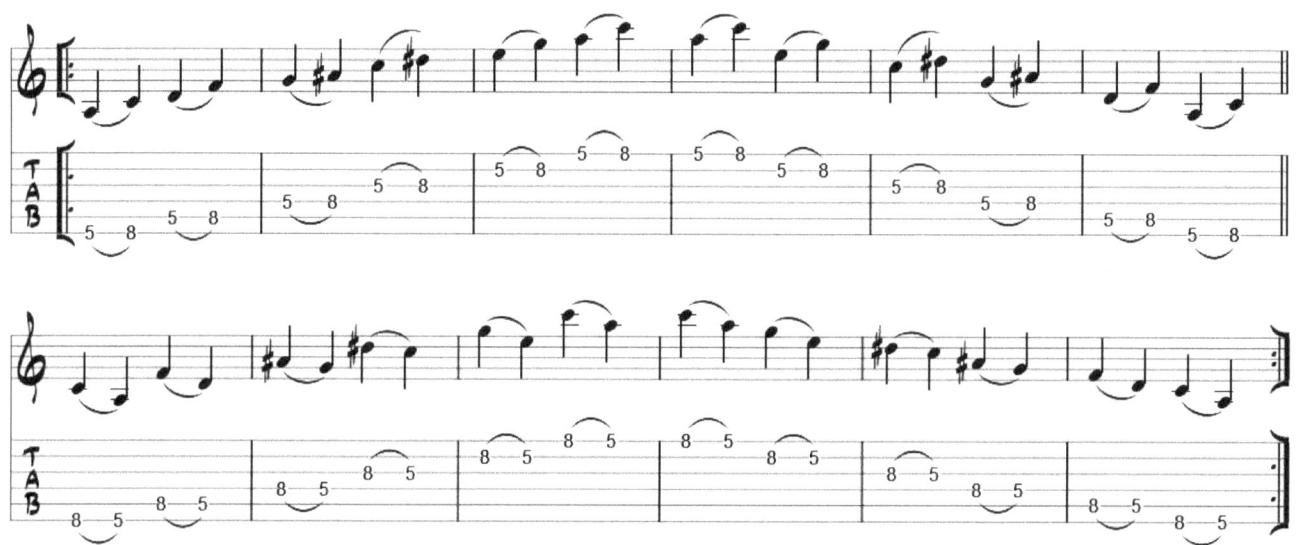

Shell 1 4 with Hammer-ons and Pull-offs (HO PO) in eighth-notes

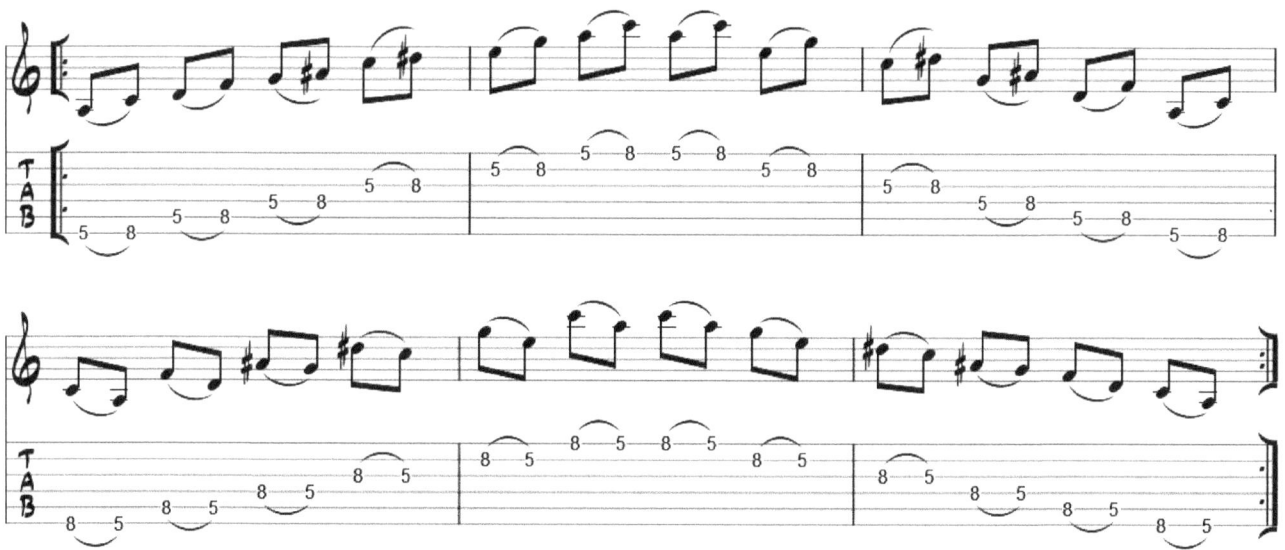

It's important to maintain the rhythm evenly. Don't let different articulations change the rhythm, they only enhance the sound. Make sure each note, whether picked, hammered on, or pulled off, has the same volume, a clear tone, and lasts the full duration of its rhythm before going to the next note.

EXERCISE

Self Generate one bar of Em chord and 1 bar Em pentatonic.
Ascend and descend for 1 octave in each of the 5 patterns.

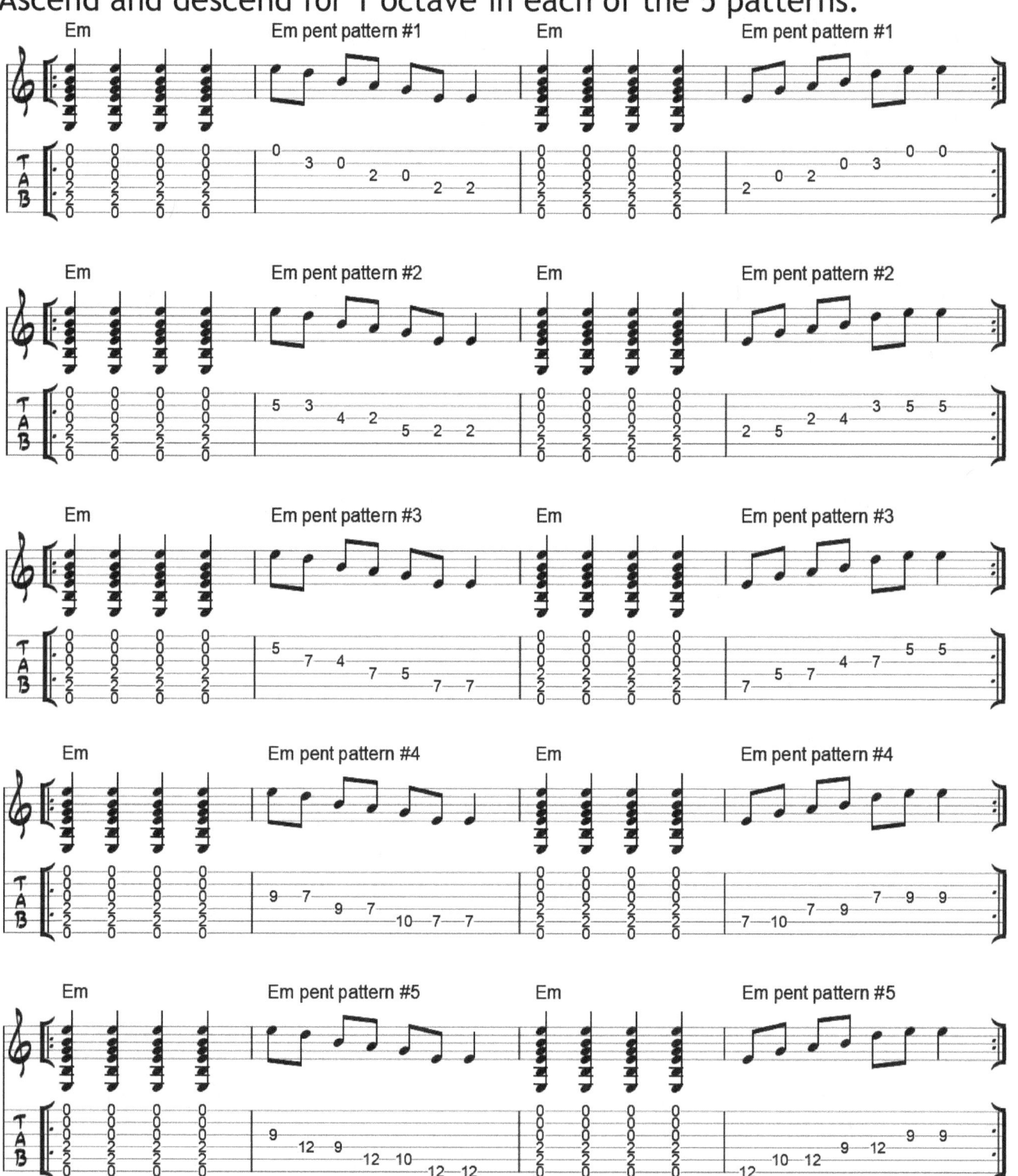

REVIEW

In the previous chapter we talked about how to play a pentatonic scale on one string on the guitar. It's really important to keep in mind that you are always operating on two levels, as a musician and as a guitar player.

Learning to play a scale on one string is a guitar player issue. It doesn't change anything about what we are doing as musicians. We are still playing a pentatonic scale. On some instruments we blow air and press valves. On some we push keys with our fingers, and we can just open our mouth and sing. The scale is the same. It just occurs in different ways on different instruments. It's only on multi stringed instruments that scales can move in multiple directions with many redundant notes.

BSSBS is for **minor** and **SSBSB** is for **Major.** You can map this on any/all of your strings. You must find the root for the scale on each string (use Neck Anatomy). The scale can ascend and descend on any string.

E minor pentatonic as BSSBS

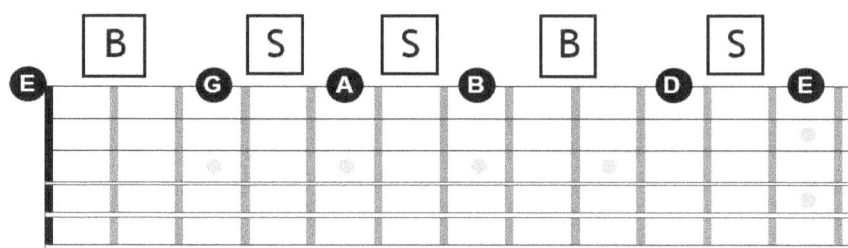

G Major pentatonic as SSBSB

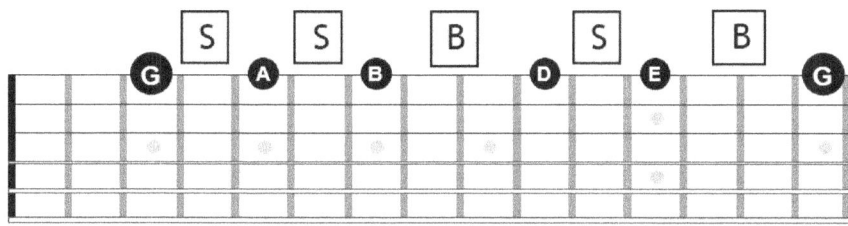

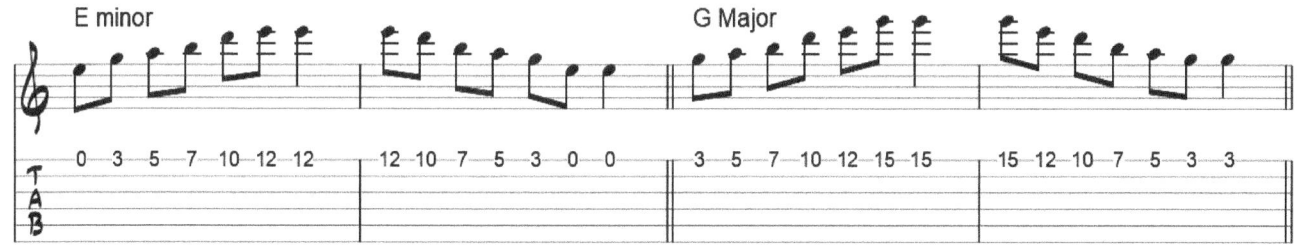

OCTAVES

In Lead Guitar Level #1 and #2 we looked at the power of Neck Anatomy. This guitar based knowledge helps us see our fretboard in a natural, musical and symmetrical way. Neck Anatomy is the term I coined to represent how OCTAVES connect on the guitar to really see how the notes move. Once you understand how other instruments move through scales (I learned this from playing flute, tenor saxophone, and even a little clarinet) you can see how the guitar does it in a really clean and clear way.

The basis for using Neck Anatomy is the actual shape of the OCTAVE. There are two shapes that will encompass the six strings. I call them SHORT and LONG. The B string is the reason the shapes on the thinner strings are larger.

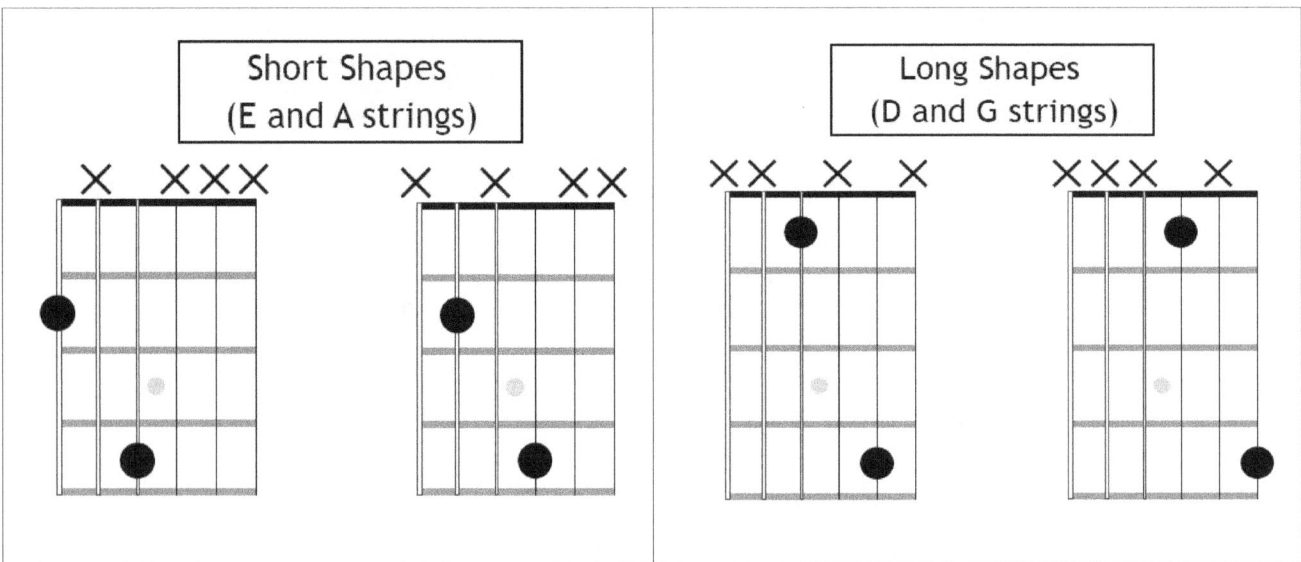

Although these shapes are the foundation for Neck Anatomy, they are also a very playable and usable sound when played together. Every shape has a muted string in between the notes. (Your index finger will most likely be the one to mute it.) I usually use my FIRST and THIRD finger for the SHORT shapes and FIRST and PINKY for the LONG shapes. Sometimes I use first and pinky for all of them. Use whichever way is easiest for you to make it happen. No one ever hears what finger you used.

It's very common to play melodies in octaves. It can really fill out the sound. From Django Reinhardt to Jimi Hendrix to Wes Montgomery octaves have been a big part of guitar playing. Any melody/solo can be played in octaves assuming you have the range available.

PRACTICE

OCTAVES IN POSITION

Play an A minor pentatonic with pattern #1 on the 5th fret. To prepare for the motion of playing in octaves, play this scale ONLY USING YOUR INDEX FINGER (1st)

Add the appropriate shape of octave for each note of Am pentatonic.

If you strum the octave (3 strings) the note in the middle with be muted (not notated).

You can also use Hybrid picking and use the pick on the lower string and middle finger for the higher octave (simultaneously plucking the two notes).

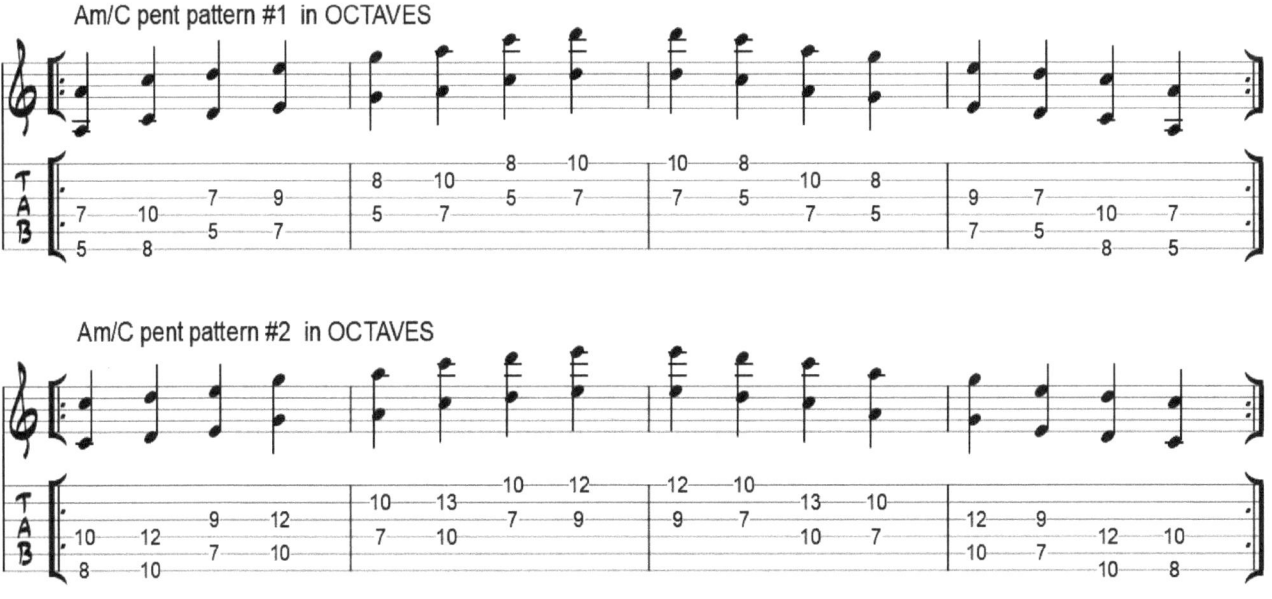

Octaves are great for following BSSBS up and down strings. BSSBS helps keep the timbre the same and helps facilitate the octave shape by keep them on the same string groups.

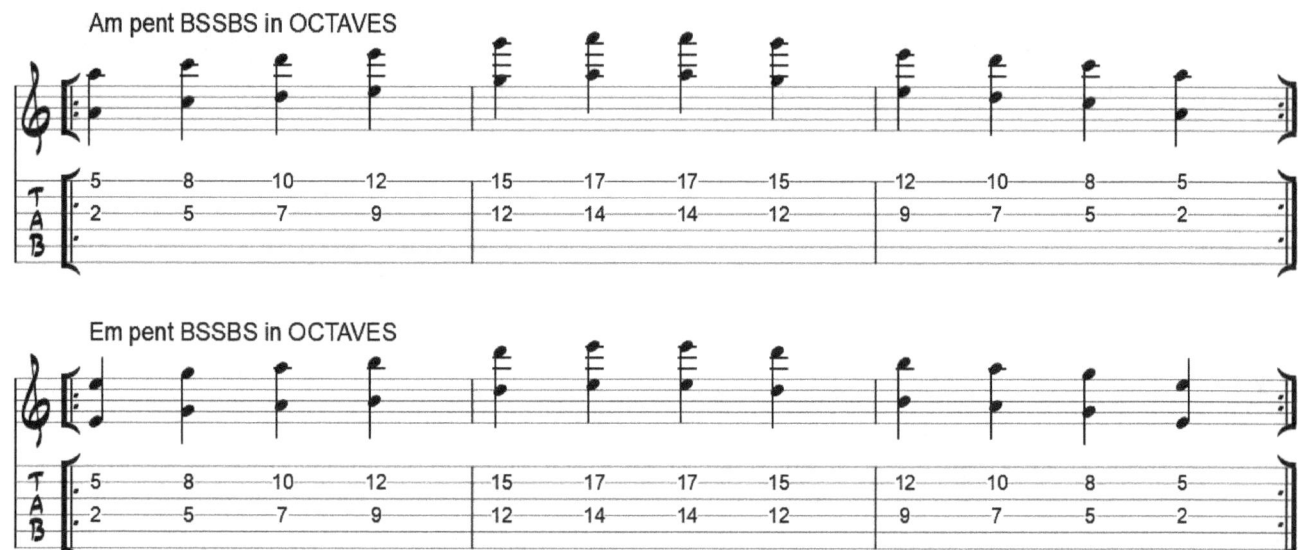

Self Generating LICKS

SUMMARY

We are musicians. We are guitar players.
We learn the language of music, Melody, Harmony, and Rhythm.
We learn the craft of playing the guitar as an instrument.

You should always remind yourself that you are learning two languages on two different levels. On one side you are learning as a musician about notes, scales, chords and keys. On the other side you are a guitar player learning scale patterns, shapes, and spacings on strings and hopefully the notes themselves on your fretboard. Always make your music decisions first and then go to your instrument (guitar).

MUSICIAN

- There are only 12 notes. (ABCDEFG are the Natural notes and there are 5 accidentals.)
- EF and BC are a ½ step apart (smallest distance).
- There are only 12 Major chords, 12 minor chords, 12 Major pentatonics, 12 minor pentatonics, each based on one of the 12 notes.
- There are two inherent sounds of a Pentatonic scale, Major and minor (to match its respective chord).
- The **Blues Scale** is playing a minor pentatonic over a Major chord.
- There is a **relative minor to every Major** (1½ steps below the Major root). This means two-for-one.
- For soloing, match a scale to its chord, **Globally** or **Playing the changes**.

GUITAR PLAYER

- The 12 notes are the first 12 frets on the guitar that we navigate on the lowest E string.
- We use the **"Rock and Roll Rule"** to put pattern #1 on the fretboard after making the music decision about what scale we need.
- There are **5 total patterns** to connect our 12 fret fretboard for all 12 keys.
- We learned how to use **BSSBS to play a minor pentatonic scale** and **SSBSB to play a Major pentatonic scale on any one string**.
- We learned how to use **OCTAVE SHAPES** as a playable sounds as well as using them to unlock the fretboard.

CHAPTER 3

TUNE IN

"I am a musician and a guitar player. Music is my language and my guitar is my voice. Music is Melody, Harmony and Rhythm. I develop my language skills and my instrument skills. They are two separate worlds working together to complete the circle of music."

Rhythm is the number one factor to sounding great as a musician.

WARM UP

Muted String Ladder (MSL) 4 strings

SHELLS

Shell 1 3 Slides as eighth-notes

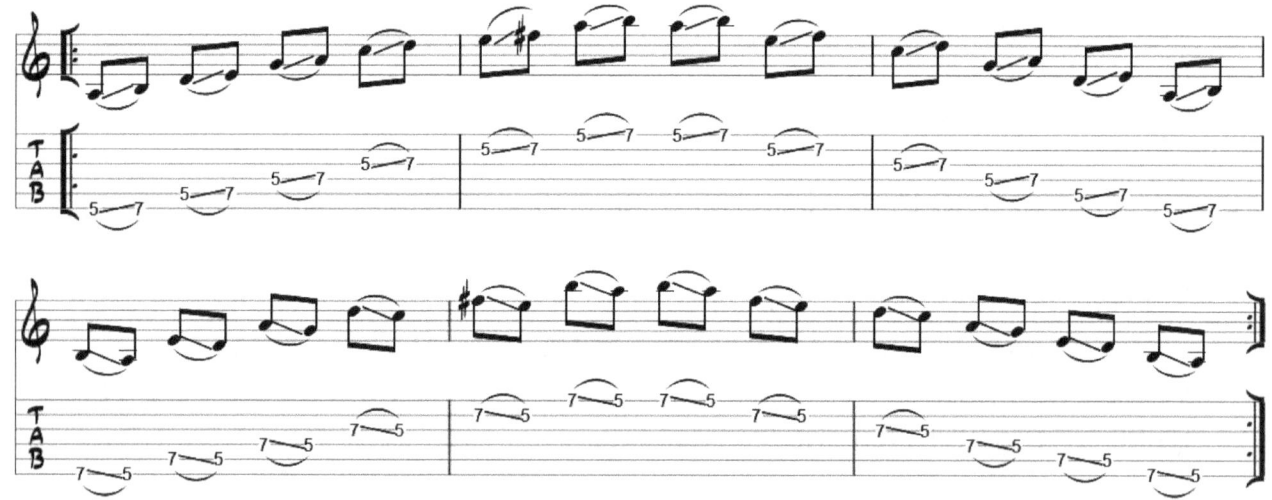

SHELLS
Shell 1 4 Slides as quarter-notes

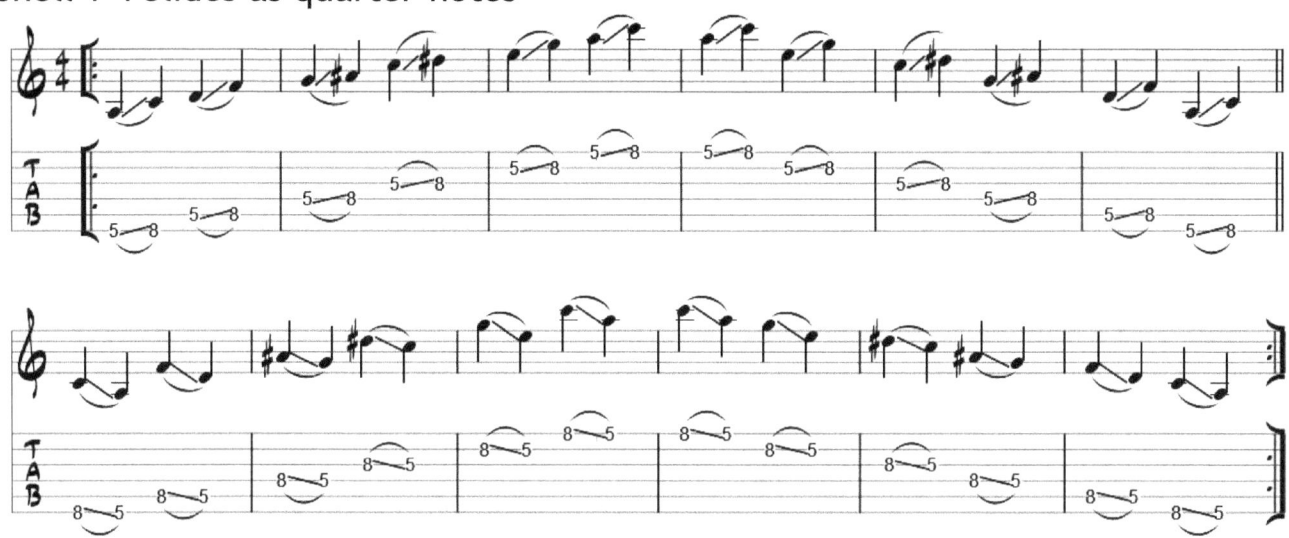

CHANGE GEARS

Change Gears on two adjacent strings

EXERCISE

Am/C Pentatonic scales pattern #1 and #2 in Octaves

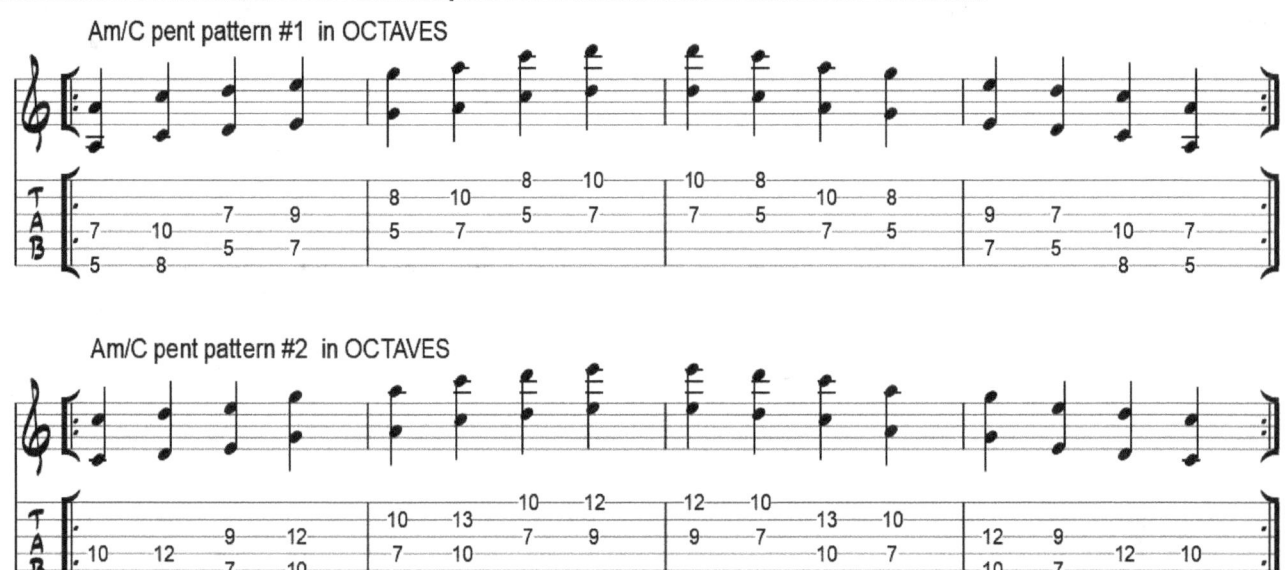

Pentatonic scale as OCTAVES monophonic

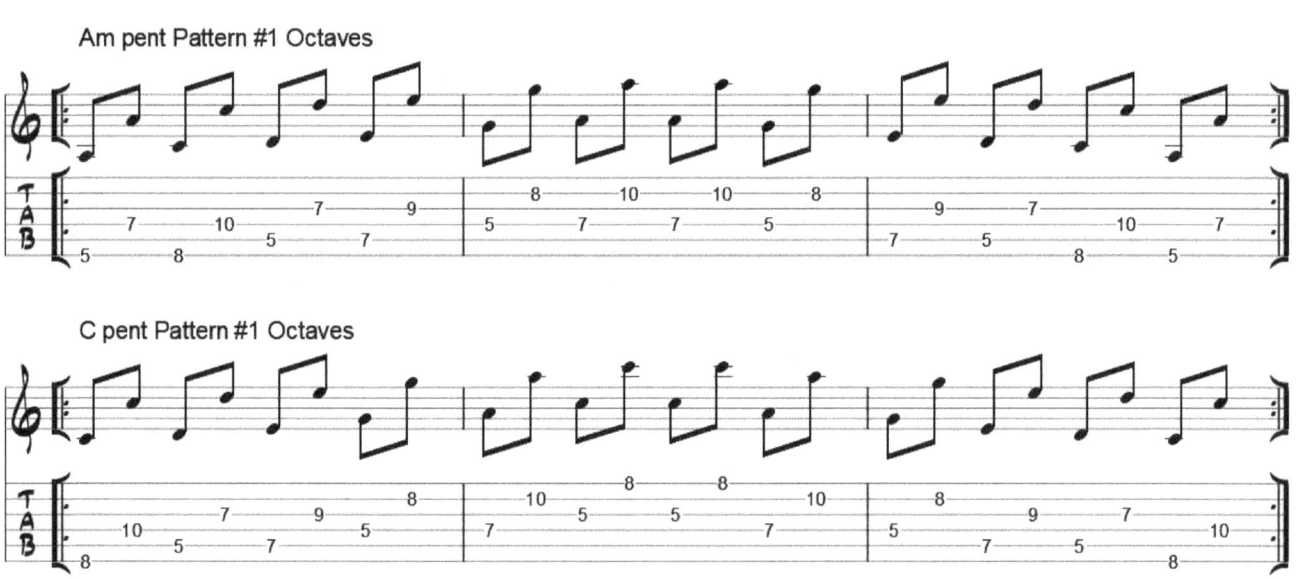

Even though it can be tricky, playing octaves monophonically is a really cool sound, especially in riffs (think "Immigrant Song"). It is a great variation in sound compared to the polyphonic way.

PLAYING THE CHANGES

When you play the changes you directly "talk" to each chord instead of globally speaking to all. This means when you play the changes you play the scale/arpeggio that directly relates to that chord. You would change scales/arpeggios for each chord. When you solo **globally**, you find and play one scale that is common to all the chords in the progression. This can allow for a consistent sound and allows the soloist to fully focus on making melodies.

When you **play the changes** and directly highlight the notes in each chord with its scale, you bring out another level in color and expressiveness that really connects to the song. One of the hardest parts when playing the changes is keeping the chords going in your head as you solo. This is crucially important.

Playing one scale on the guitar can be challenging enough. The idea of changing scales each time the chord changes can seem impossible. Even though changing scales on the guitar can seem like looking for a straight line through a kaleidoscope it can offer some extreme conveniences.

Using Pattern #1 you can play all 12 Major and minor pentatonic scales by sliding the pattern up and down to match it's respective root note on the E string.

C Major and C minor pentatonic scale with Pattern #1

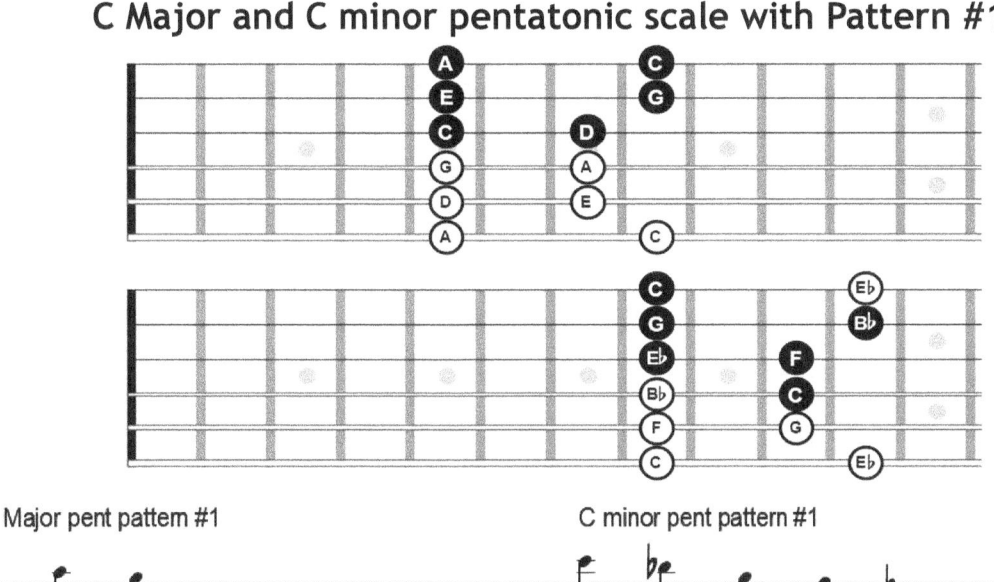

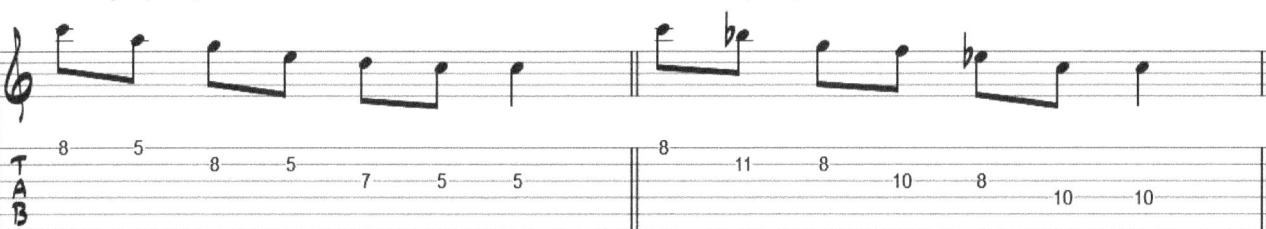

PRACTICE

There are only 12 keys in music and there are only 12 Major pentatonics, one for each note. Two of the most common ways to go through the 12 notes is by using the Circle of 5ths and the Circle of 4ths.

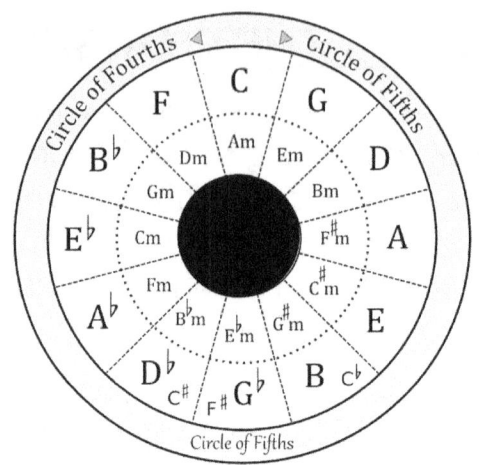

The idea is to start on C and move either a 4th or 5th interval through the 12 tones. On guitar, there are 2½ steps (5 frets) up on one string for a 4th and 3½ steps (7 frets) for a 5th.

Playing in 4ths is a very common sound in music. Chord progressions often move in 4ths. You should get to know the 12 notes in order of the Circle of 5ths and the Circle of 4ths. Start with the 4ths. When you get to Gb/F# that is half way around the clock (counter clockwise) and the keys flip from flat to sharp. TIP: Look for the word BEAD. You see it in the flats first, then in the sharps. Seeing those four letters always help me remember it.

CIRCLE OF 4ths

C F Bb Eb Ab Db Gb/F# B E A D G

Practice finding the notes on the high E string. If you are going to use pattern #1 for Major then play the root notes with your pinky (4th finger). If you are going to use pattern #1 as minor play the root notes with your index finger (first finger/pointer).

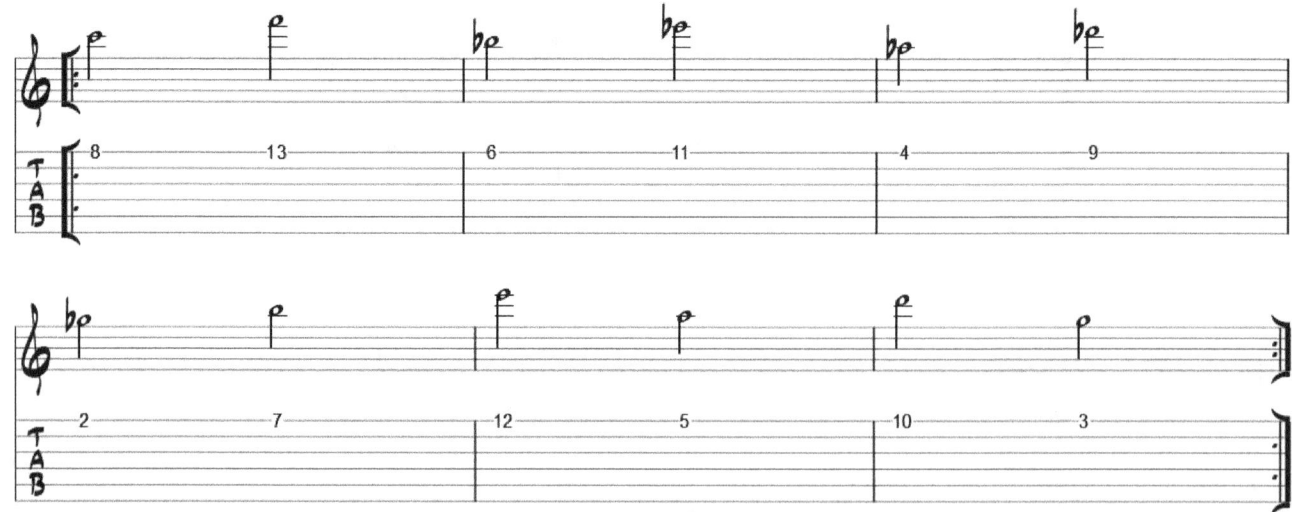

Play a 1 octave descending **Major pentatonic scale** from each root in the circle of 4ths. You will start each time with the pinky on the high E string.

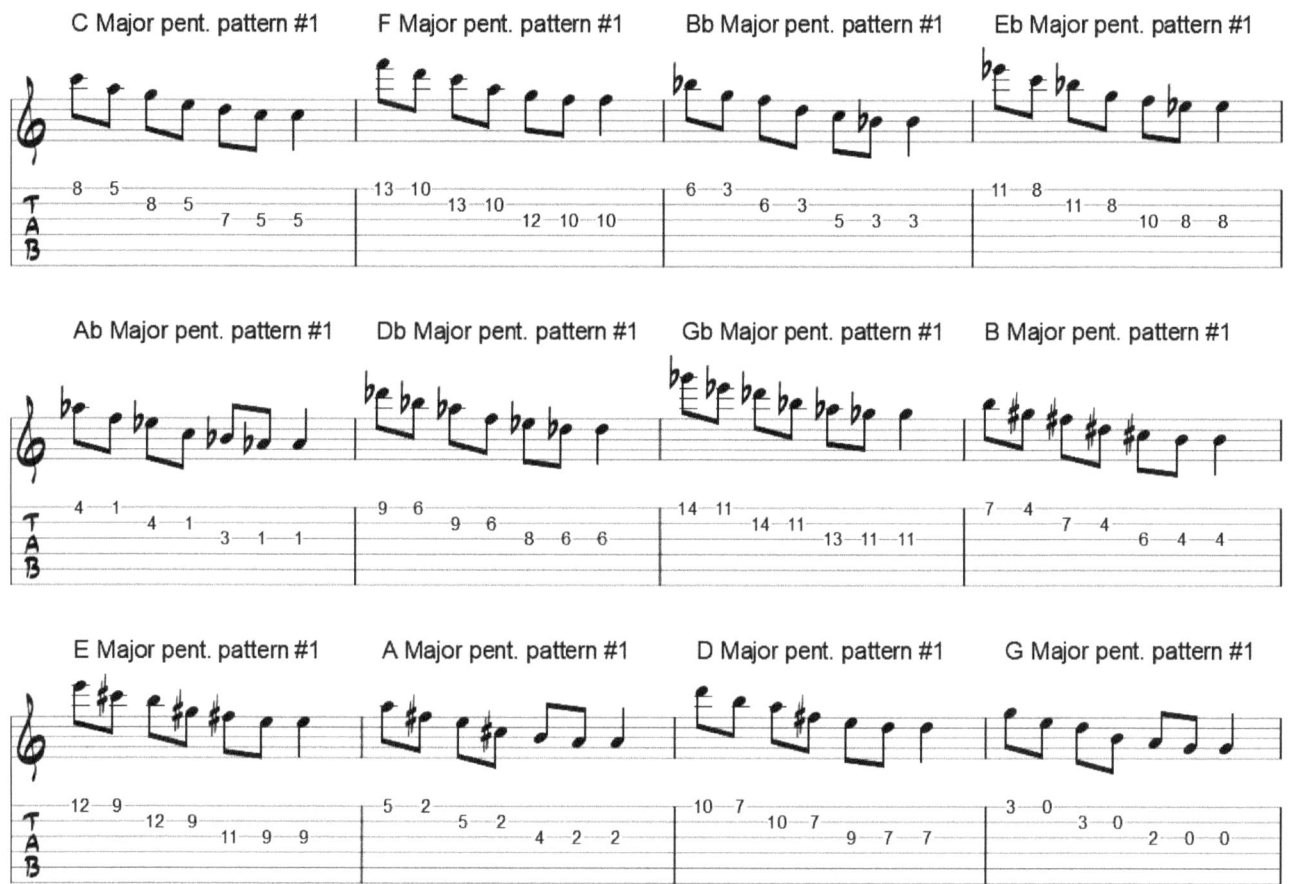

You should also ascend the scale. You can navigate from the root on the G string. Remember that the full octave of the scale encompasses the same space as the LONG octave shape (from the G to high E string).

You should also play the scale ascending and descending from the lowest octave in pattern #1. Navigate from the root notes on the LOW E string. Start with your pinky to ascend. Descending you would navigate from the root note on the G string back to the root note on the low E string.

Play a 1 octave descending **minor pentatonic scale** for each root note in the circle of 4ths. You will start with the index (pointer/1st) finger each time.

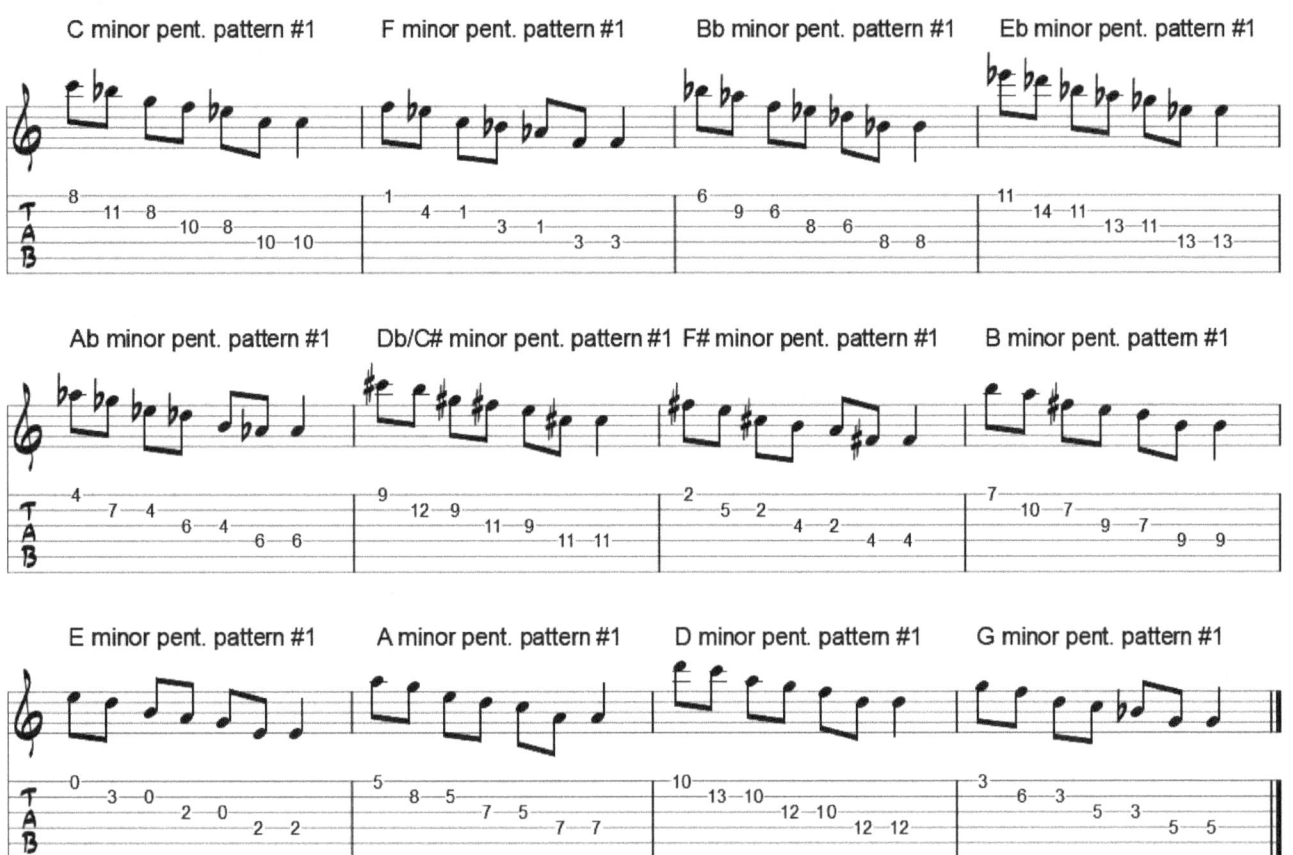

You should also ascend the scale. Navigate from the root on the D string back to the root on the high E string.

You should also play the scale ascending and descending from the lowest octave in pattern #1. Navigate the root notes from the LOW E string and start with your index (1st/pointer) finger to ascend. Descending you would navigate from the root note on the D string. Look for the SHORT octave shape from the Low E string to help find the root note on the D string.

PLAY PATTERN #1 for each chord. Match chord and scale quality. Major chord gets a Major pentatonic and a minor chord gets a minor pentatonic.

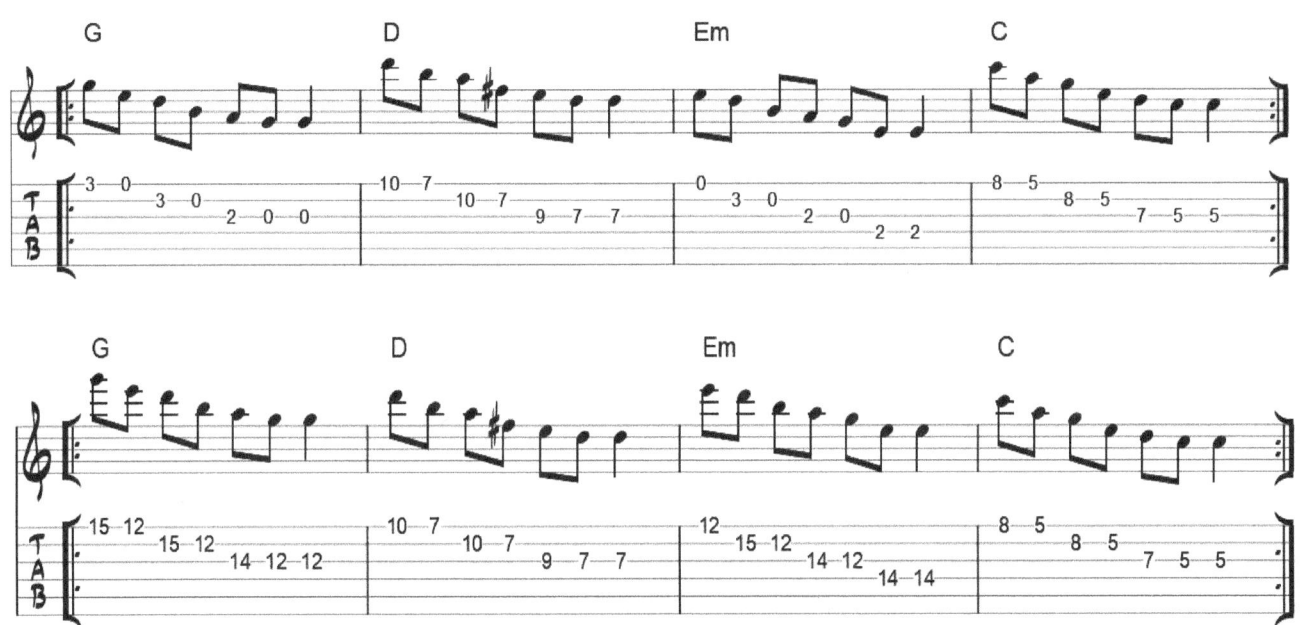

Play LICKS in pattern #1 for each chord.

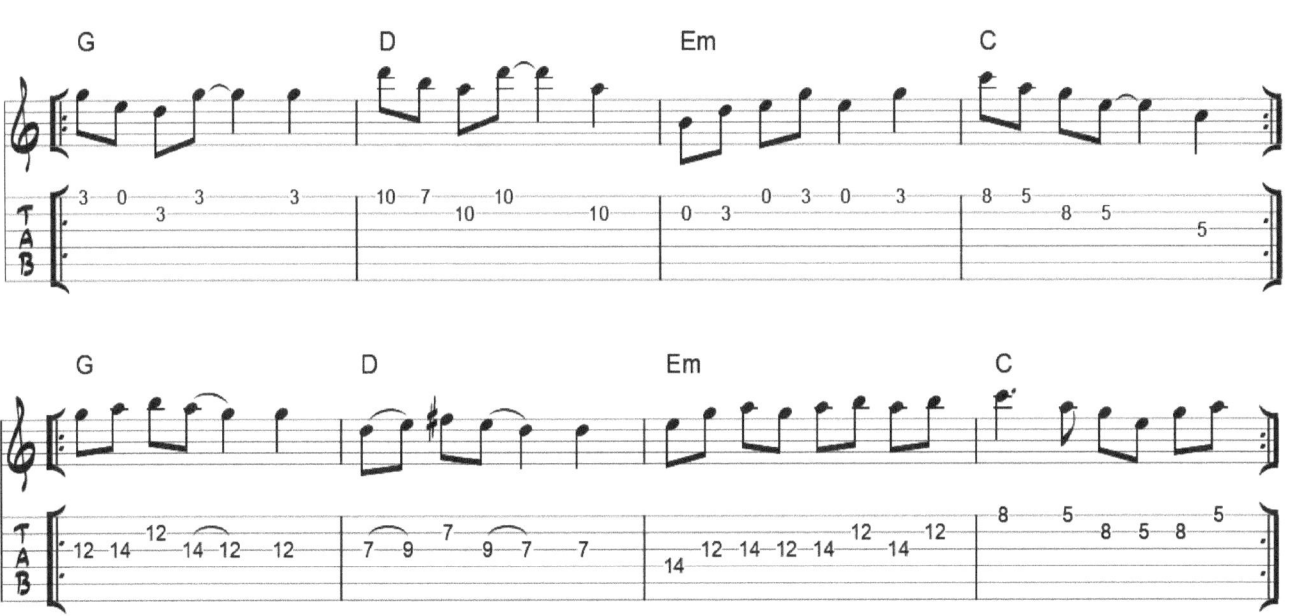

PLAY PATTERN #1 for each chord. Match chord and scale quality. Major chord gets a Major pentatonic and a minor chord gets a minor pentatonic.

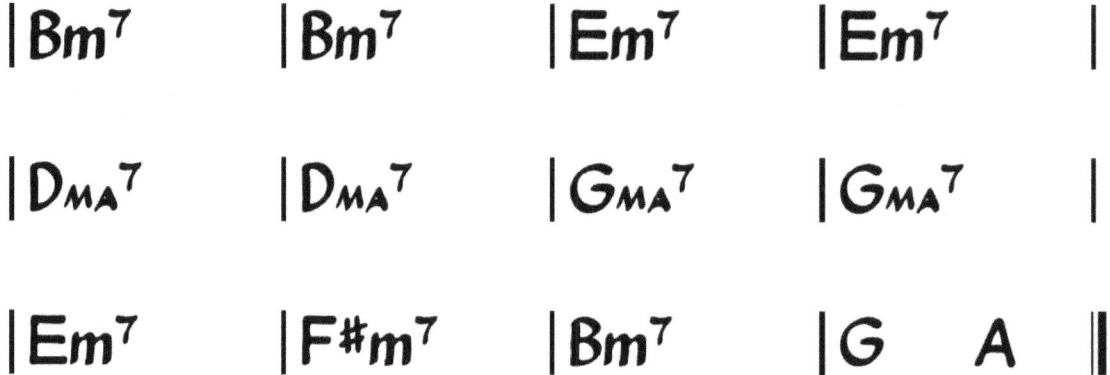

Play the Changes with LICKS in pattern #1 for each chord of the progression.
This is the same progression as before. Some of these licks are sequences.

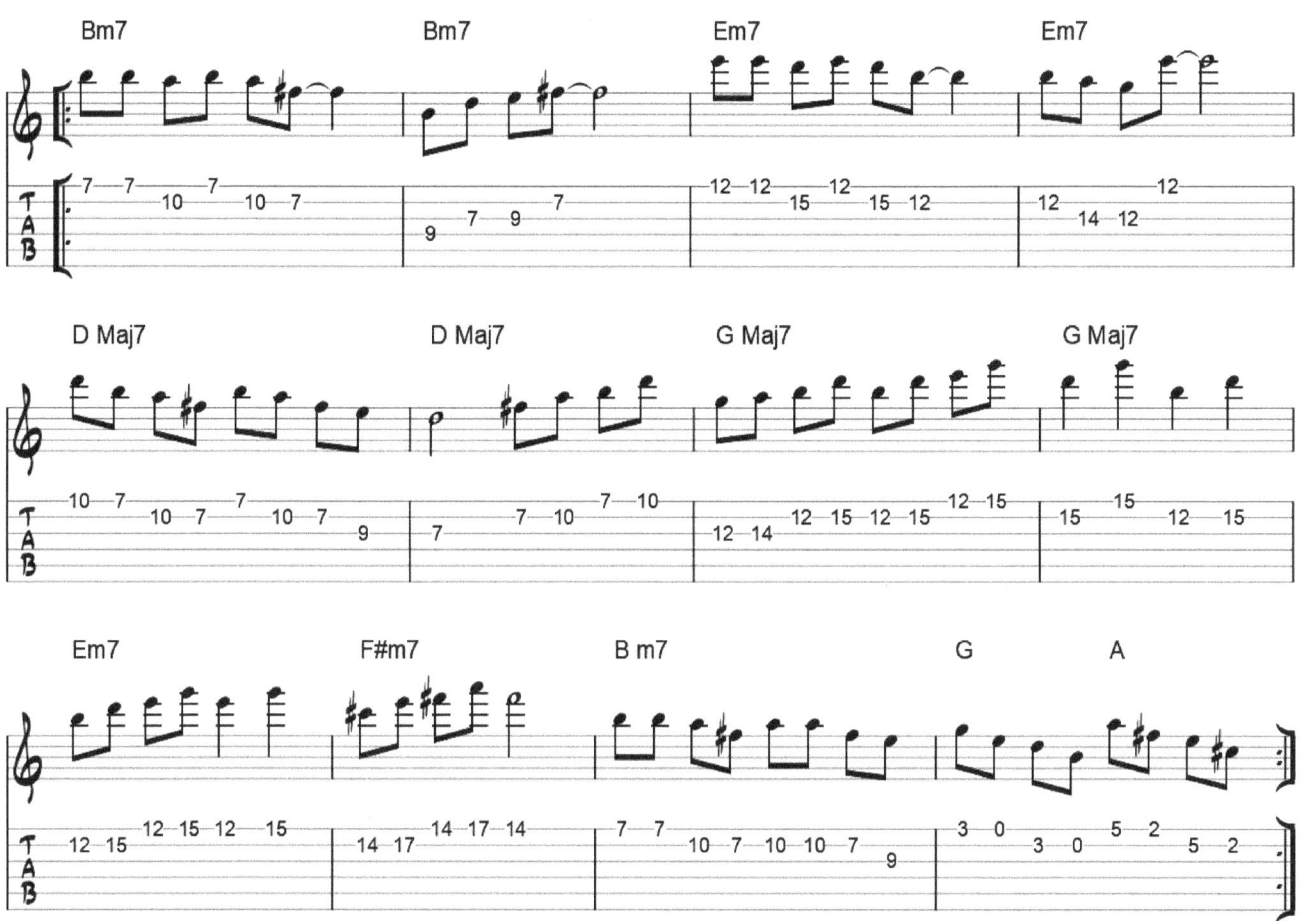

Follow-along Backing Tracks
www.LeadGuitarWorkshop.com

SUMMARY

We are musicians. We are guitar players.
We learn the language of music, Melody, Harmony, and Rhythm.
We learn the craft of playing the guitar as an instrument.
Always make your music decisions first and then go to your instrument/guitar.

MUSICIAN

- There are only 12 notes. (ABCDEFG are the Natural notes and there are 5 accidentals.)
- EF and BC are a ½ step apart (smallest distance).
- There are only 12 Major chords, 12 minor chords, 12 Major pentatonics, 12 minor pentatonics, each based on one of the 12 notes.
- There are two inherent sounds of a Pentatonic scale, Major and minor (to match its respective chord).
- The **Blues Scale** is playing a minor pentatonic over a Major chord.
- There is a **relative minor to every Major** (1½ steps below the Major root). This means two-for-one.
- For soloing, match a scale to its chord.
- Playing **Globally** equals 1 scale for all the chords.
- **Playing the changes** equals playing a scale for each chord. This "talks" directly to each chord, giving you its chord tones and color tones.

GUITAR PLAYER

- The 12 notes are the first 12 frets on the guitar that we navigate on the lowest E string.
- We use the "**Rock and Roll Rule**" to put pattern #1 on the fretboard after making the music decision about what scale we need.
- There are **5 patterns** to connect our 12 fret fretboard for all 12 keys.
- We learned how to use **BSSBS to play a minor pentatonic scale and SSBSB to play a Major pentatonic scale on any one string**.
- We learned how to use **OCTAVE SHAPES** as a playable sounds as well as using them to unlock the fretboard.
- Use pattern #1 to get started with **PLAYING THE CHANGES**.

CHAPTER 4

TUNE IN

"I am a musician and a guitar player. Music is my language and my guitar is my voice. Music is Melody, Harmony and Rhythm. I develop my language skills and my instrument skills. They are two separate worlds working together to complete the circle of music."

Rhythm is the number one factor to sounding great as a musician.

WARM UP

Muted String Ladder (MSL) 4 Strings

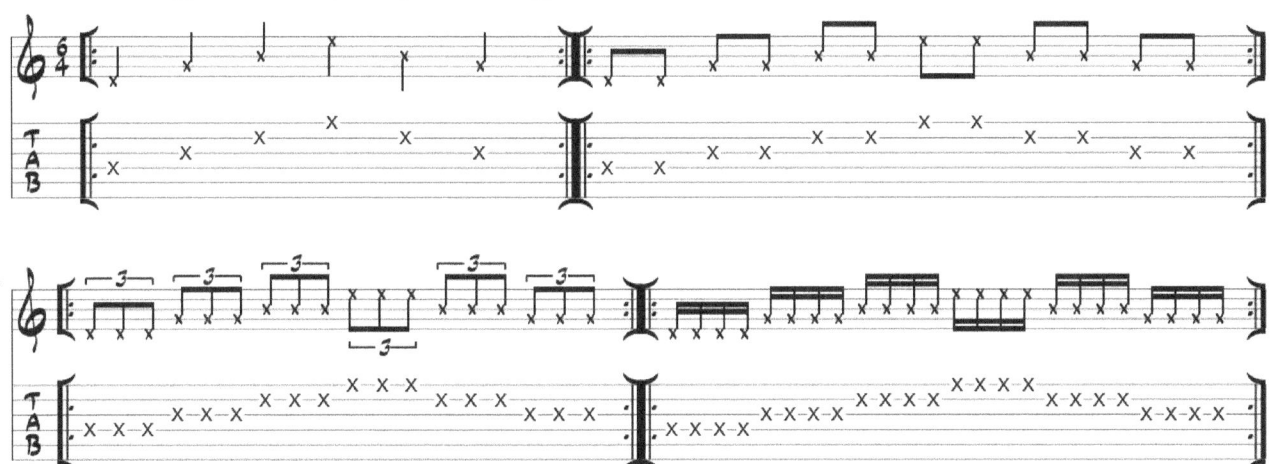

SHELLS

SHELL 1 3 4 quarter-notes

SHELLS

SHELL 1 3 4 eighth-notes

CHANGE GEARS

Alternating on two adjacent strings. Tempo 60-90 BPM

EXERCISE

Play pattern #1 as a Major pentatonic and play through the 12 keys in the circle of 4ths. Descend the scale for one octave.

CIRCLE OF 4ths

C F Bb Eb Ab Db Gb/F# B E A D G

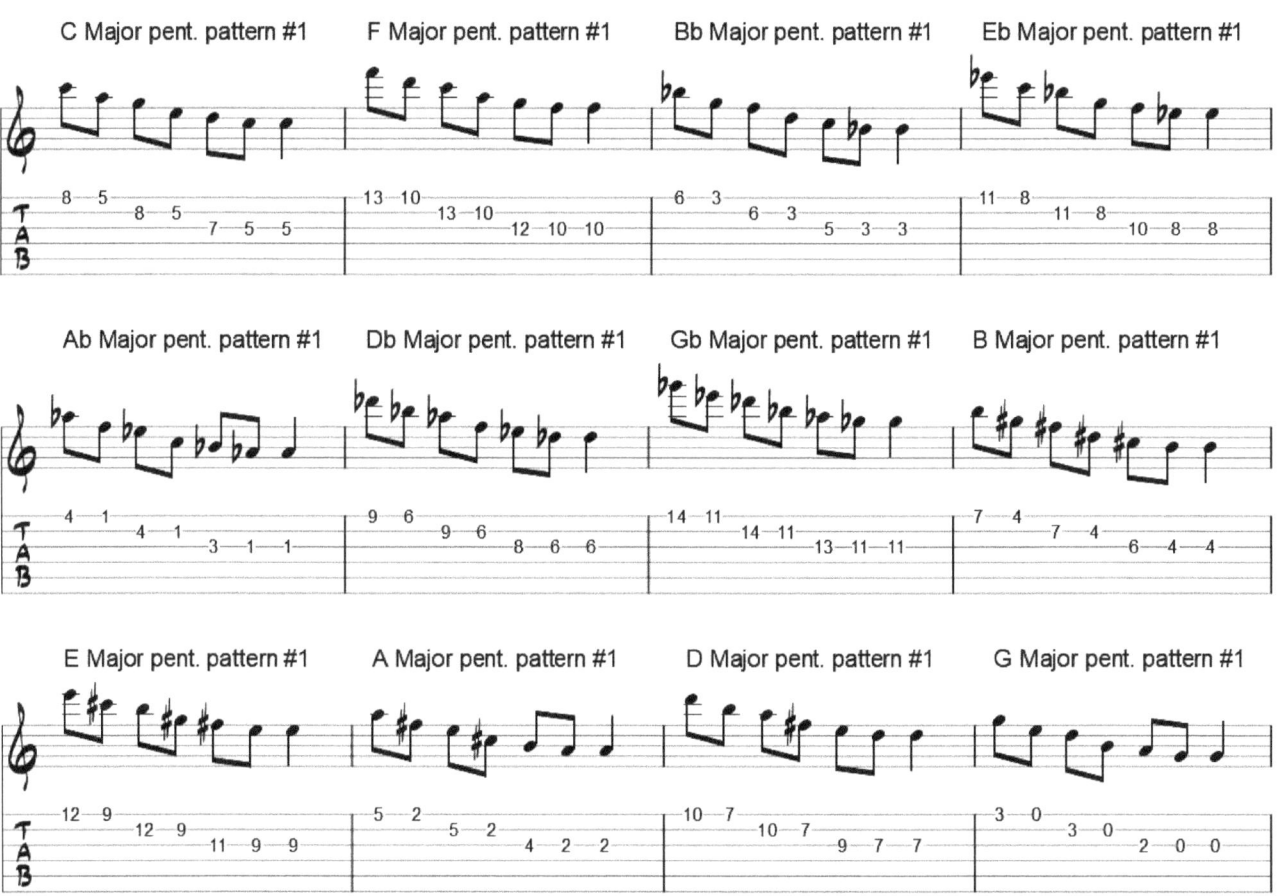

The 5 Patterns of C Major/A minor pentatonic are on the following page, starting with #1 at the top, all the way down to pattern #5. At the bottom is the summation of the 5 patterns across the 12 fret fretboard.

5 Patterns for C Major/A minor

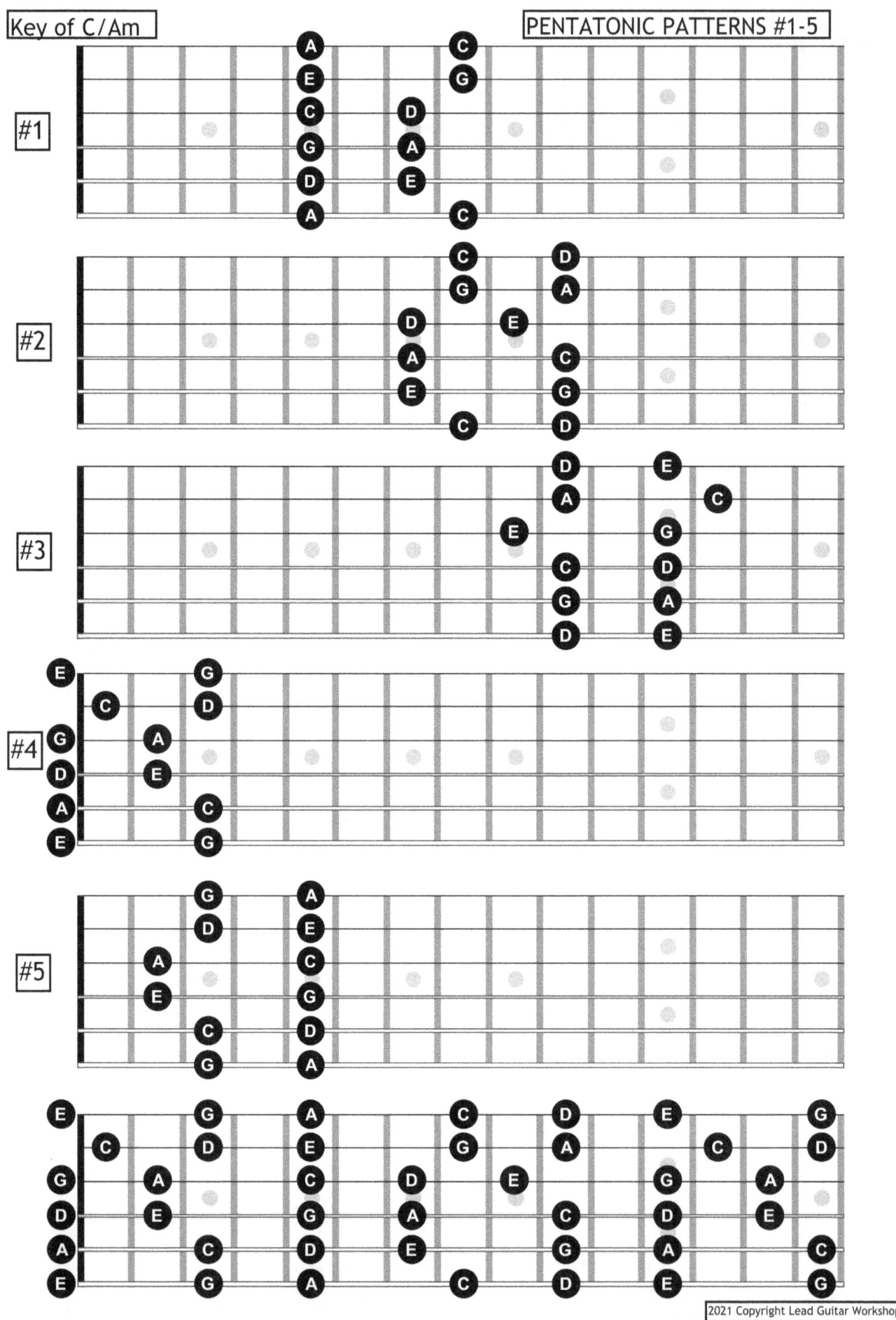

REVIEW

When we solo or create melodies we usually have two options: we can play "globally" and use one scale for all the chords or "play the changes" and directly relate to each chord with its own scale/chord tones. We can mix an match the two strategies as well. There is no rule as to when to play the changes (although it is often necessary when the chords are not in the same key).

As a musician one of the hardest things to do when playing the changes is to constantly keep track of the chords in your head. They have to be there. You have to know where you are at all moments if you wish to take advantage of each chord's sound.

When playing the changes, you simply match a scale to the chord. Major chord gets a Major pentatonic and a minor chord gets a minor pentatonic. Remember that each pentatonic has the three notes of the chord plus two color tones. The Blues Scale (minor pentatonic over a major chord) is usually is reserved for the "main" chord of the song, although you can work it on other chords. You just have to try it out. Stevie Ray Vaughn does this in "Couldn't Stand the Weather" where he plays a B minor pentatonic over the B minor chord (main chord) then an A minor pentatonic over an A7 chord and G minor pentatonic over the G7 chord.

As a guitar player you can think of playing the changes like moving bar chords. At first you learn one shape (bar chord) that can play all 12 Major chords. (You probably first learned E form bar chord to use as the full F bar chord). But you soon realize you have to slide up and down a lot when using one shape. This is the same feeling when we use pattern #1 for all chords, Major and minor. You end up moving the same shape (pattern #1) up and down the fretboard. This is easy to look at and follow, but can sometimes feel tedious and monotonous. Later in the book we will discuss the advantages and challenges of using different pentatonic patterns to play the changes.

No matter what instrument and what style, playing the changes just sounds right. You could argue that you do play the changes when you play globally by resolving to different notes in the scale that best relate to the chord of the moment. How ever you look at it, when you directly "talk" to each chord as you solo/play melodies, it sounds fantastic. You will find there are so many approaches to playing the changes, both musically and instrumentally.

CAGED

The CAGED system is a method for guitar players that helps associate chord shapes with scale positions. It helps connect your whole fretboard. This doesn't change the sound at all. CAGED is not a music thing, but a guitar thing. There are 5 chord shapes on the guitar that connect the 12 frets. You use the five CAGED shapes to make the SAME chord (musically). We can correlate them to the five pentatonic shapes (and even the MODE shapes).

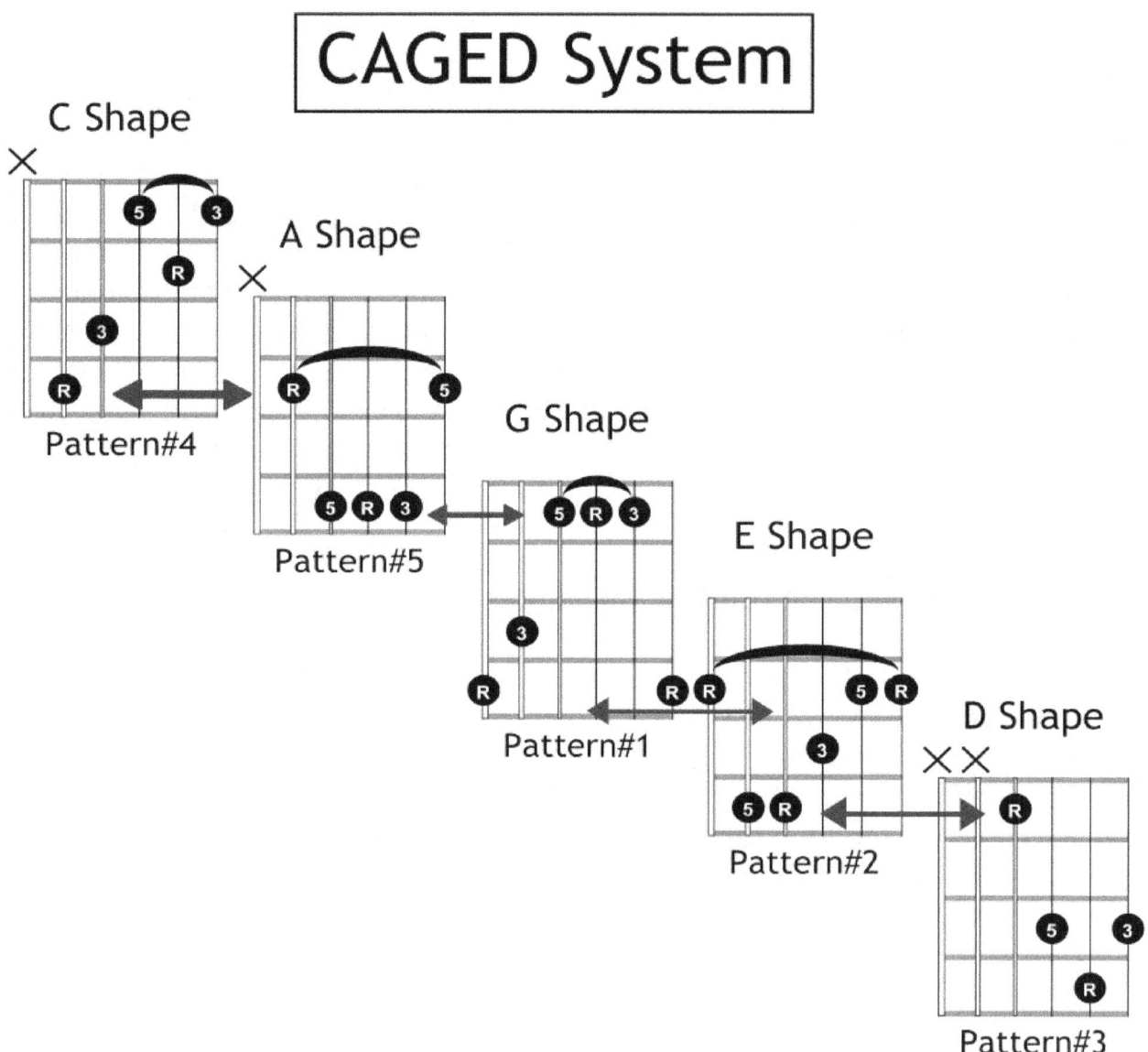

Here is a more detailed look at each chord shape and its correlating pentatonic pattern. Each shape and scale has some pros and cons

Chord Shape/Pentatonic Pattern	Comments
C Shape Pattern #4	CHORD: Although this is hard to play it is a great sounding chord to add to your vocabulary. You will also use parts of this as inversions (3 strings at a time). SCALE: To me pattern #4 is like Pattern #1 starting on the A string.
A Shape Pattern #5	CHORD: This is one of your two most used bar chords. The straight 3 notes in the shape are a great guide to help connect to the G shape, and it is also used for its inversion shape. SCALE: Pattern #5 is the easiest to remember. It is always available under your A form bar chord.
G Shape Pattern #1	CHORD: This chord shape is tricky. You will rarely play the whole shape. You will play sections of it. The inner four strings are an inversion that Hendrix used all of the time. SCALE: Even though this is our most recognizable pattern, it is so often overlooked as a Major pentatonic because of the awkwardness of having the pinky be the root note on the E strings.

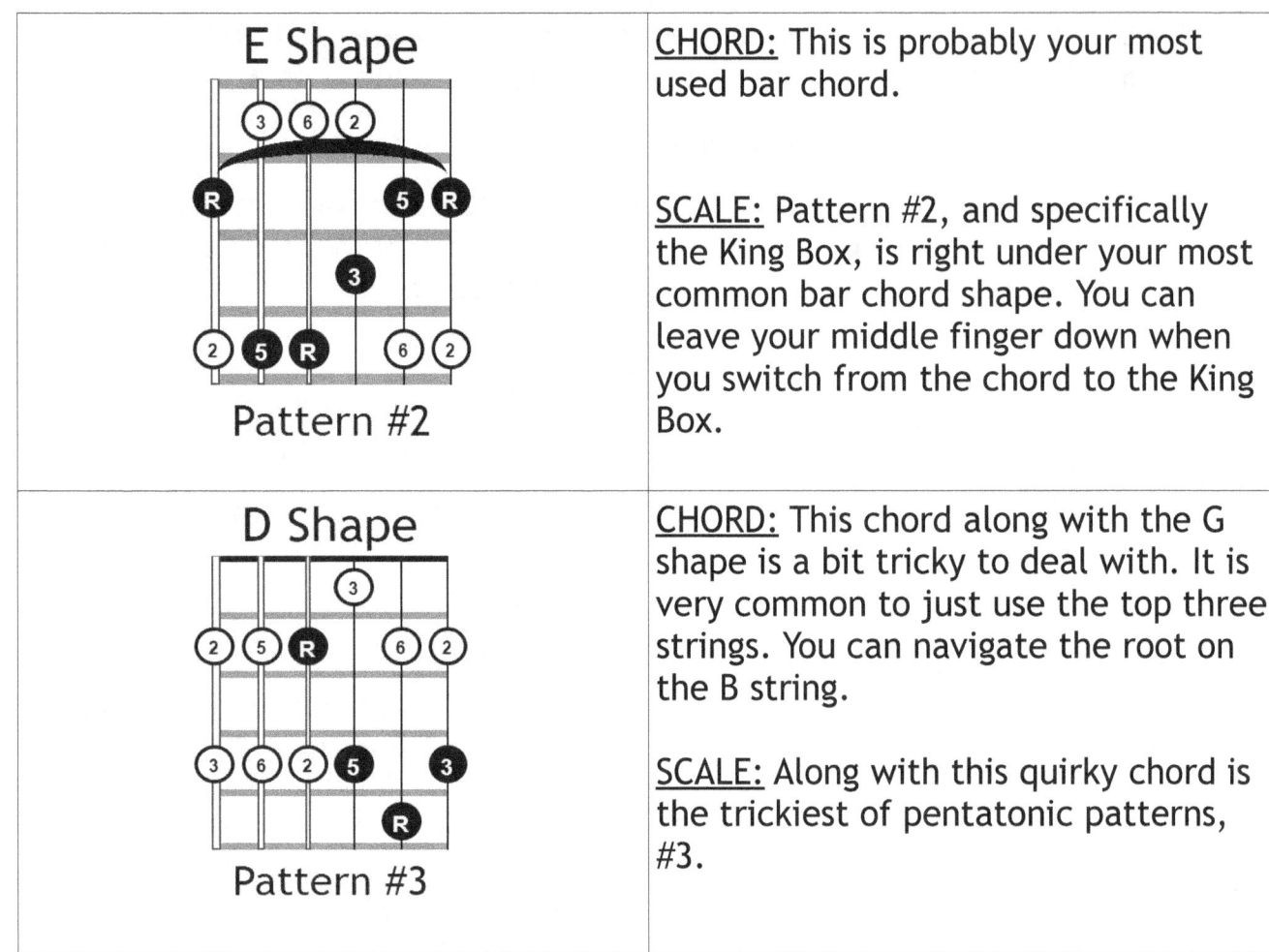

| E Shape — Pattern #2 | CHORD: This is probably your most used bar chord.

SCALE: Pattern #2, and specifically the King Box, is right under your most common bar chord shape. You can leave your middle finger down when you switch from the chord to the King Box. |
| D Shape — Pattern #3 | CHORD: This chord along with the G shape is a bit tricky to deal with. It is very common to just use the top three strings. You can navigate the root on the B string.

SCALE: Along with this quirky chord is the trickiest of pentatonic patterns, #3. |

Focus on the shapes you use the most. Most likely the E and A shape bar chords are the most used. They are Pattern #2 and Pattern #5 respectively.

Arpeggios are more than the physical chord shape. The arpeggio is R 3 5. It is not possible to play more than 1 note per string. This limits us in our ability to play the complete triad simultaneously. You have to remember that any R, 3, and 5 are the chord tones (arpeggio) not just the ones in your fingering for your chord.

On the following page are the five CAGED shapes. Each shape is shown with its correlating pentatonic pattern.

It is really helpful to keep in mind that chords and scales are part of the same information and share the same space.

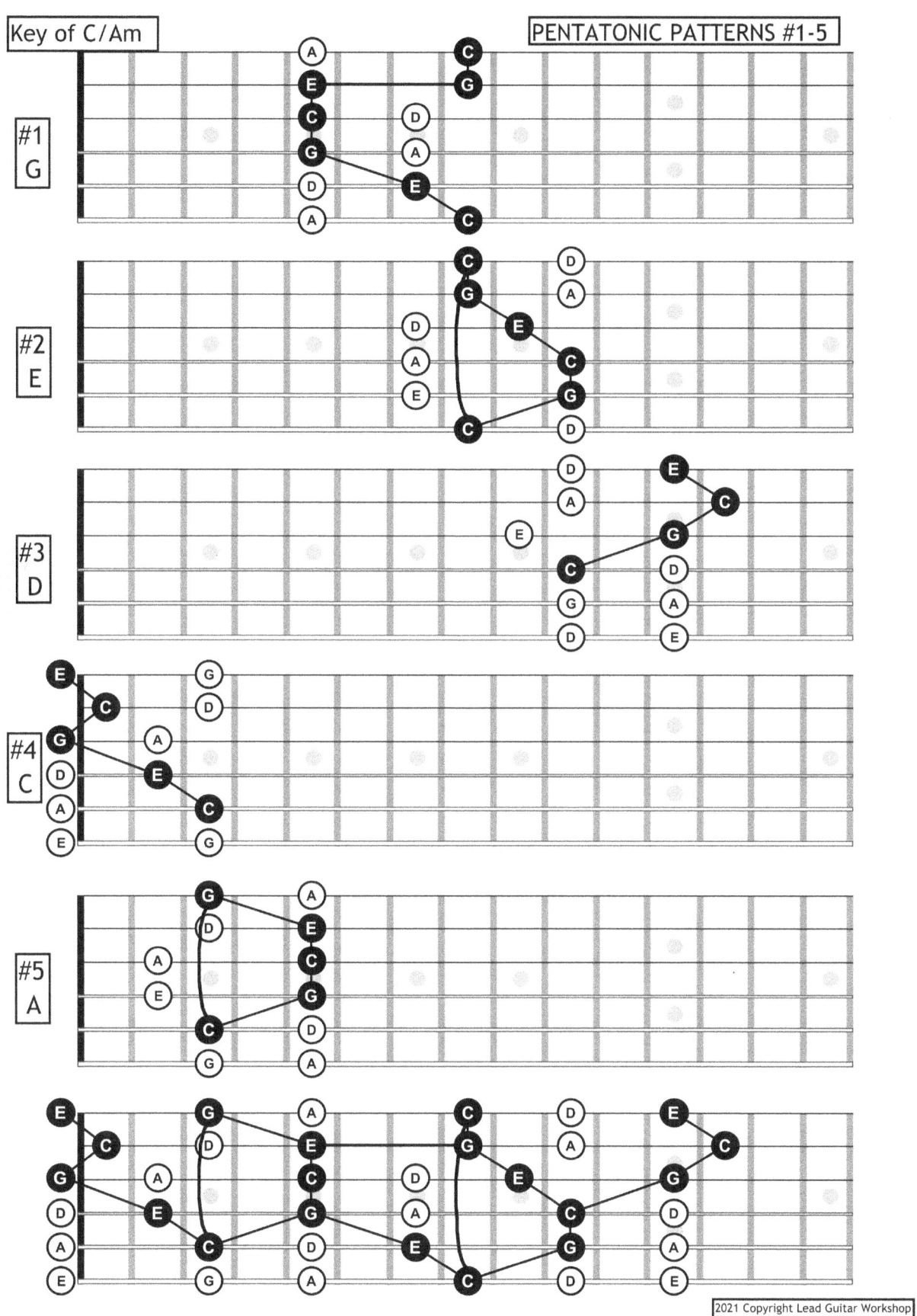

CAGED Relative minor

There is also the relative minor. Each minor chord for CAGED also has a pentatonic pattern that it is associated with.

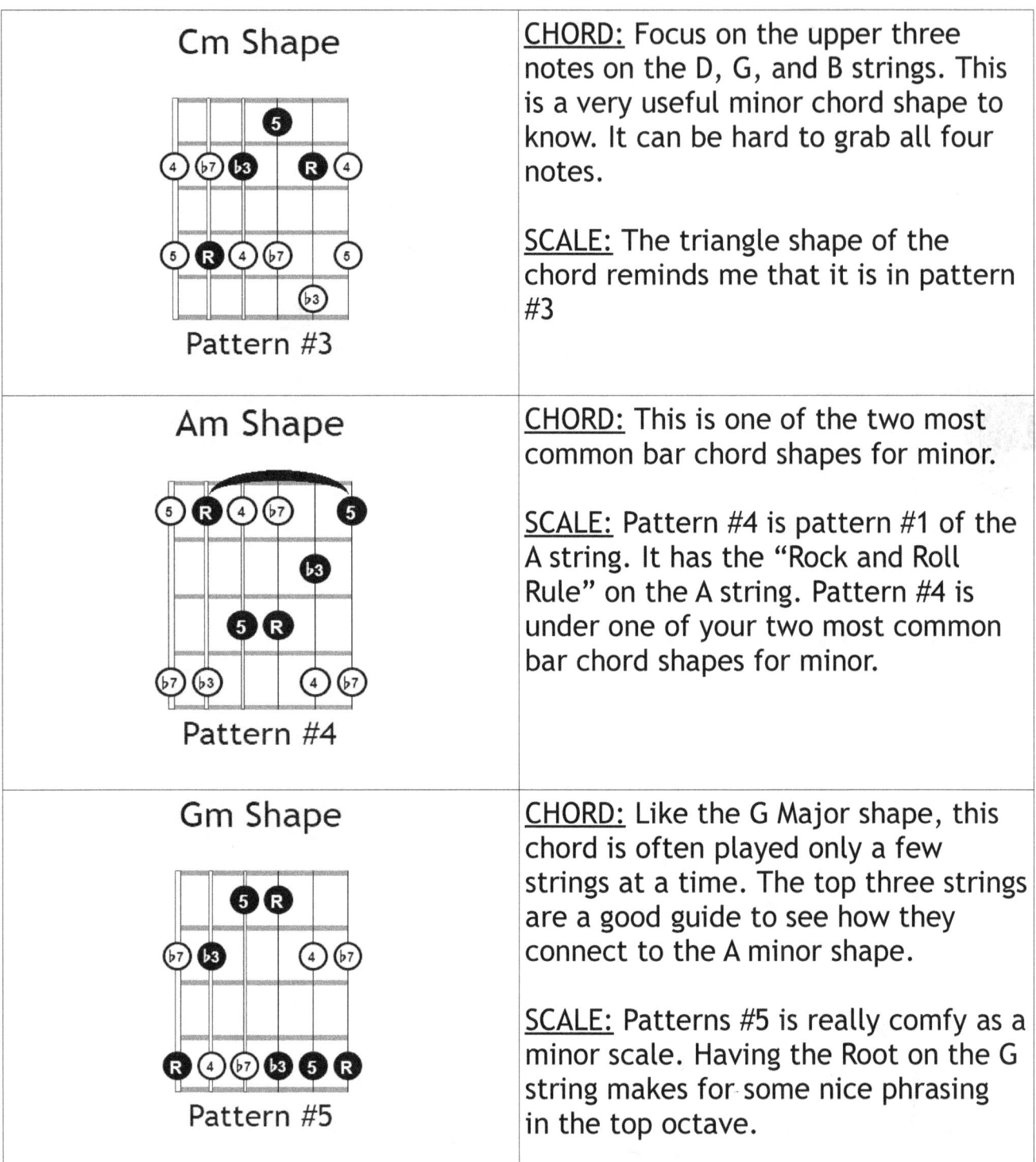

Cm Shape (Pattern #3)	**CHORD:** Focus on the upper three notes on the D, G, and B strings. This is a very useful minor chord shape to know. It can be hard to grab all four notes.
	SCALE: The triangle shape of the chord reminds me that it is in pattern #3
Am Shape (Pattern #4)	**CHORD:** This is one of the two most common bar chord shapes for minor.
	SCALE: Pattern #4 is pattern #1 of the A string. It has the "Rock and Roll Rule" on the A string. Pattern #4 is under one of your two most common bar chord shapes for minor.
Gm Shape (Pattern #5)	**CHORD:** Like the G Major shape, this chord is often played only a few strings at a time. The top three strings are a good guide to see how they connect to the A minor shape.
	SCALE: Patterns #5 is really comfy as a minor scale. Having the Root on the G string makes for some nice phrasing in the top octave.

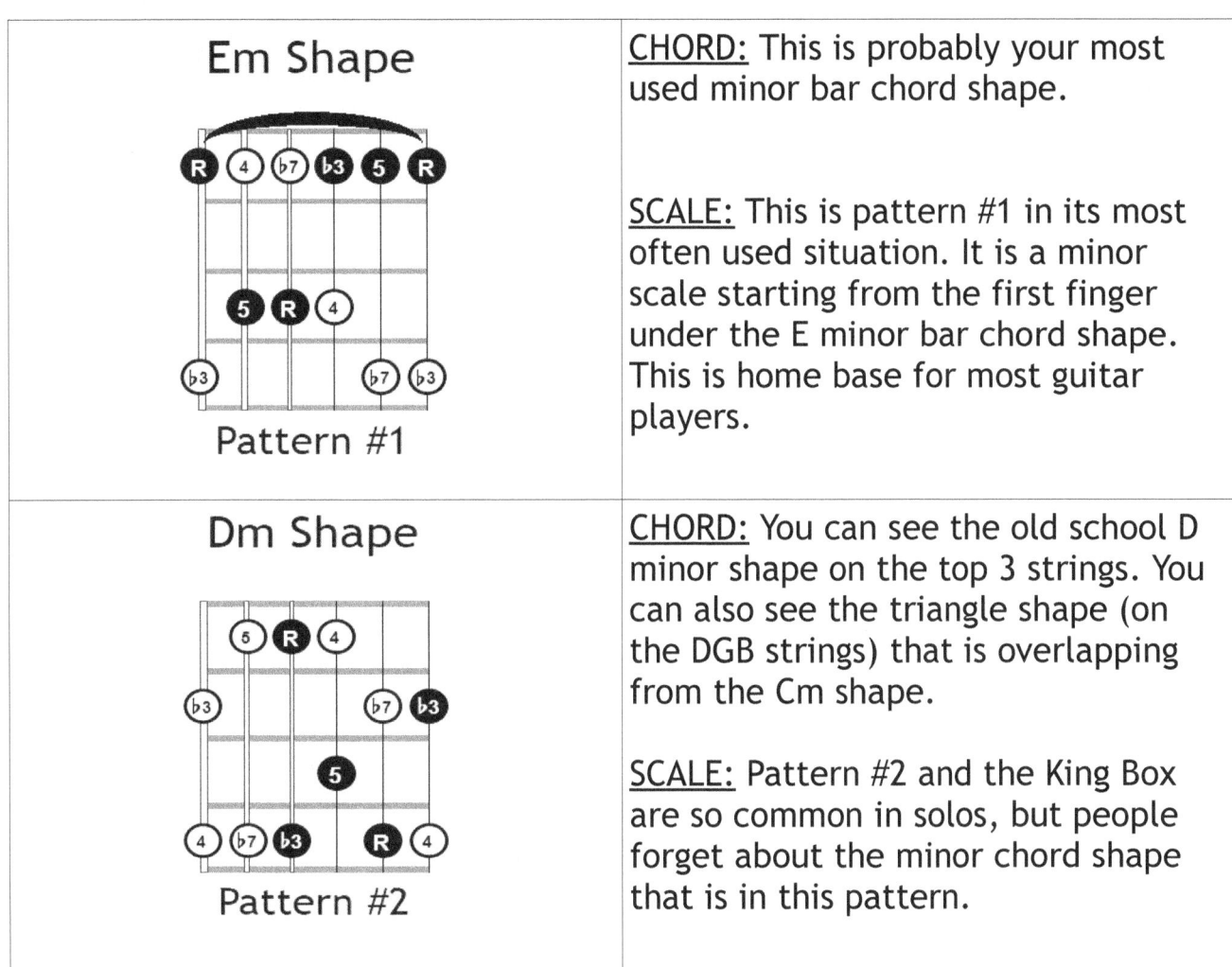

Em Shape (Pattern #1)	**CHORD:** This is probably your most used minor bar chord shape. **SCALE:** This is pattern #1 in its most often used situation. It is a minor scale starting from the first finger under the E minor bar chord shape. This is home base for most guitar players.
Dm Shape (Pattern #2)	**CHORD:** You can see the old school D minor shape on the top 3 strings. You can also see the triangle shape (on the DGB strings) that is overlapping from the Cm shape. **SCALE:** Pattern #2 and the King Box are so common in solos, but people forget about the minor chord shape that is in this pattern.

Focus on the E and A forms. These are the bar chord shapes you use the most. Get to know which scales go with each shape.

E Major BAR FORM	Pattern #2
E minor BAR FORM	Pattern #1
A Major BAR FORM	Pattern #5
A minor BAR FORM	Pattern #4

On the following page are the five minor shapes of CAGED shown with its correlating pentatonic patterns.

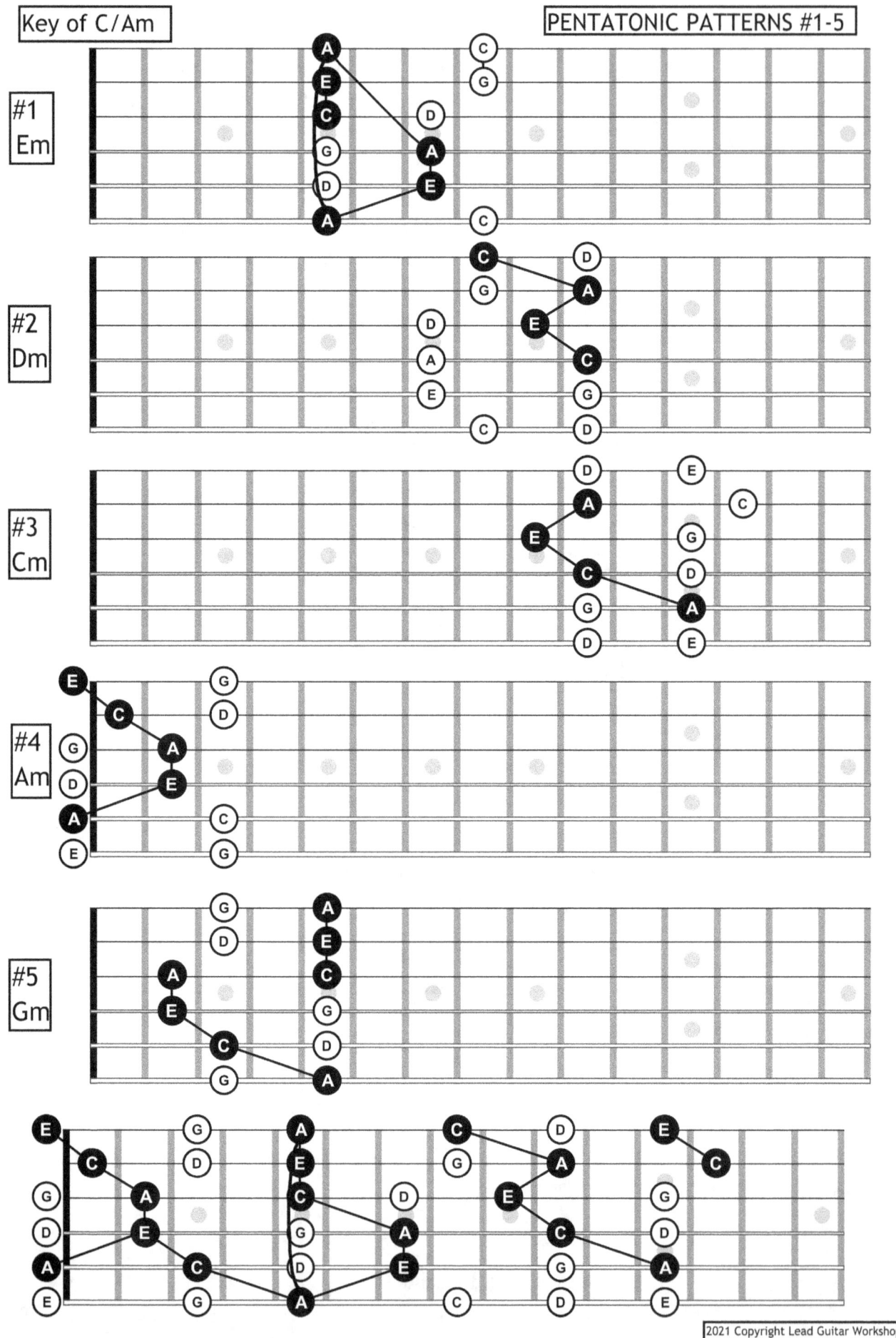

Key of C / Am

PENTATONIC PATTERNS #1-5

#1
Em

#2
Dm

#3
Cm

#4
Am

#5
Gm

PRACTICE

Self generate CAGED with C Major pentatonic. Use the CAGED chord shape and its corresponding scale pattern. Descend from highest note in the pattern.

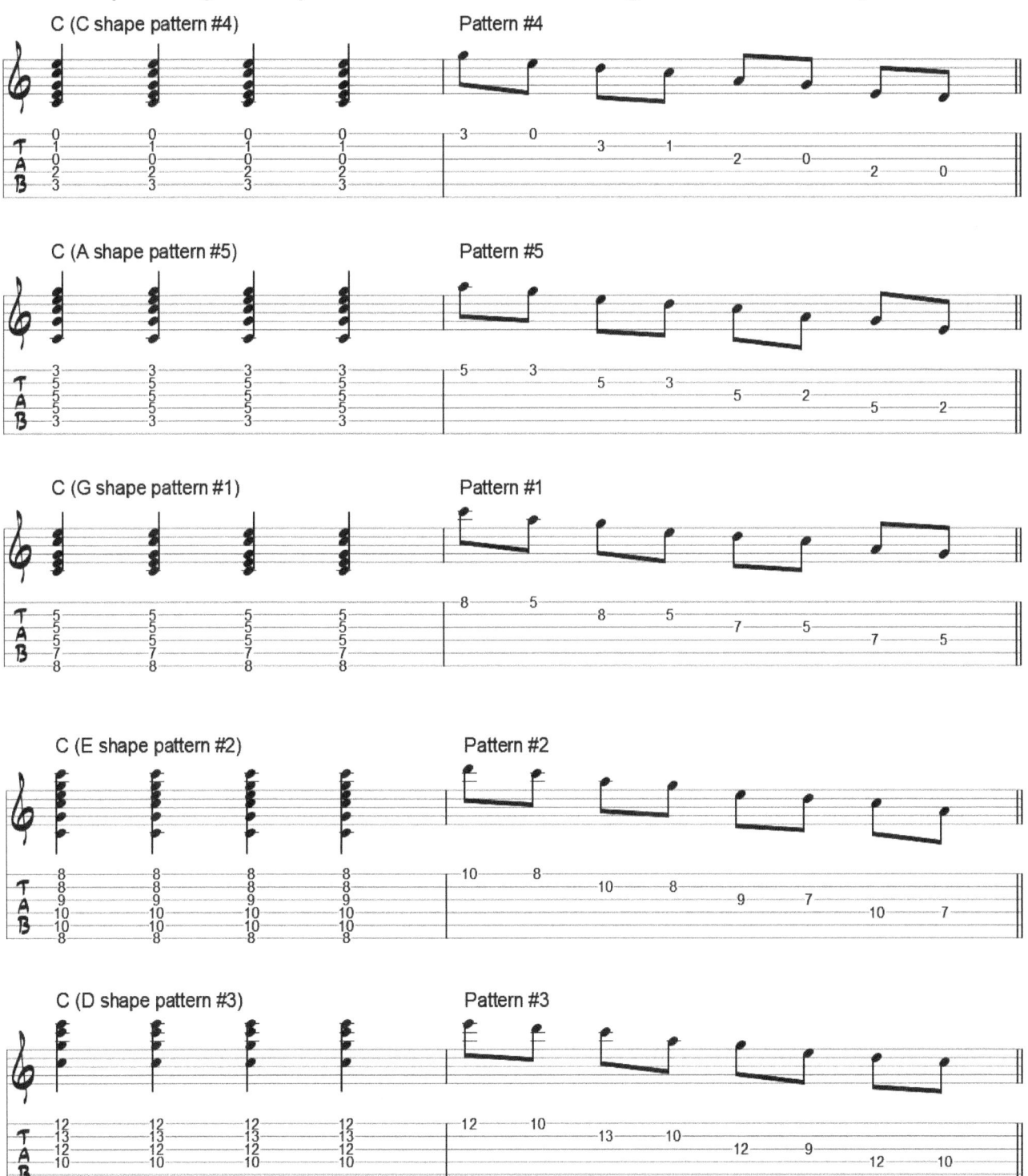

Self-Gen CAGED with A minor pentatonic

Self generate CAGED with A minor pentatonic. Use the CAGED chord shape and its corresponding scale pattern. Descend from highest note in pattern.

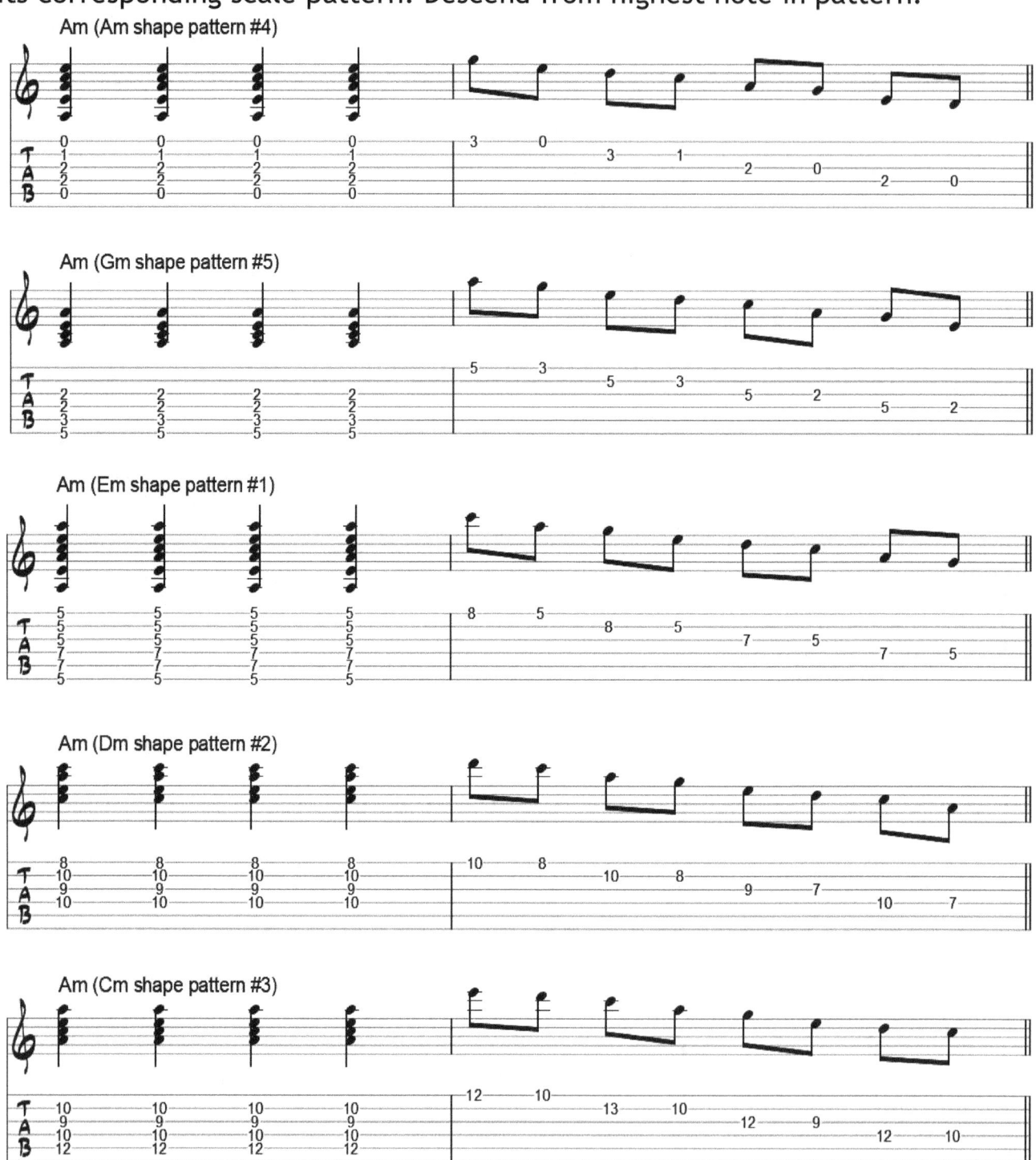

SUMMARY

We are musicians. We are guitar players.
We learn the language of music, Melody, Harmony, and Rhythm.
We learn the craft of playing the guitar as an instrument.
Always make your music decisions first and then go to your instrument/guitar.

MUSICIAN

- There are only 12 notes. (ABCDEFG are the Natural notes and there are 5 accidentals.)
- EF and BC are a ½ step apart (smallest distance).
- There are only 12 Major chords, 12 minor chords, 12 Major pentatonics, 12 minor pentatonics each based on one of the 12 notes.
- There are two inherent sounds of a Pentatonic scale, Major and minor (to match its respective chord).
- The **Blues Scale** is playing a minor pentatonic over a Major chord.
- There is a **relative minor to every Major** (1½ steps below the Major root). This means two-for-one.
- For soloing, match a scale to its chord.
- Playing **Globally** equals 1 scale for all the chords.
- **Playing the changes** equals a scale per chord. This "talks" directly to each chord, giving you its chord tones and color tones.

GUITAR PLAYER

- The 12 notes are the first 12 frets on the guitar that we navigate on the lowest E string.
- We use the "**Rock and Roll Rule**" to put pattern #1 on the fretboard after making the music decision about what scale we need.
- There are **5 patterns** to connect our 12 fret fretboard for all 12 keys.
- We learned how to use **BSSBS** to play a minor pentatonic scale and **SSBSB** to play a Major pentatonic scale on any one string.
- We learned how to use **OCTAVE SHAPES** as a playable sounds as well as using them to unlock the fretboard.
- Use pattern #1 to get started with **PLAYING THE CHANGES**.
- Use the **CAGED** system to connect chord shapes to scale shapes.

CHAPTER 5

TUNE IN

"I am a musician and a guitar player. Music is my language and my guitar is my voice. Music is Melody, Harmony and Rhythm. I develop my language skills and my instrument skills. They are two separate worlds working together to complete the circle of music."

Rhythm is the number one factor to sounding great as a musician.

WARM UP

Muted String Ladder (MSL) All 6 strings.

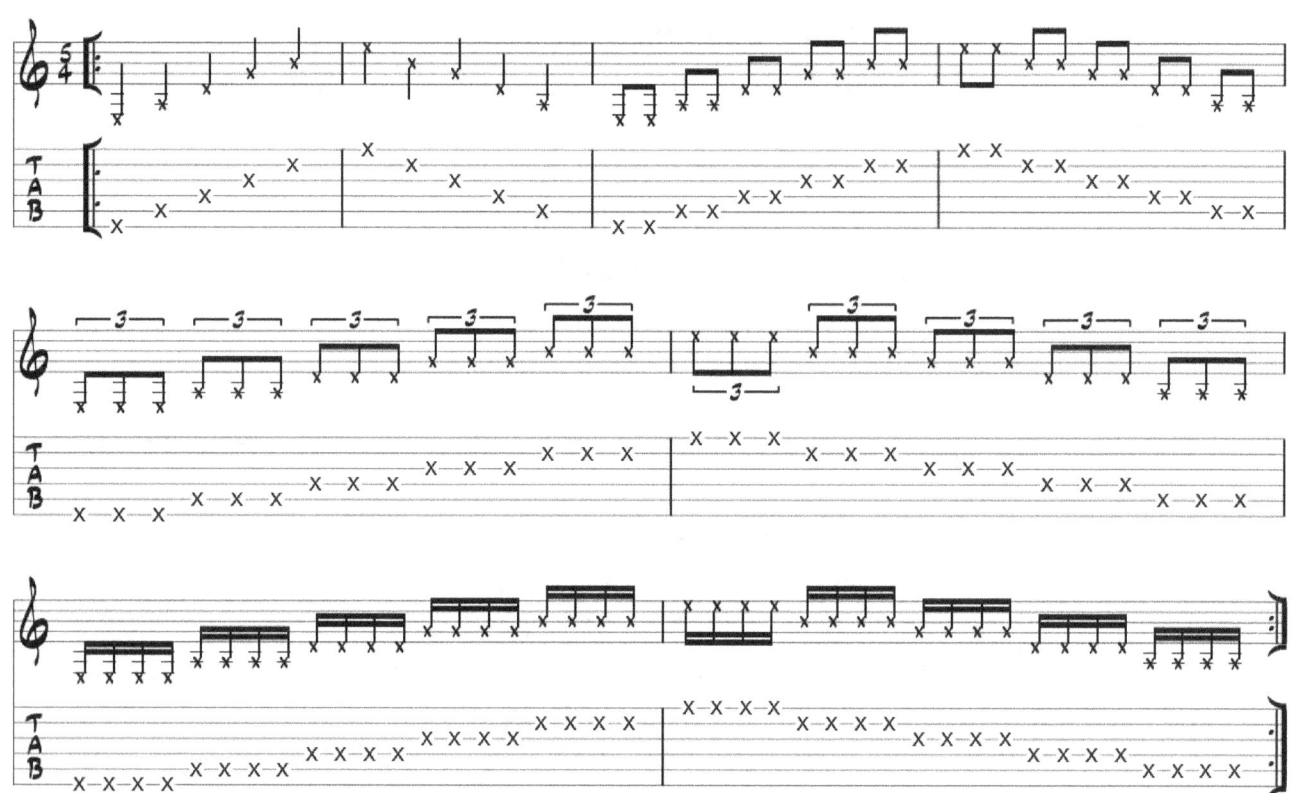

SHELLS

1 3 4 as triplets.

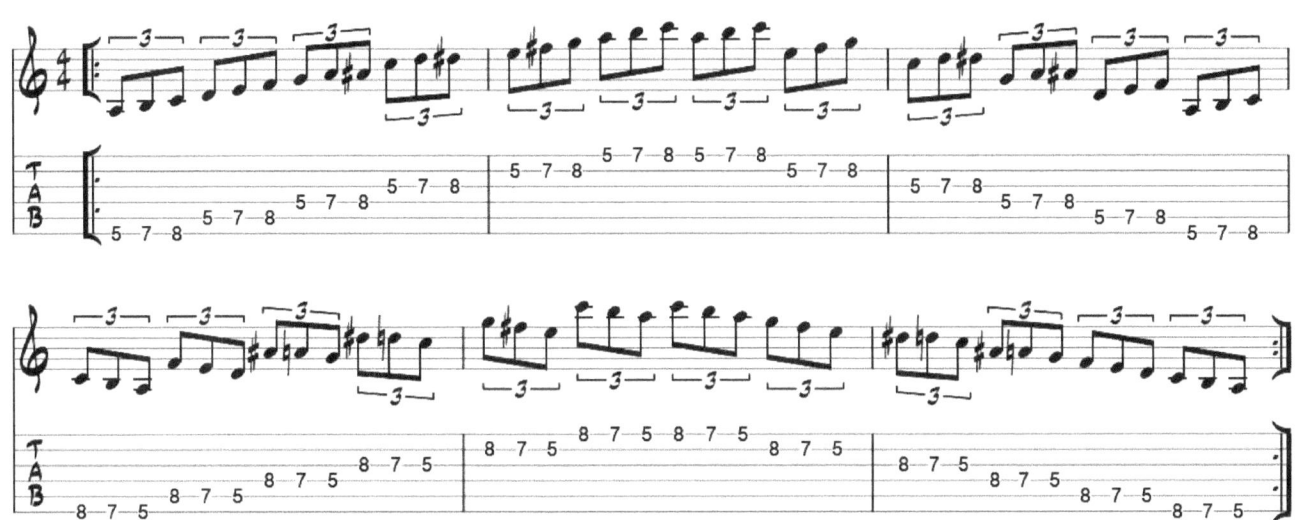

CHANGE GEARS

QUARTER-NOTE LADDER

Play a quarter-note on the B string and Change Gears every other beat on the high E string.

EIGHTH-NOTE LADDER

Play eighth-notes on the B string and Change Gears on the high E string.

EXERCISE

Self generate CAGED with C Major pentatonic. Use the CAGED chord shape and its corresponding scale pattern. Descend from highest note in the pattern.

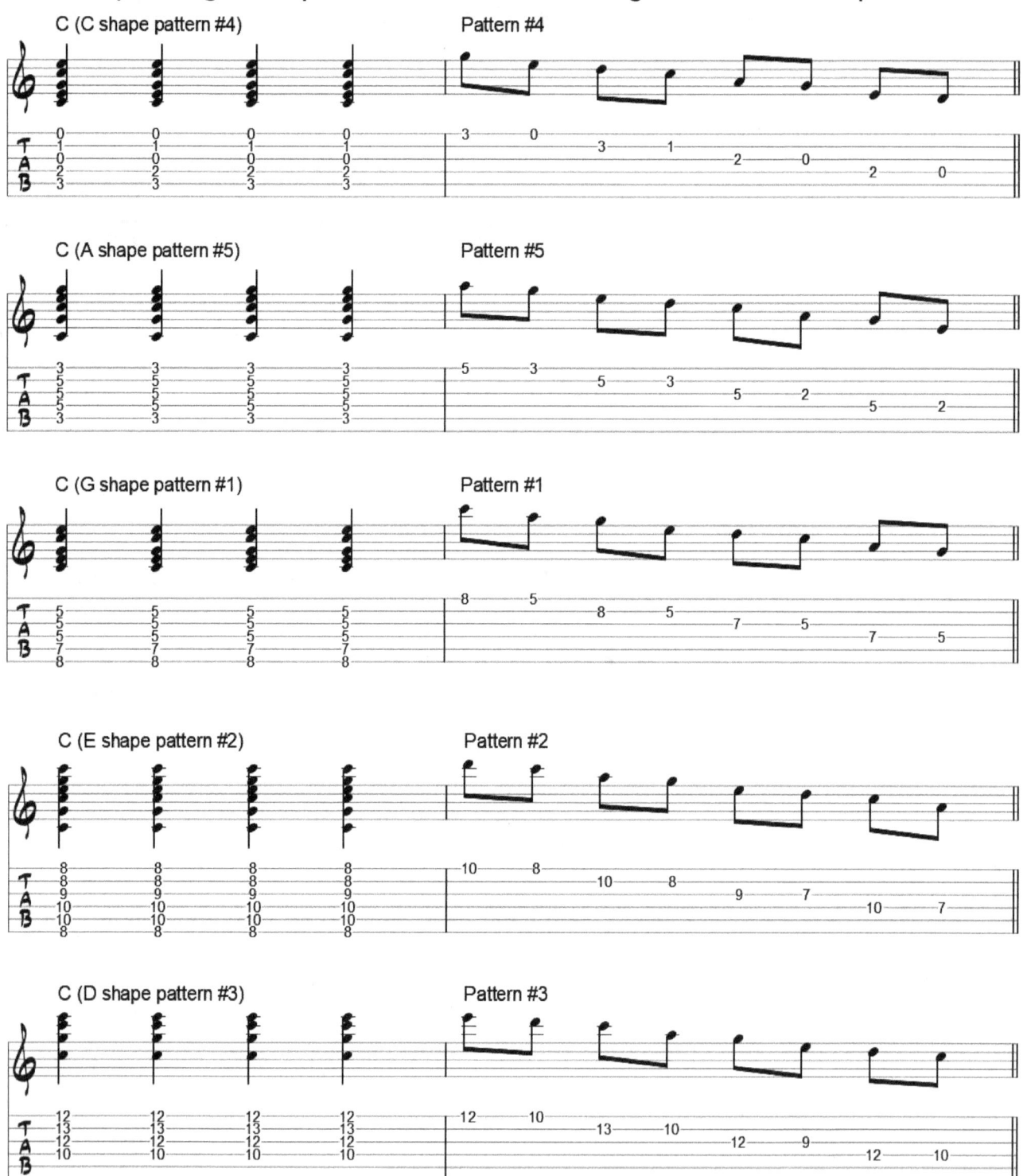

REVIEW

CAGED is a great tool for guitar players to help keep track of chord shapes and scale shapes. CAGED represents the five open chord shapes used; C chord, A chord, G chord, E chord, and D chord. All of them are the open position shape, but when you move the shape you need to appropriately bar any open strings relative to the chord shape. I like to think of this as "Mother Nature's capo."

CAGED System

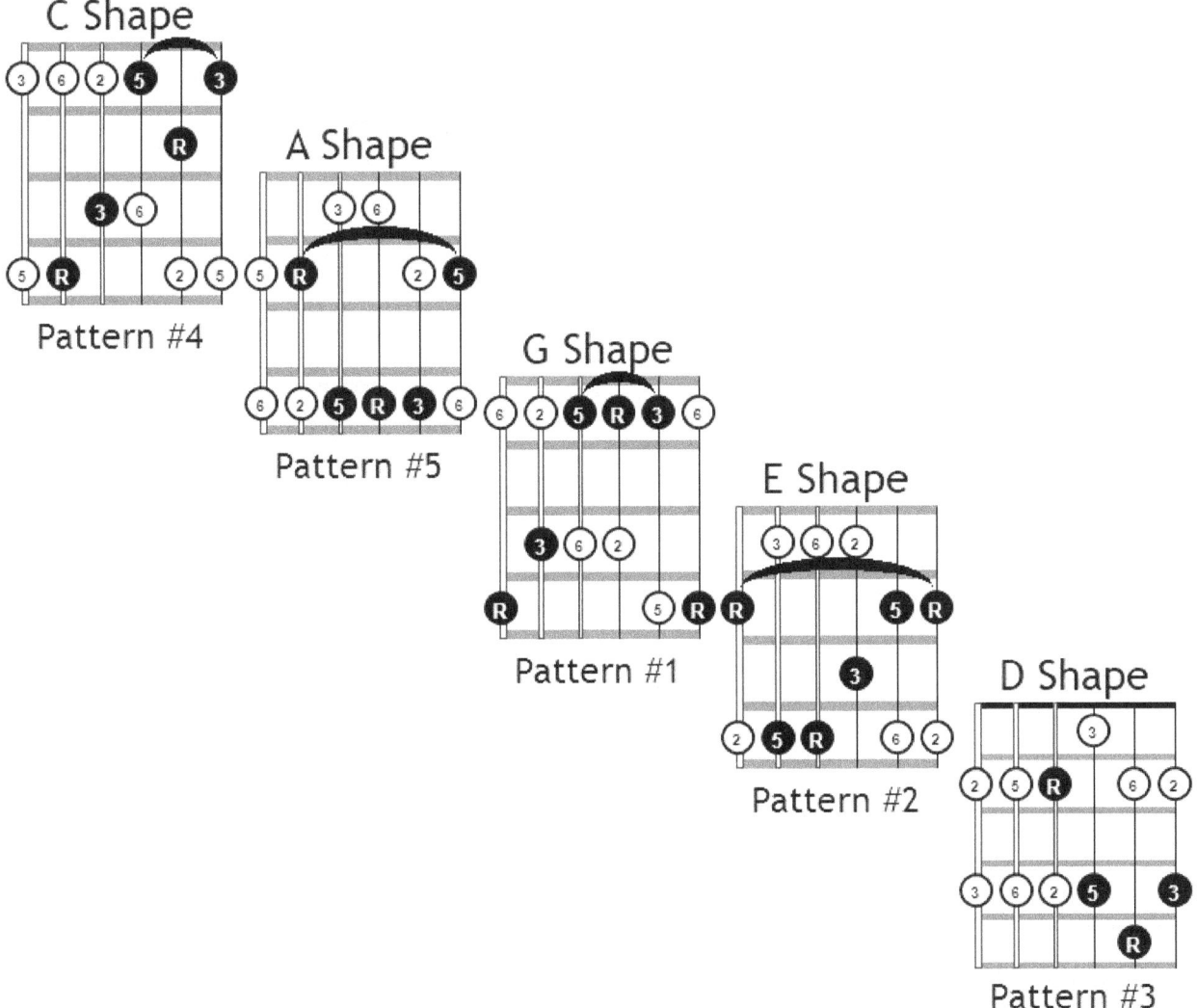

Watch CAGED video
www.LeadGuitarWorkshop.com

There are 5 chord shapes for the Major chords and 5 for the minor chords. The relative Major/minor relationship reminds us that any one of the pentatonic shapes has both the relative Major and relative minor chord and scale in it.

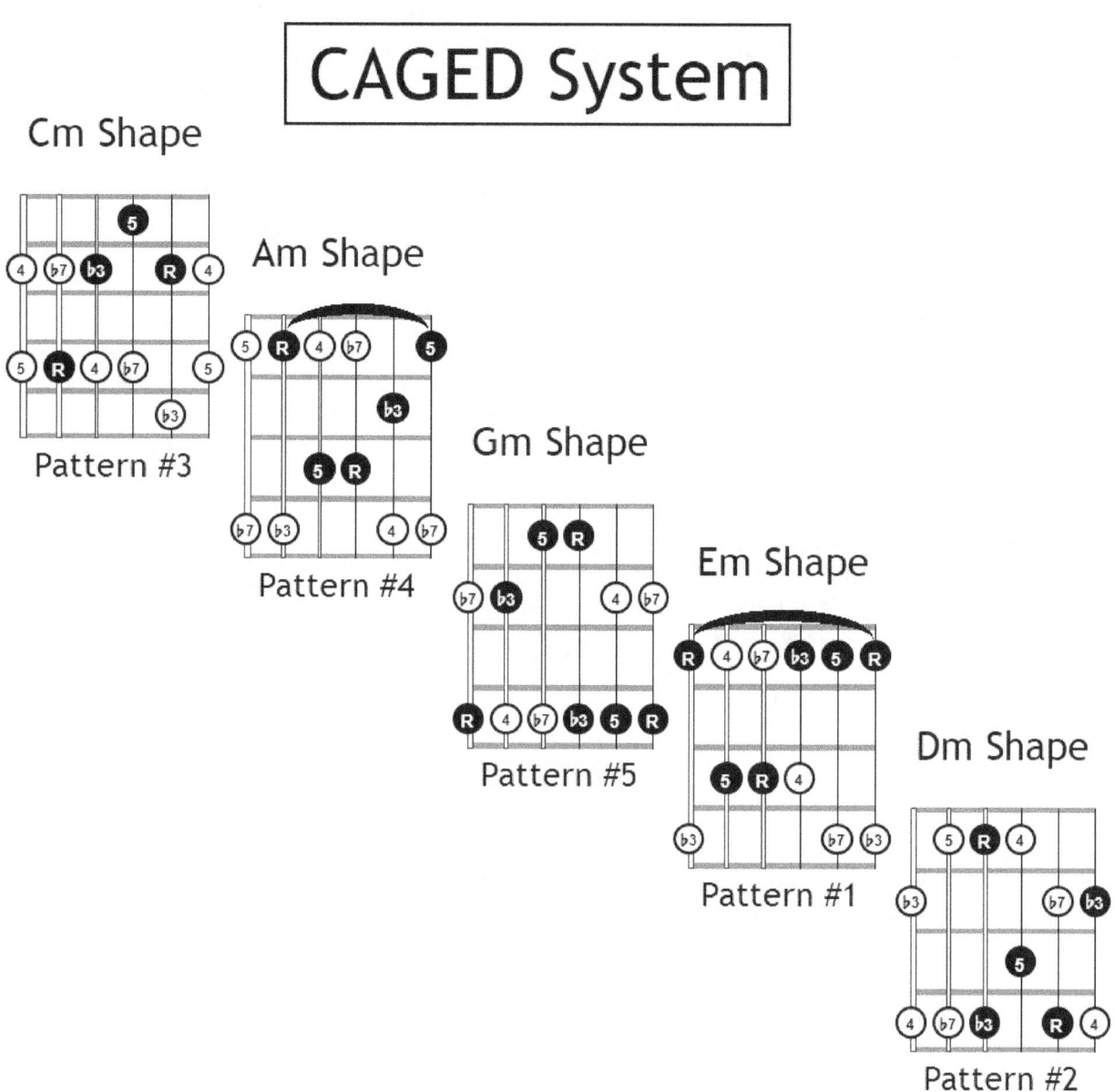

CAGED System

Cm Shape — Pattern #3

Am Shape — Pattern #4

Gm Shape — Pattern #5

Em Shape — Pattern #1

Dm Shape — Pattern #2

SEQUENCES

A sequence is a musical idea that refers to the patterns we apply to groups of notes and scales. As we have seen, one of the most often used sequence is a 3 note sequence. If you simply numbered every note in a scale, a 3 note sequence would be 123, 234, 345, 456, 567, and continuing through the scale.

There are endless possibilities with sequences. They are so useful because they are very musical to listen to, and that makes them great for composing and soloing. They are great for your ear, they give you an aural expectation. They are fantastic for your instrumental chops (abilities), as they get you playing all the combinations of notes, not just the ones that are easy for your fingers.

4 Note Sequence

After the 3 note sequence, the next most common one I see is simply a 4 note sequence. If you think of the scale in numbers then this would translate to 1234, 2345, 3456, 4567, and continuing to the end of the scale.

Leap Frog Sequence

This is a fantastic and familiar sounding sequence. In terms of numbers it would be: 1 3, 2 4, 3 5, 4 6, 5 7, and continuing until the end of the scale.

General Ideas about Sequences

- Any musical phrase can be sequenced.

- Sequences can ascend and descend.

- They can be played with any rhythm (for example, eighth-notes, triplets, sixteenth-notes).

- They sound especially cool when the rhythm doesn't match the number of notes in the sequence. For example, try playing a 3 note sequence as eighth-notes or sixteenth-notes.

- You can "flip-flop" groups in a sequence. For example, in a 3 note sequence it would be 123, *432*, 345, *654*. You can see that every other group is reversed.

- You can mix and match groups. For example, alternate between a 3 and 4 note group to sequence 1234, 234, 3456, 456.

- Anytime you learn a new instrument, sequence scales!

PRE-BEND

When you think about bending a note on the guitar, it really involves two parts; the bend and the release of the bend. Once a bend is "up" you can hold that note as long as you want, especially if it is still sustaining (proper distortion and compression). As always, you have to think musically about bends to really take advantage of them. You are changing notes when you bend (assuming it's more than a ¼ step bend).

BEND

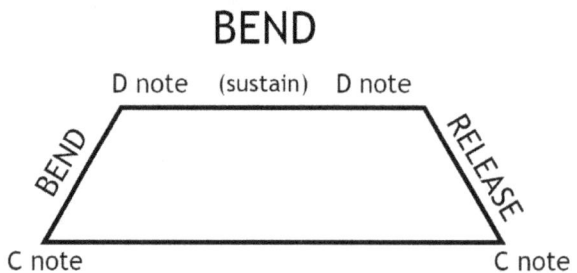

Pre-bend/Ghost bend

Bends usually go up in sound, regardless of which way you push the string. There is a way to just make the note go down in sound, and it is a pre-bend, also known as a ghost bend. For every bend there must be a release. (You can play either, or both.)

The idea is that you bend the string WITHOUT STRIKING IT. This is really hard because you have to have a very good feel for bends to do this properly. Once the note is bent, you strike the note and at some point just release the bend. The result is that you hear a note and then it descends to the next note.

Here is the notation for a whole-step bend and release, a whole-step pre-bend, and a whole-step pre-bend and release. A straight arrow UP indicates a PRE-BEND.

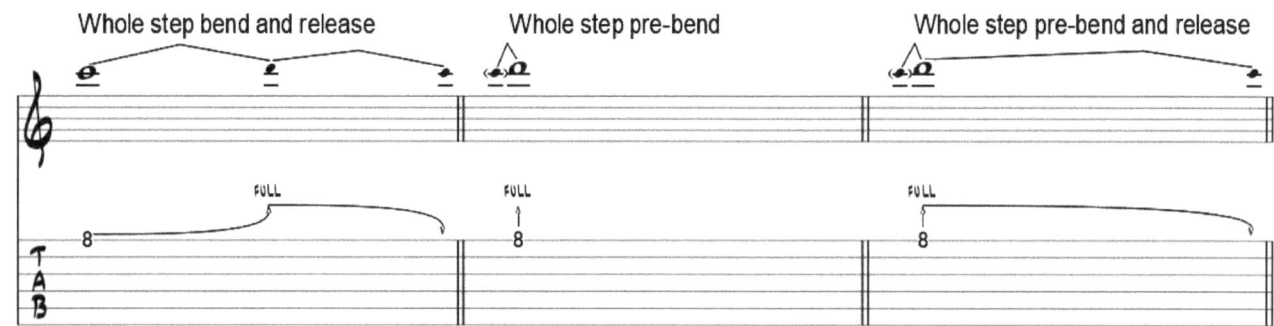

PRACTICE

Using pattern #1 C/Am pentatonic, play a 4 note sequence descending in quarter-notes. Each bar represents a 4 note sequence. Notice how each bar begins with the scale tones in order. Focus on that first note of each sequence to help you see the scale and remember where to start next group of four.

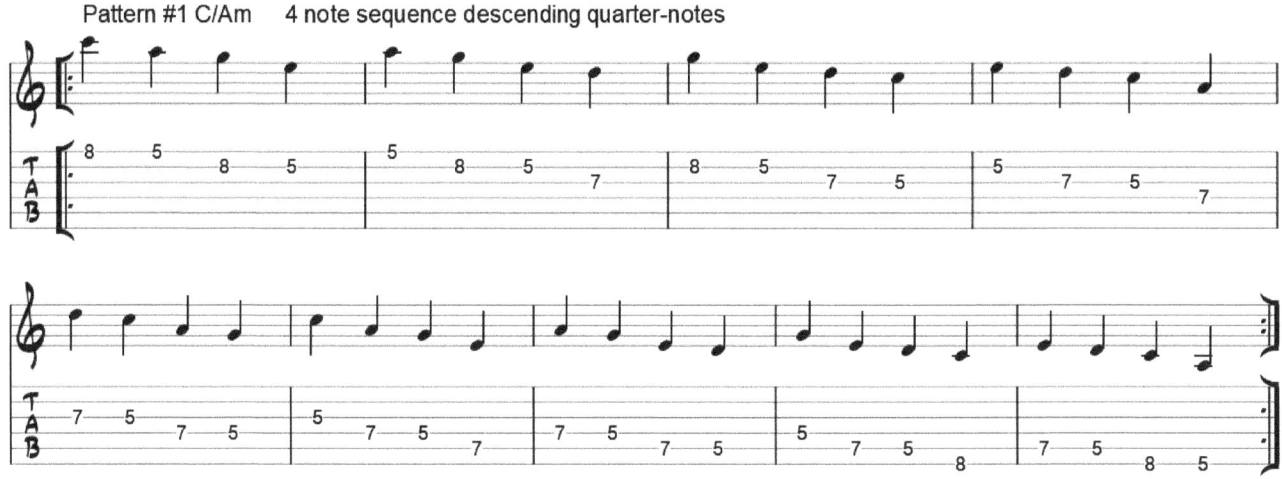

Using pattern #1 C/Am pentatonic, play a 4 note sequence ascending in quarter-notes.

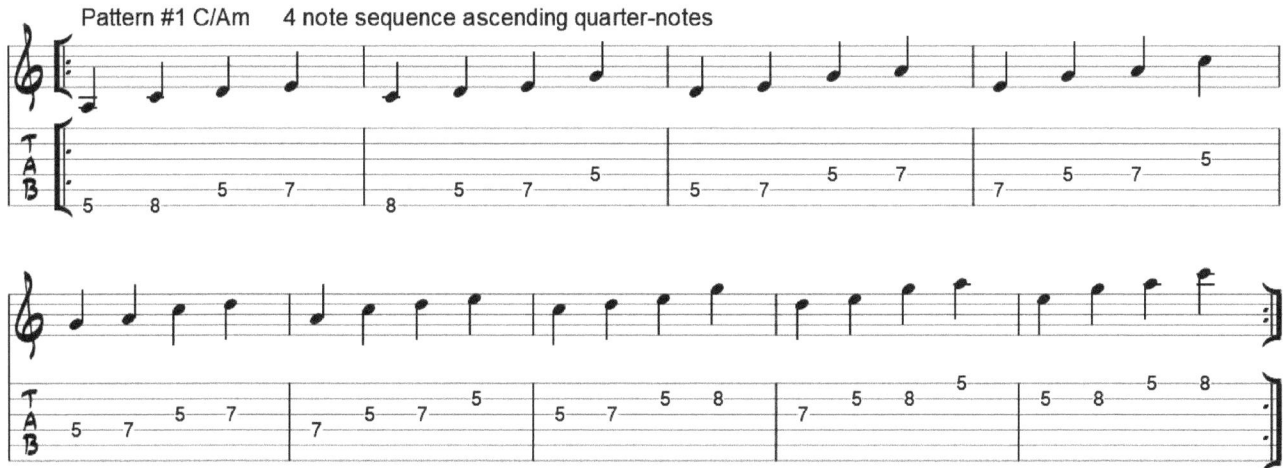

Self generate a 4 note Sequence. Use pattern #1 C/Am pentatonic and its respective chord.

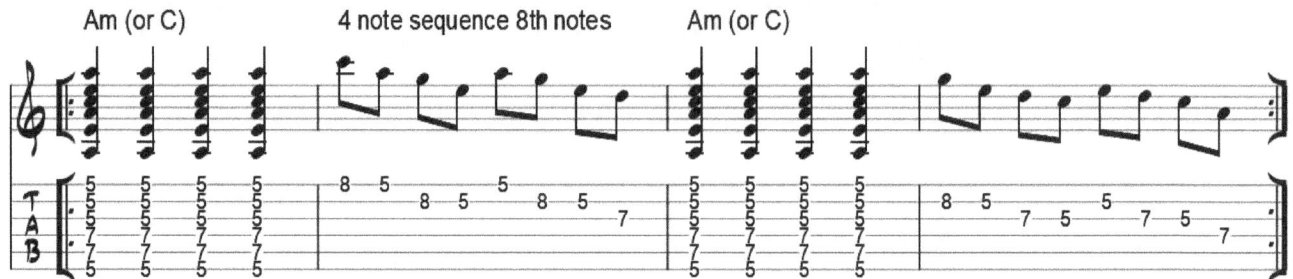

Using pattern #1 C/Am pentatonic, play a Leapfrog sequence descending and ascending in quarter-notes. There is a lot of finger rolling involved in this.

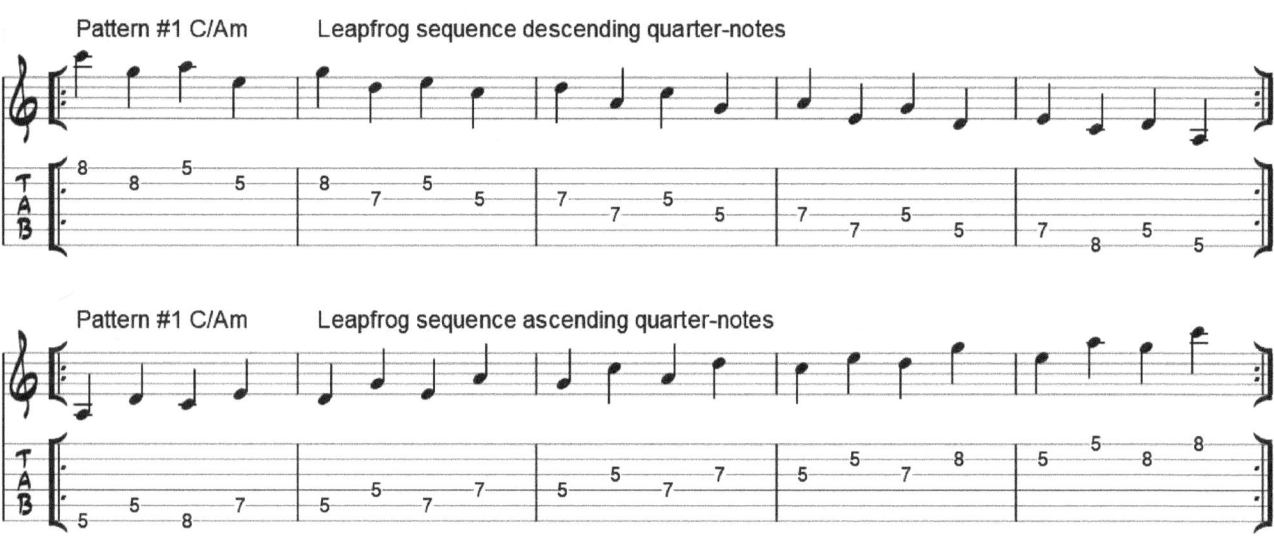

Self generate with Leapfrog Sequence. Use pattern #1 C/Am pentatonic and its respective chord.

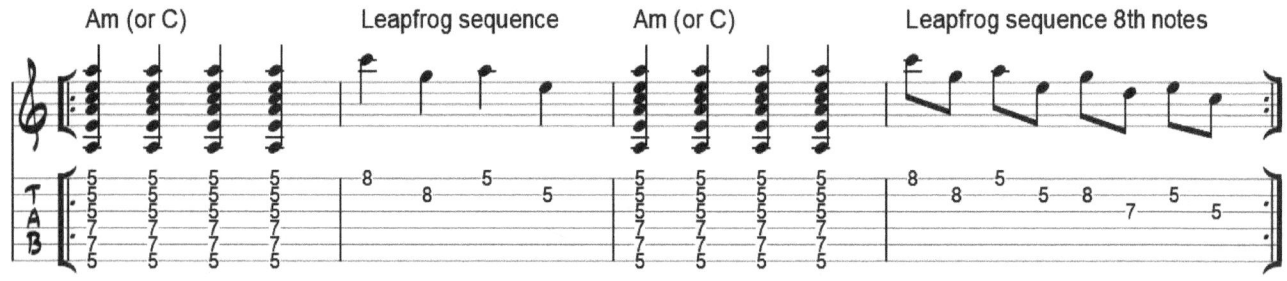

Practice the pre-bend by first playing a phrase without a pre-bend. Follow it with the same sounding phrase but do it with the pre-bend. This example can be thought of as pattern #1 and #2 of C/Am.

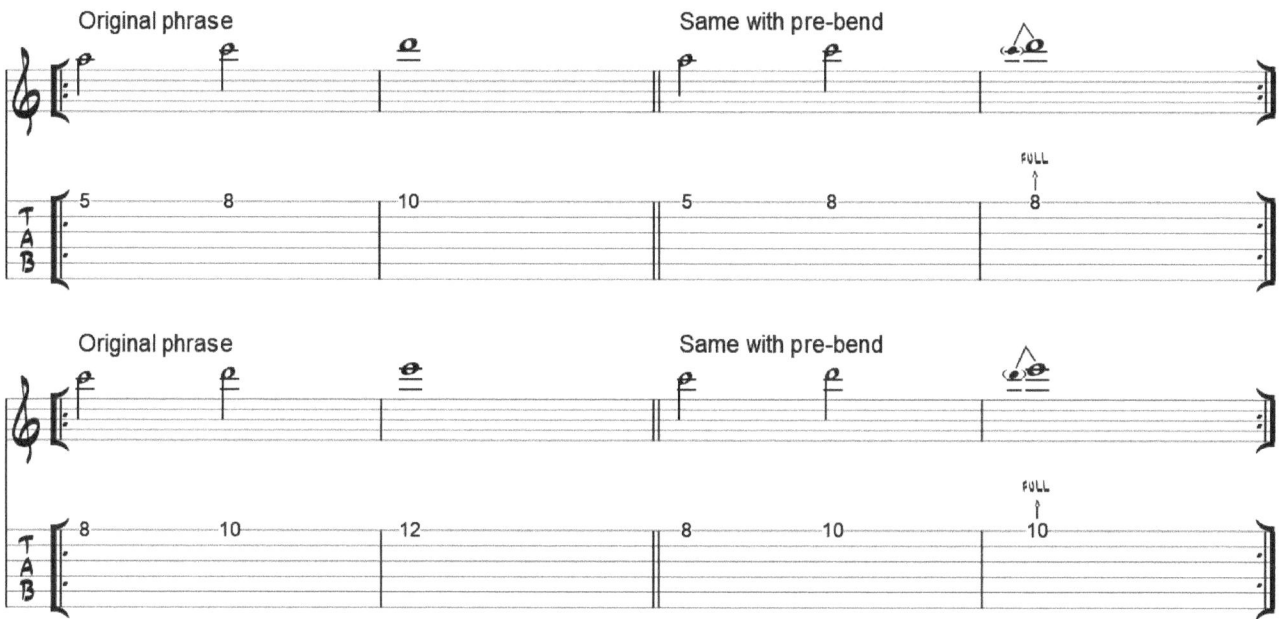

Self Generate Am (or C) pattern #1 and #2. Use pre-bend and release.

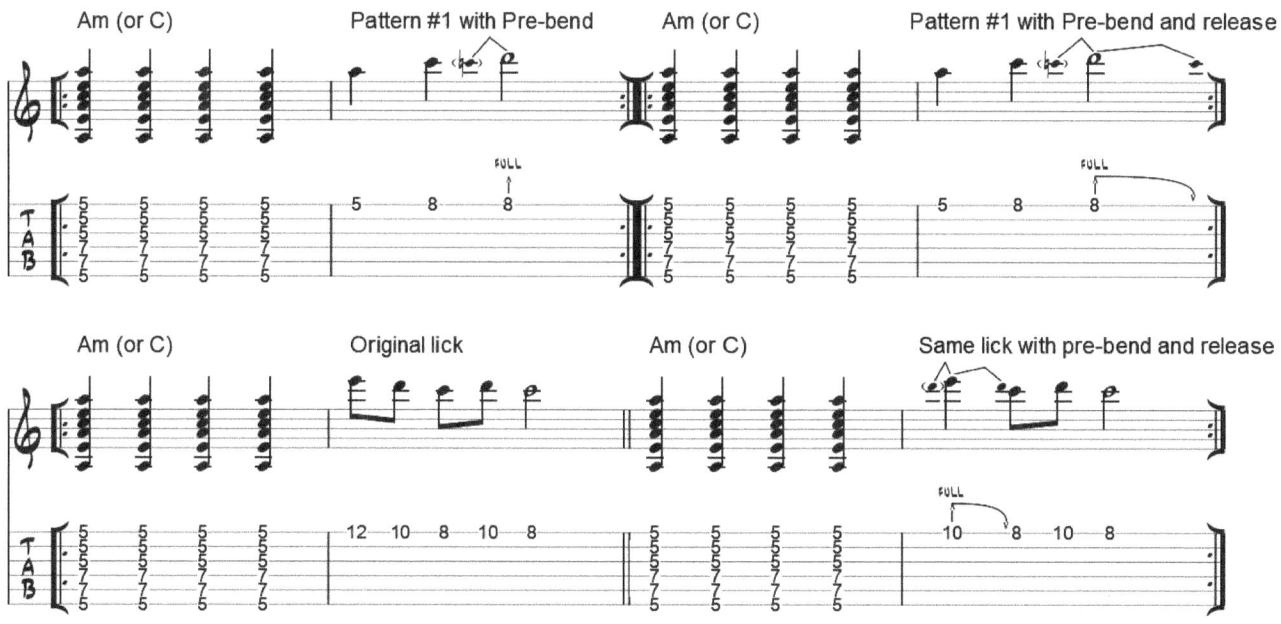

SUMMARY

We are musicians. We are guitar players.
We learn the language of music, Melody, Harmony, and Rhythm.
We learn the craft of playing the guitar as an instrument.
Always make your music decisions first and then go to your instrument/guitar.

MUSICIAN

- There are only 12 notes. (ABCDEFG are the Natural notes and there are 5 accidentals.)
- EF and BC are a ½ step apart (smallest distance).
- There are only 12 Major chords, 12 minor chords, 12 Major pentatonics, 12 minor pentatonics each based on one of the 12 notes.
- There are two inherent sounds of a Pentatonic scale, Major and minor (to match its respective chord).
- The **Blues Scale** is playing a minor pentatonic over a Major chord.
- There is a **relative minor to every Major** (1½ steps below the Major root). This means two-for-one.
- For soloing, match a scale to its chord.
- Playing **Globally** equals 1 scale for all the chords.
- **Playing the changes** equals a scale per chord. This "talks" directly to each chord, giving you its chord tones and color tones.
- **Sequences** are a powerful musical sound. They are really natural to listen to and great for composing and improvising.

GUITAR PLAYER

- The 12 notes are the first 12 frets on the guitar that we navigate on the lowest E string.
- We use the **"Rock and Roll Rule"** to put pattern #1 on the fretboard after making the music decision about what scale we need.
- There are **5 patterns** to connect our 12 fret fretboard for all 12 keys.
- We learned how to use **BSSBS** to play a minor pentatonic scale and **SSBSB** to play a Major pentatonic scale on any one string.
- We learned how to use **OCTAVE SHAPES** as a playable sounds as well as using them to unlock the fretboard.
- Use pattern #1 to get started with **PLAYING THE CHANGES.**
- Use the **CAGED** system to connect chord shapes to scale shapes.
- Bends are the most advanced of our legato techniques. We can see the power of **pre-bends** as they are the only way to allow the notes to bend "down."

CHAPTER 6

TUNE IN

"I am a musician and a guitar player. Music is my language and my guitar is my voice. Music is Melody, Harmony and Rhythm. I develop my language skills and my instrument skills. They are two separate worlds working together to complete the circle of music."

Rhythm is the number one factor to sounding great as a musician.

WARM UP

Muted String Ladder (MSL)
This is a new variation I call "One Pluck Per String" (OPPS). This involves moving the rhythm across strings instead of multiple attacks on the same string.
In this example we are using two strings (B E) and changing gears from quarter-notes to sixteenth-notes.

- Play quarter-notes with ALL DOWN, then ALL UP, and ALTERNATE picking.
- Change to eighth-notes and repeat.
- Do the same for triplets and sixteenth-notes.

MSL OPPS 2 strings

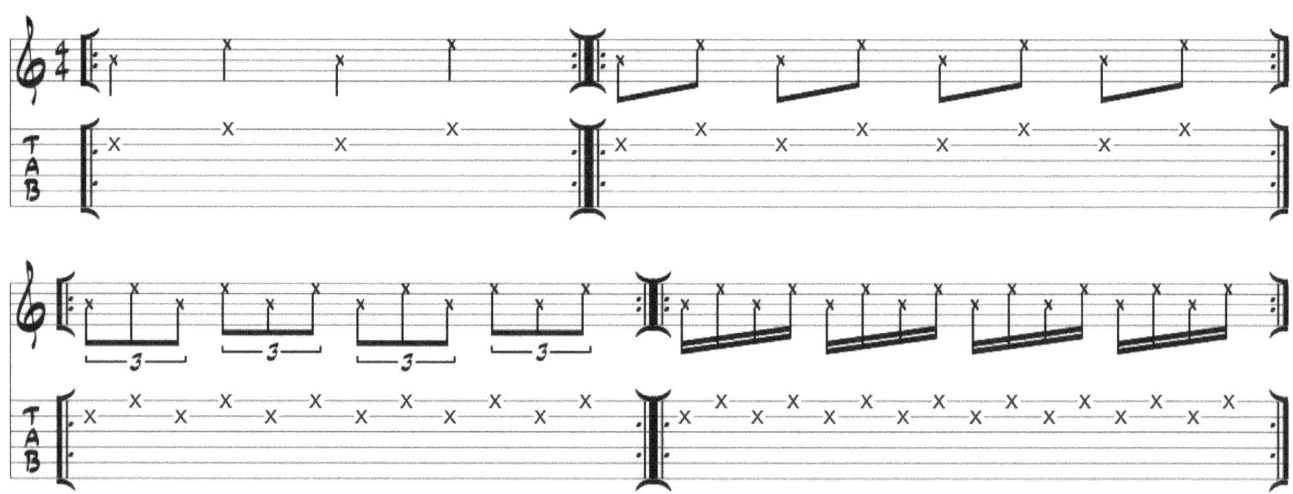

SHELLS

SHELL 1 2 4 as eighth-notes

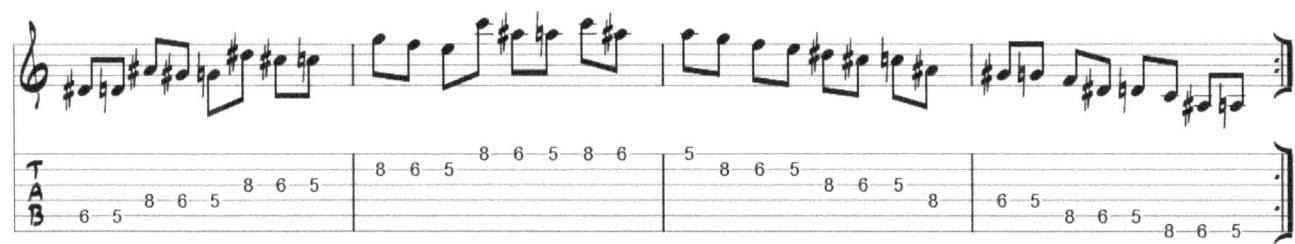

SHELL 1 2 4 as triplets

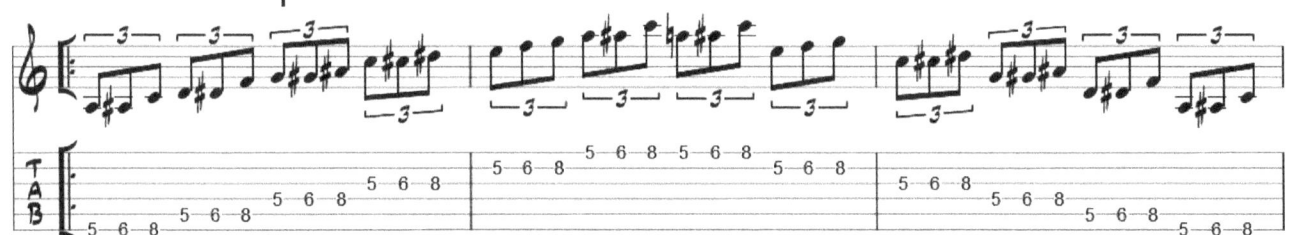

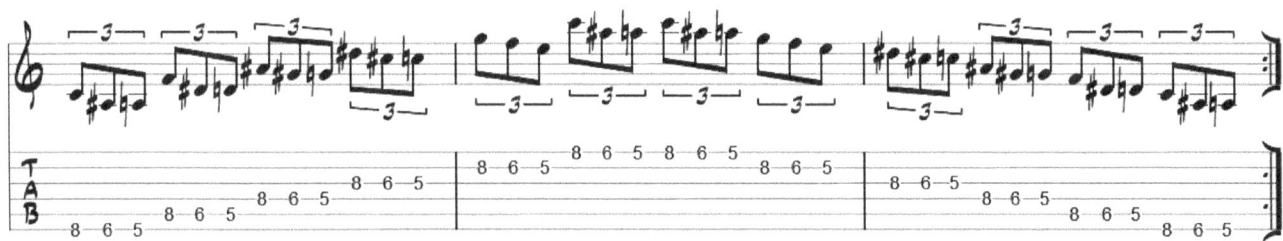

CHANGING GEARS

Chang Gears with ladders. On the B string play first gear, and every other beat go to the E string and Change Gears. It goes by fast, so you have to concentrate really hard to lock in with the gears. Use quarter-notes, eighth-notes, and triplets as gears on the B string.

Quarter-note Ladder

Eighth-note Ladder

Triplet Ladder

EXERCISE

Pattern #1 C/Am   4 note sequence descending quarter-notes

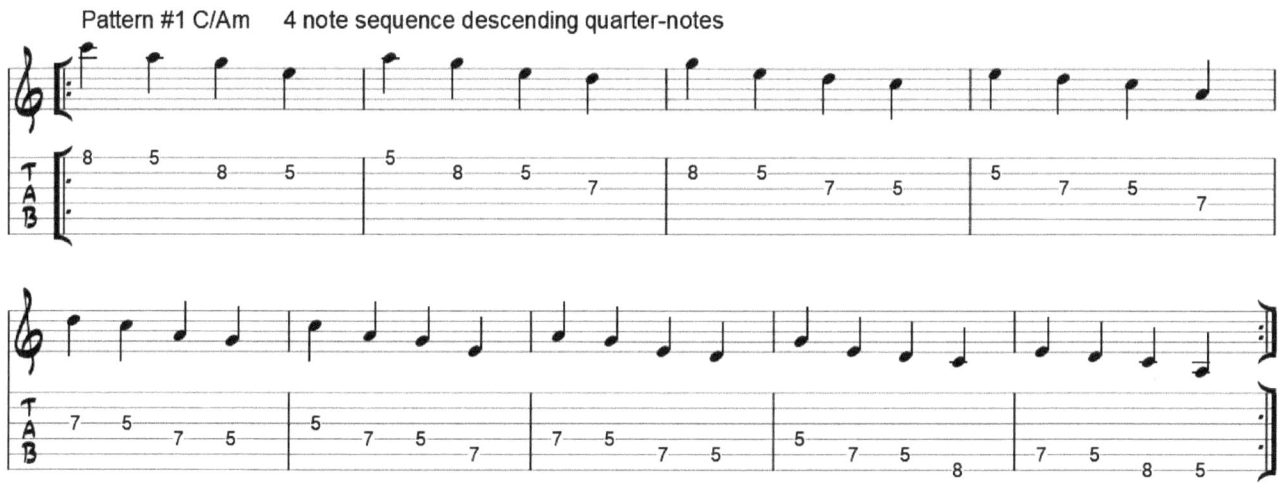

Pattern #1 C/Am   Leapfrog sequence descending quarter-notes

Pattern #1 C/Am   Leapfrog sequence ascending quarter-notes

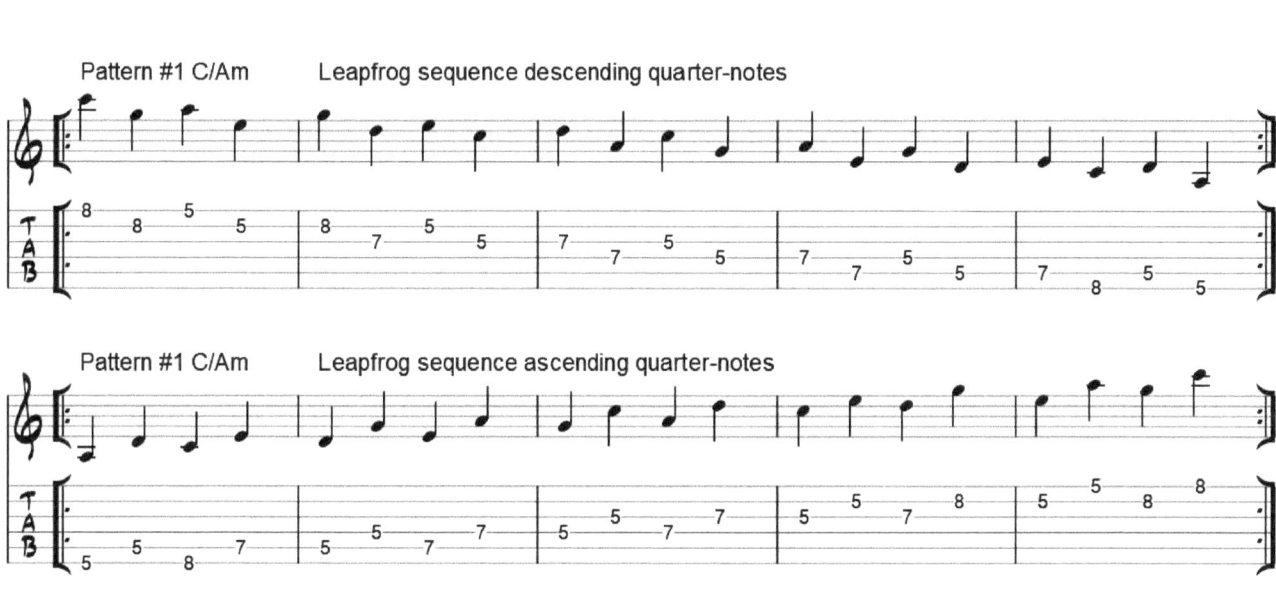

REVIEW

Sequences

The beauty of sequences is that they are equally good for you as a musician as well as a guitar player (instrumentalist). As a musician they can be used for composing melodies. They can also be used in solos as you improvise. They are very natural to listen to and make sense to your brain. They allow for a flow in music, and even work with call and response types of ideas.

Sequences are a natural way to move notes in music. As a guitar player sequences are great for evening out the fretboard hand's abilities. They force you to follow the notes regardless of how awkward it may feel. With time the sequences will build your dexterity and "chops." They really help you hear music on the guitar. They help your ear, in a natural way, to expect what is coming next.

General Ideas about Sequences

- Any musical phrase/scale can be sequenced. Sequences can have multiple notes and intervals.

- Sequences can ascend and descend.

- Sequences can be played with any rhythm (for example eighth-notes, triplets, sixteenth-notes).

- Sequences sound especially cool when the rhythm doesn't match the number of notes in the sequence. For example try a 3 note sequence as eighth-notes or sixteenth-notes.

- You can "flip-flop" groups in a sequence. For example, in a 3 note sequence groups could be 123, *432*, 345, *654*. You can see that every other group is reversed.

- You can mix and match groups. For example, you can alternate between a 3 and 4 note group to sequence. Try 1234, 234, 3456, and 456.

- Anytime you learn a new instrument, sequence scales! It is a great way to develop on your new instrument.

- Sequences work in all aspects of music. They work as bass lines, as melodies, in background accompaniment, in solos, as improvisational ideas, and more.

ACCENTS

There are many factors in music that help us be expressive. Accents are one of the most effective tools we have to express ourselves as musicians. Accents are part of the world of DYNAMICS.

In music, dynamics vary the intensity and volume of musical phrases. They are natural to listen to, just like the dynamics when we speak. Any instrument can vary dynamics. This is one of the most deciding factors in making you sound like yourself on an instrument compared to other people.

Within dynamics are accents. Accents are just like they sound (pun intended). They add a loud sound as compared to a softer sound. They are rhythm-based ideas, and drummers and percussionists are very at home with accents when compared to musicians playing melodic based instruments. Think about it. If you are clapping you have two options, clap or don't clap. When you clap you do it in rhythm. That's the only thing you need/have. (There are no notes or chords.) Adding accents allows one sound (clap) to have at least two different sounds (regular and loud) creating a natural call and response. This actually creates a second rhythm on top of the original.

The accent symbol looks like a sideways "V." It's positioned over the note you accent. This example is an eighth-note rhythm with accents on each of the four downbeats.

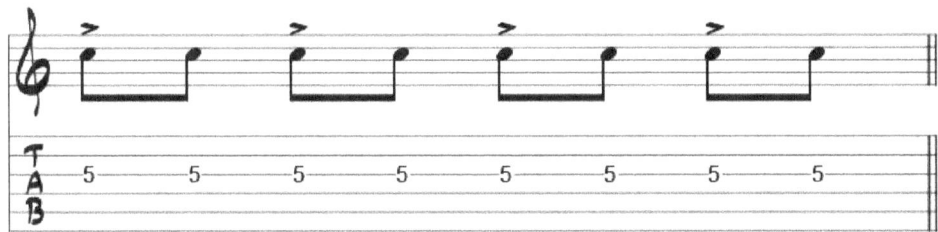

If you think about it, the rhythm of the accents is just quarter-notes. This creates a different feel than just straight evenly sounding eighth-notes.

If you take this a little further, you can make rhythms on top of other rhythms. Here is an example of eighth-notes with accents. The accents create a very common strumming pattern. When you strum you usually "air guitar" all of the gear, in this case all of the eighth-notes (all the downs and ups). You usually make contact with the strings in the rhythm of the accents (the second bar).

You can do this with your two hands; Left (L) and Right (R). If you just played eighth-notes on your thighs with your two hands it would be:

LR LR LR LR

The left hand becomes the down beat and the right hand becomes the off/up beat. If you apply accents (in bold) you would get this:

LR **LR LR LR**

This is all from drummers. Drummers spend their whole lives mastering beats, tempo, gears, permutations and doing it all using up to four limbs. Thinking in L and R is a great foundation in basic rhythm. Remember rhythm is time. It is everywhere and anything can be rhythmic, an alarm, a cars turn signal, and you! You are a rhythmic instrument. When you walk down the street you are being rhythmic. I practice a lot of rhythms while I walk. My left and right feet provide the quarter-note and my hands and mind are free to be rhythmic.

SUBGROUPS

When you match note groups to accents you get what I call "subgroups."
One of the most common examples of this is what I call 332. It is three eighth-notes, another three eighth-notes, and two more to make eight eighth-notes.

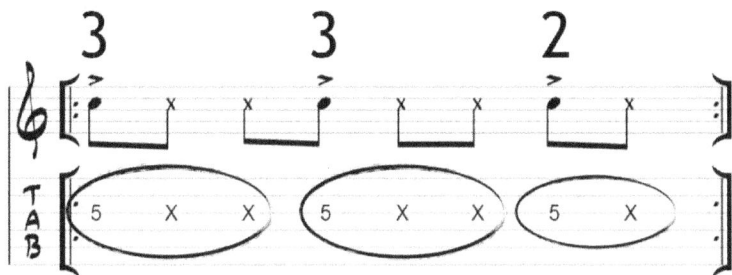

When you add notes you can see how it works. Every accent on the 332 is the C note (8th fret) of the three notes. To keep it in 4/4 you have to drop the last of the three notes to make it eight and not nine eighth-notes.

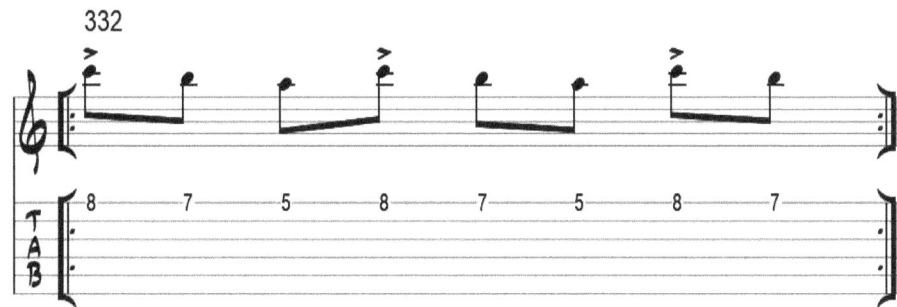

If you kept playing every third eighth-note and didn't truncate it to fit into one bar, it would take three full bars before the same note starts over again on the downbeat of one. And cool enough, there are 3 accents in the first bar, 3 in the second bar and 2 in the third bar.

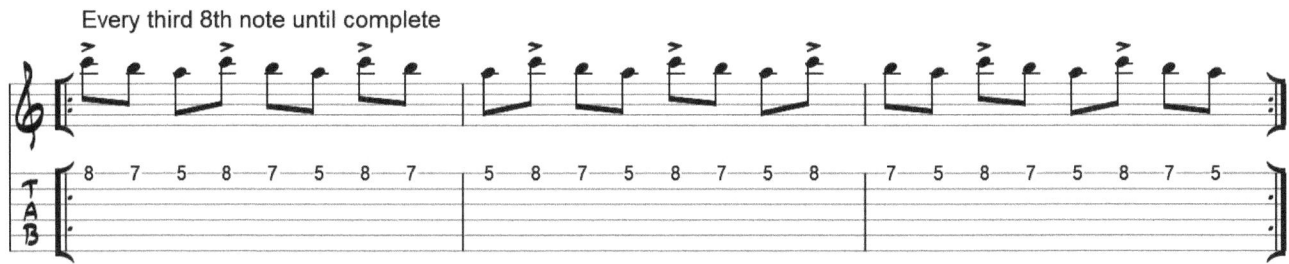

Subgouping sounds the coolest when the number of notes DOES NOT match the rhythmic gear. For example try 3 notes as eighth-notes or sixteenth-notes, or 2 or 4 notes as triplets.

PRACTICE

In each gear practice accenting different beats and combinations. Use a muted G string and press down on the 5th fret for each accent.

Quarter-notes

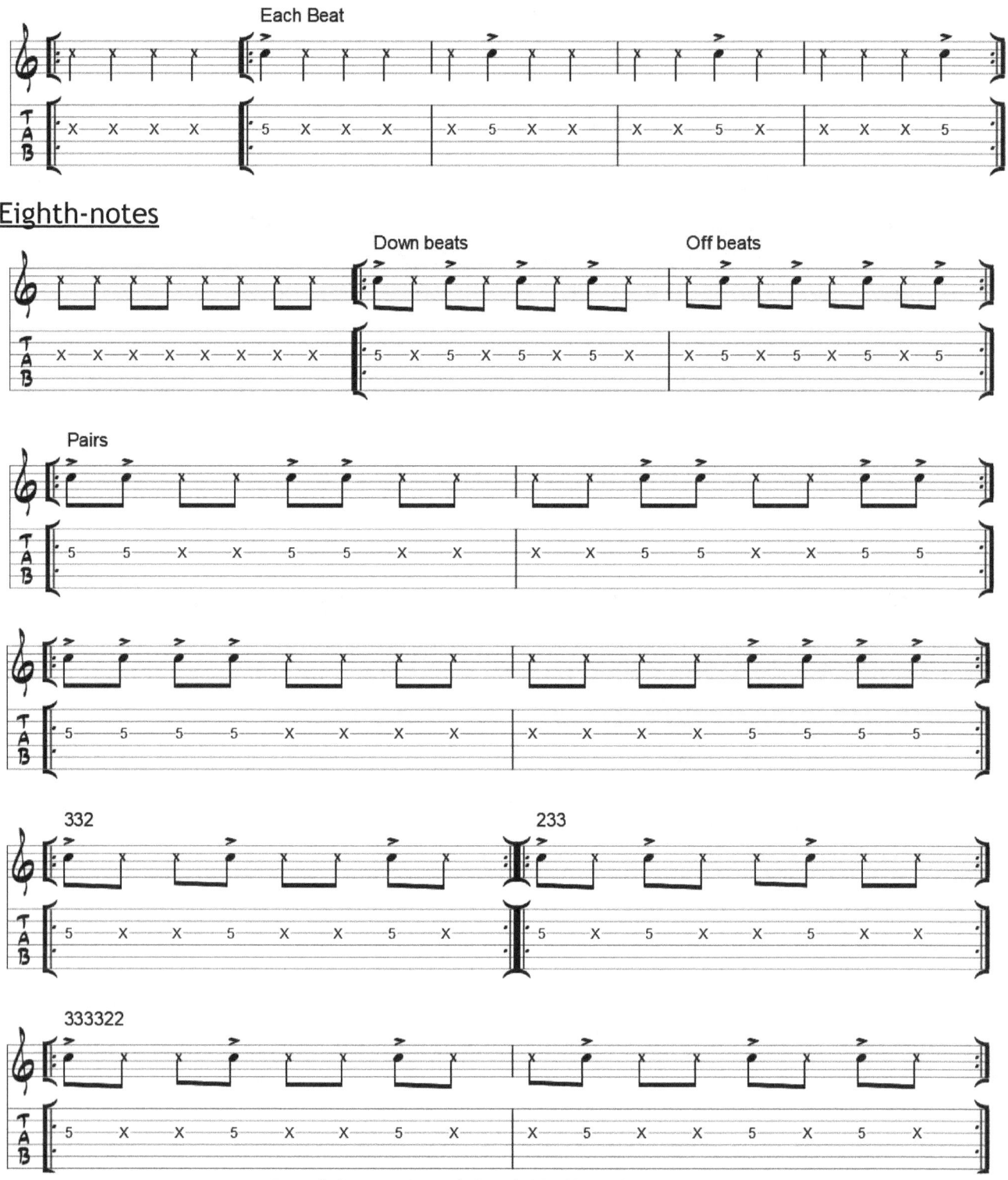

Eighth-notes

Triplets

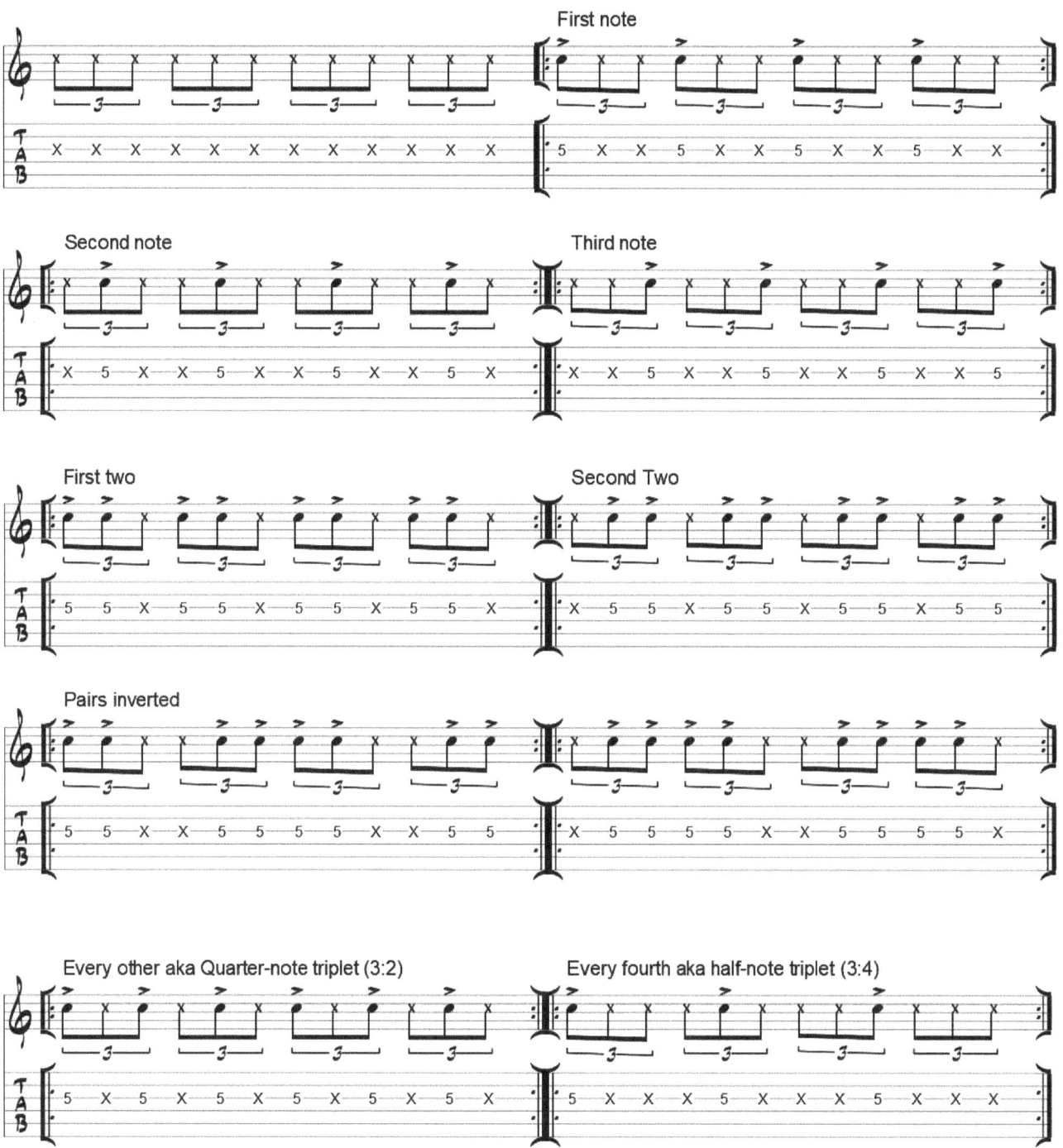

Sixteenth-notes

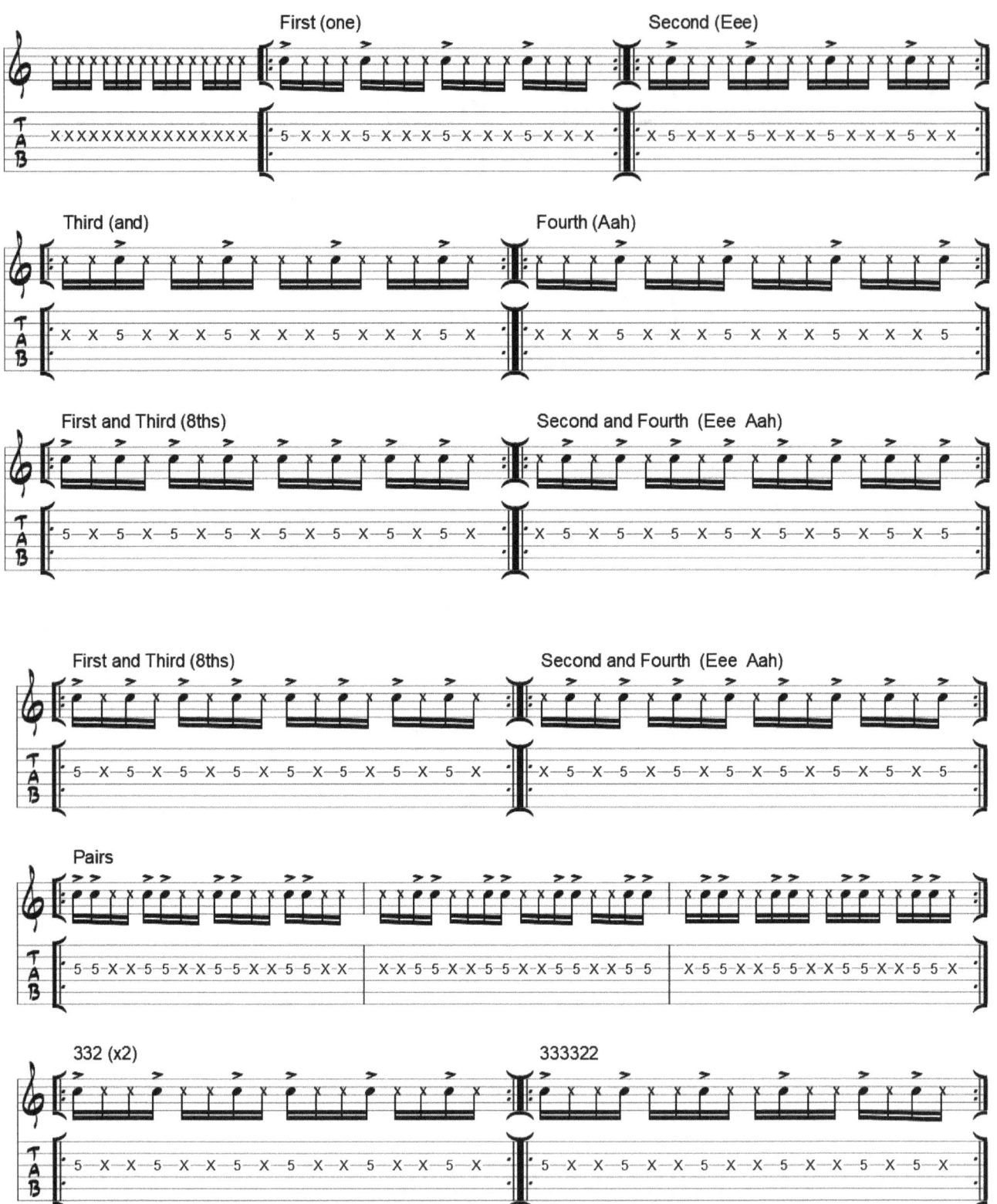

LICKS

Eighth-note ideas with 332

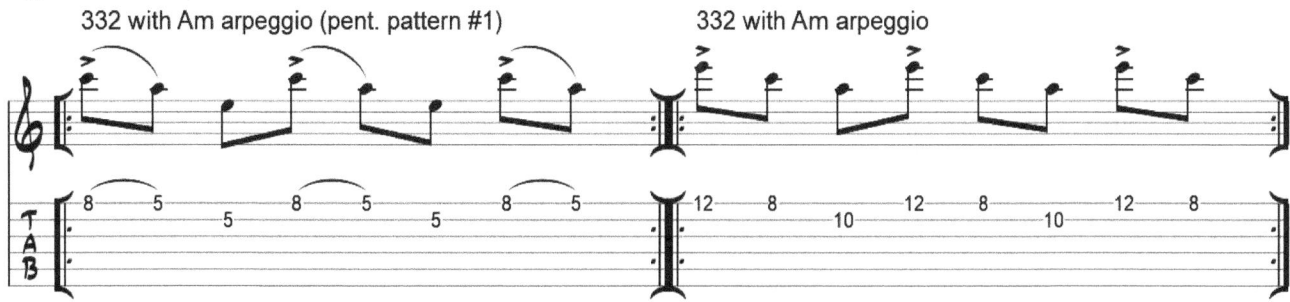

332 with Am arpeggio (pent. pattern #1)   332 with Am arpeggio

Triplet ideas with subgroups

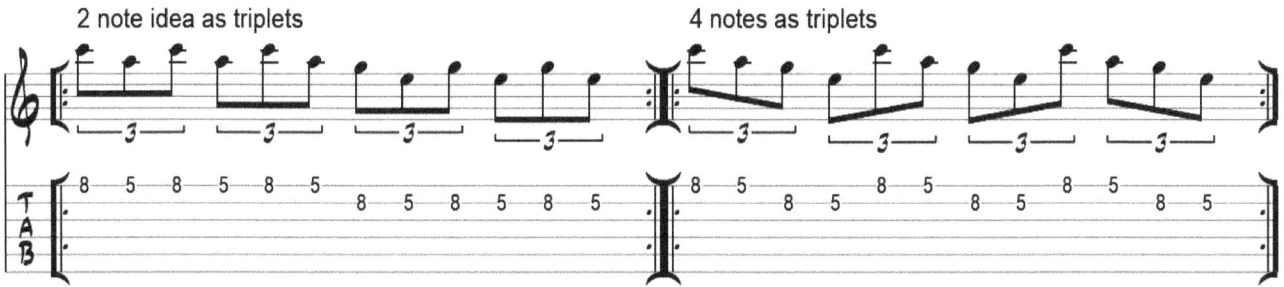

2 note idea as triplets   4 notes as triplets

Sixteenth-note ideas with subgroup and accents

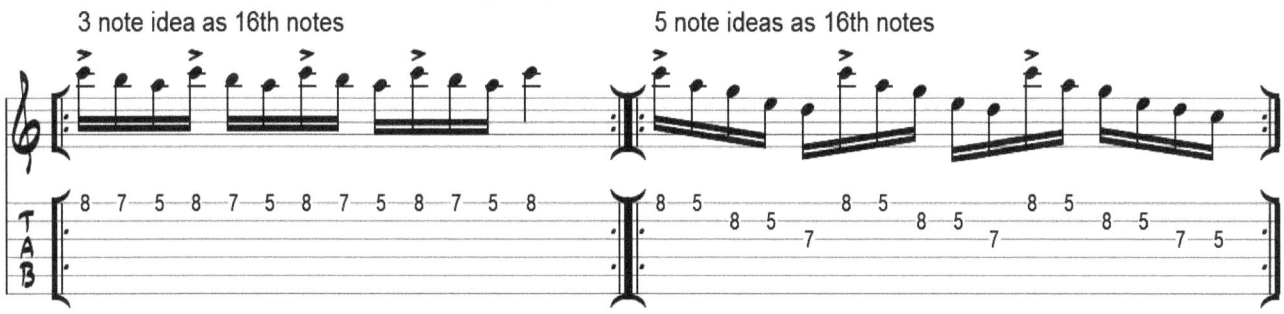

3 note idea as 16th notes   5 note ideas as 16th notes

SUMMARY

We are musicians. We are guitar players.
We learn the language of music, Melody, Harmony, and Rhythm.
We learn the craft of playing the guitar as an instrument.
Always make your music decisions first and then go to your instrument/guitar.

MUSICIAN
- There are only 12 notes. (ABCDEFG are the Natural notes and there are 5 accidentals.)
- EF and BC are a ½ step apart (smallest distance).
- There are only 12 Major chords, 12 minor chords, 12 Major pentatonics, 12 minor pentatonics each based on one of the 12 notes.
- There are two inherent sounds of a Pentatonic scale, Major and minor (to match its respective chord).
- The **Blues Scale** is playing a minor pentatonic over a Major chord.
- There is a **relative minor to every Major** (1½ steps below the Major root). This means two-for-one.
- For soloing, match a scale to its chord.
- Playing **Globally** equals 1 scale for all the chords.
- **Playing the changes** equals playing a scale per chord. This "talks" directly to each chord, giving you its chord tones and color tones.
- **Sequences** are a powerful musical sound. They are really natural to listen to and great for composing and improvising.
- **Accents** give dimension to rhythm. Accents allow multiple rhythms to exist simultaneously. There is so much potential expressiveness with accents.

GUITAR PLAYER

- The 12 notes are the first 12 frets on the guitar that we navigate on the lowest E string.
- We use the **"Rock and Roll Rule"** to put pattern #1 on the fretboard after making the music decision about what scale we need.
- There are **5 patterns** to connect our 12 fret fretboard for all 12 keys.
- We learned how to use **BSSBS** to play a minor pentatonic scale and **SSBSB** to play a Major pentatonic scale on any one string.
- We learned how to use **OCTAVE SHAPES** as a playable sounds as well as using them to unlock the fretboard.
- Use pattern #1 to get started with **PLAYING THE CHANGES**.
- Use the **CAGED** system to connect chord shapes to scale shapes.
- Bends are the most advanced of our legato techniques. We can see the power of **pre-bends** as they are the only way to allow the notes to bend "down."
- Knowing how hard and soft to pluck is essential to properly playing with **dynamics**. **Accents** can happen in the pick hand (hard and soft picking) as well as in the fretboard hand (when you play notes versus mutes).

CHAPTER 7

TUNE IN

"I am a musician and a guitar player. Music is my language and my guitar is my voice. Music is Melody, Harmony and Rhythm. I develop my language skills and my instrument skills. They are two separate worlds working together to complete the circle of music."

Rhythm is the number one factor to sounding great as a musician.

WARM UP

Muted String Ladder (MSL) using One Pick Per String (OPPS) for 3 strings

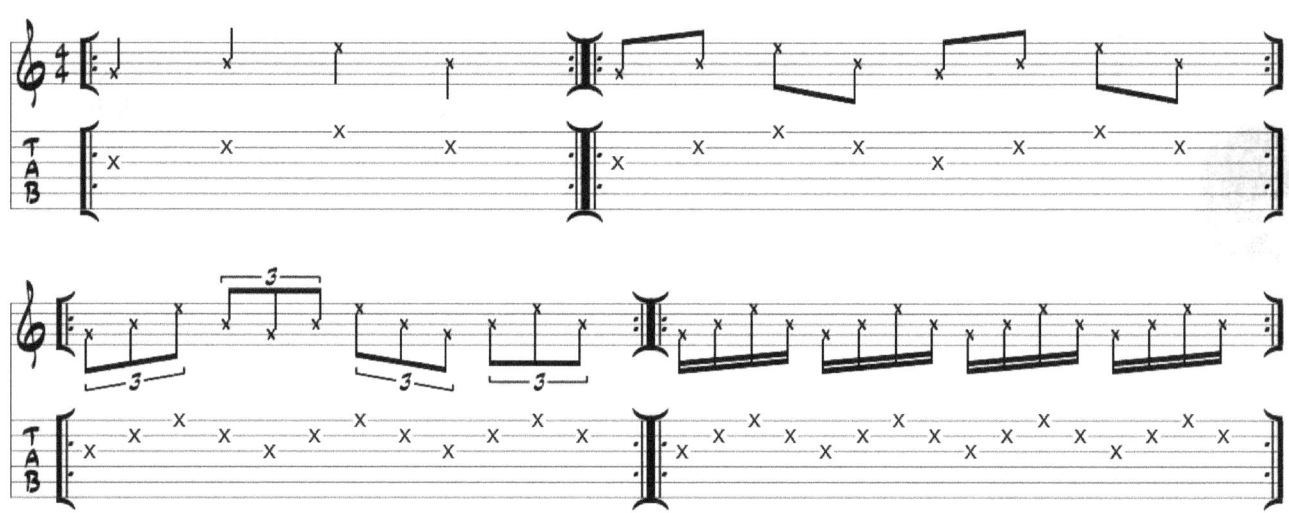

Here are some different picking methods. With economy/sweep picking, let the pick land on the next string and follow through, don't re-pick it. It should feel as if it is one motion.

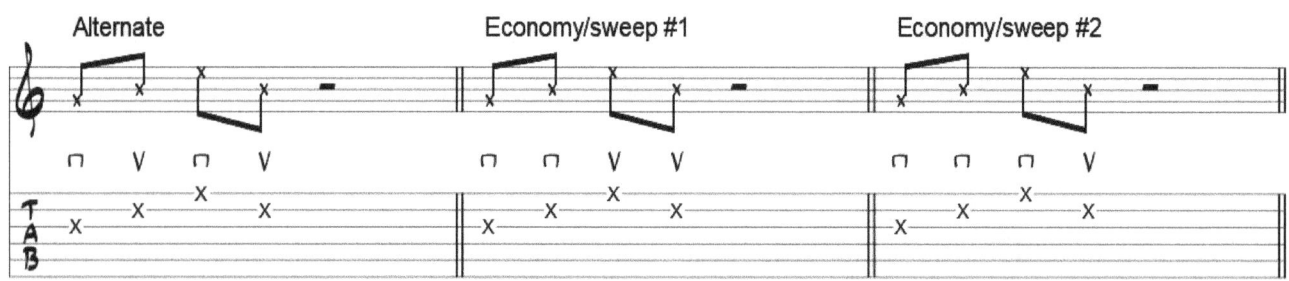

SHELL-ROTATIONS

With 2 finger shells there are naturally only two options for the order in which to play them. This is exercised completely with the shell concept. But, when you have a 3 or even 4 finger shell there can be more combinations. This is where ROTATIONS happen. If you have a 1 3 4 shell, it's opposite is 4 3 1. With a ROTATION you would start on the 3rd finger. For example it could be 3 4 1, and its counter part 1 4 3, or it could be 3 1 4 (4 1 3).

CHANGING GEARS

Using the same 1 3 4 fingering we used for the first four gears, you can go higher into fifth and sixth gears. For fifth gear (quintuplets) you use 1 3 4 3 1. For sixth gear (sextuplets) the fingering could be 1 3 4 1 3 4. You can think of it as the triplet fingering played twice in a beat (which could also be thought of as sixteenth-note triplets).

Change Gears 1-6

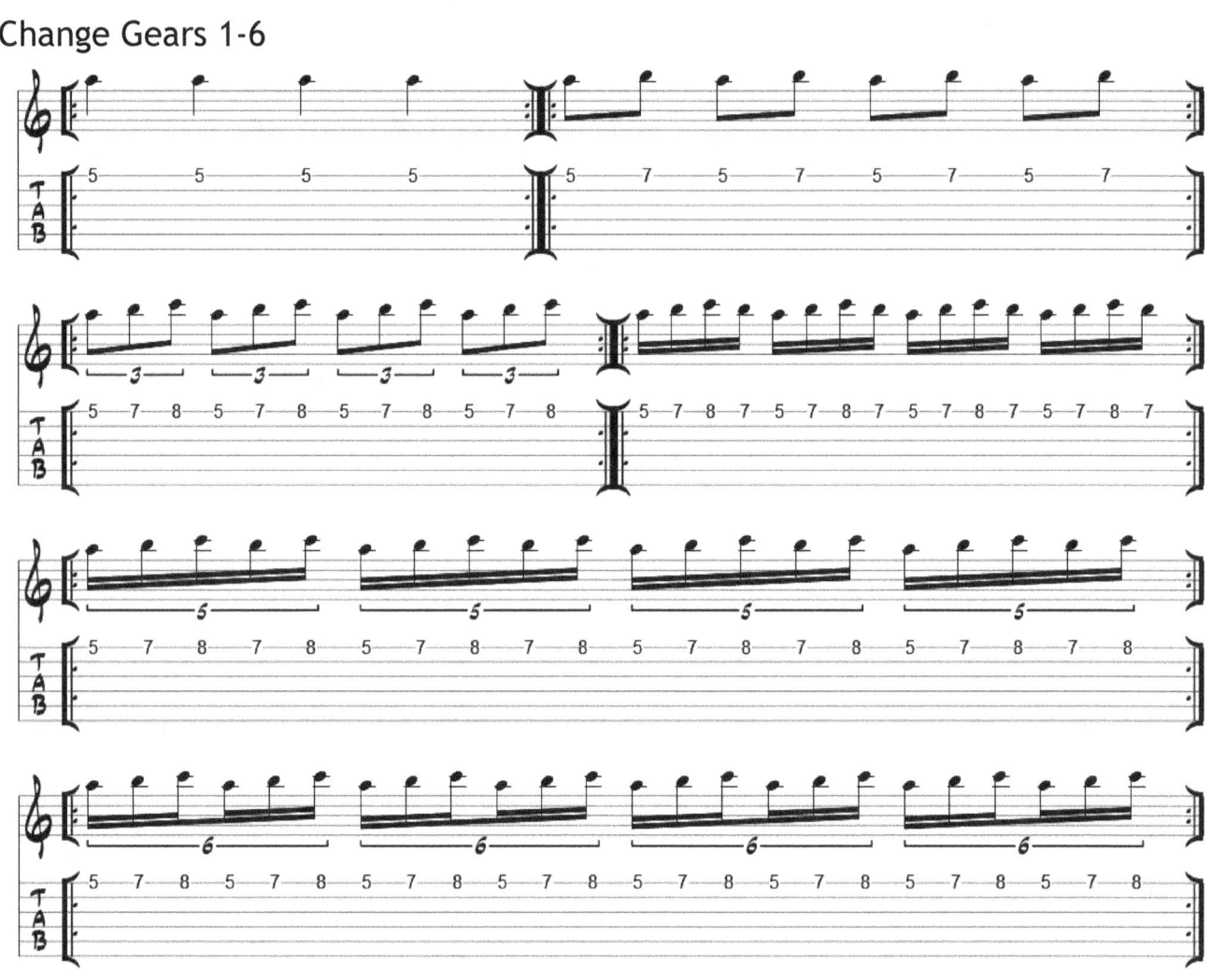

EXERCISE

Play pentatonic pattern #1 and #2 in the key of D/Bm. Play it as Round the Block. Ascend pattern #1, shift up, and descend pattern #2 from its highest note.

There are accents on the downbeats, the offbeats, and every 3rd eighth-note.

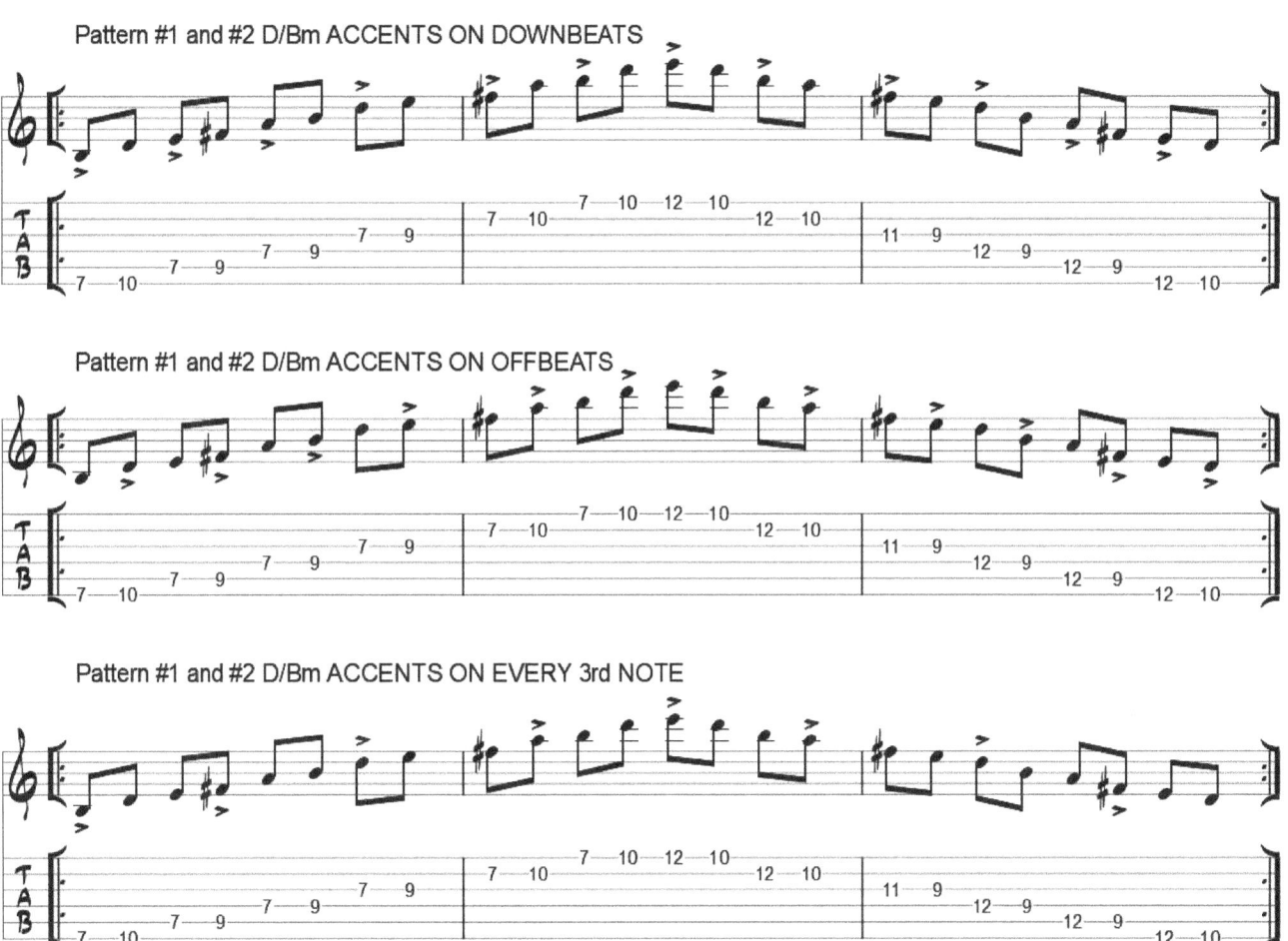

REVIEW

Accents

Dynamics are so important to our expressive abilities as musicians. They are important for us humans as well, and that's why they translate so strongly to music. Think of the teacher in the movie, "Ferris Bueller's Day Off." He spoke in a monotone voice. It completely lacked emotion, passion or any sort of expressiveness. We don't want that in music, it sounds unnatural.

Dynamics are an overall change in level of volume and intensity. Accents are very specific increases in volume and intensity, based on rhythm, to bring about a new level of rhythmic expression. Accents will create a new layer of rhythmic interest above the original rhythm. Now, even with a single sound (like a clap) we have multiple sounds instead of clap or no clap. Clap this example of 332.

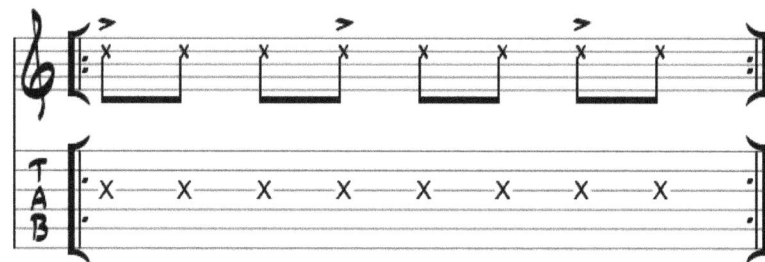

Subgroups

Subgroups are an aspect of accents accompanied by note groups to help reinforce the spacings of the accents. Here is the above example with notes.

332 as sequence in Patten #1 D/Bm

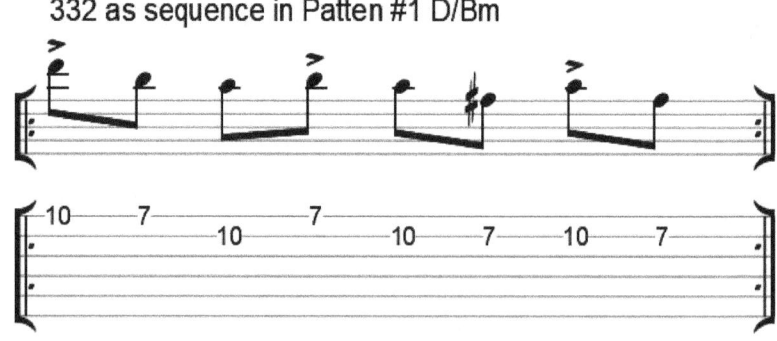

NECK ANATOMY 3 OCTAVE SCALES

The octave shapes are the foundation to neck anatomy.

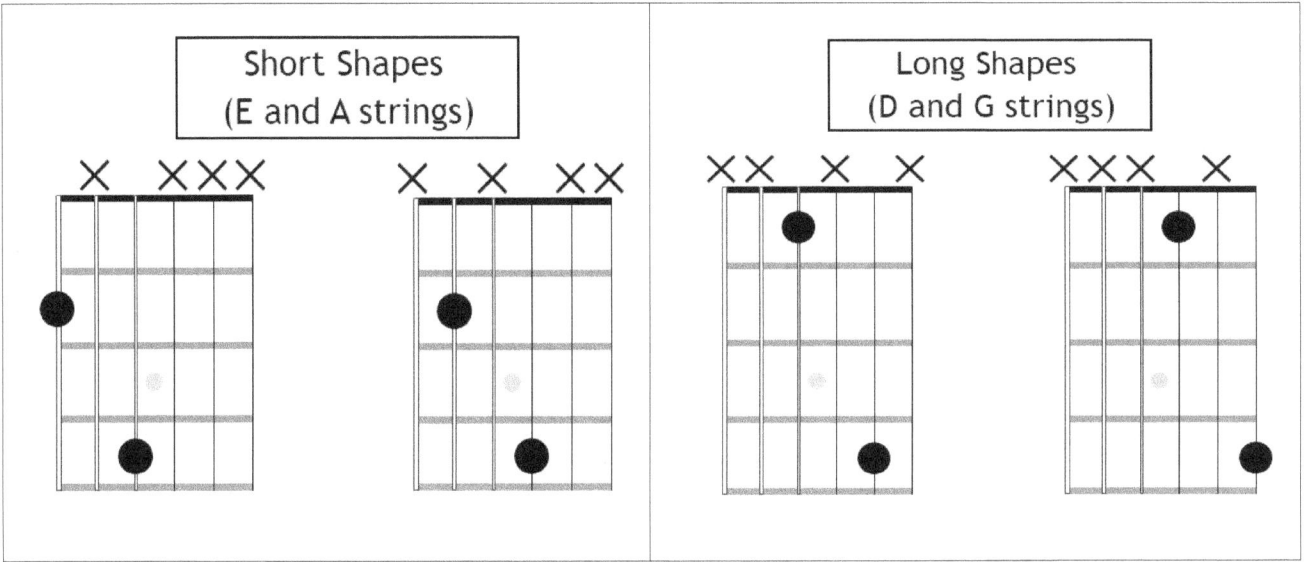

Connecting the Octave with *Short to Long shape* is the Keystone.

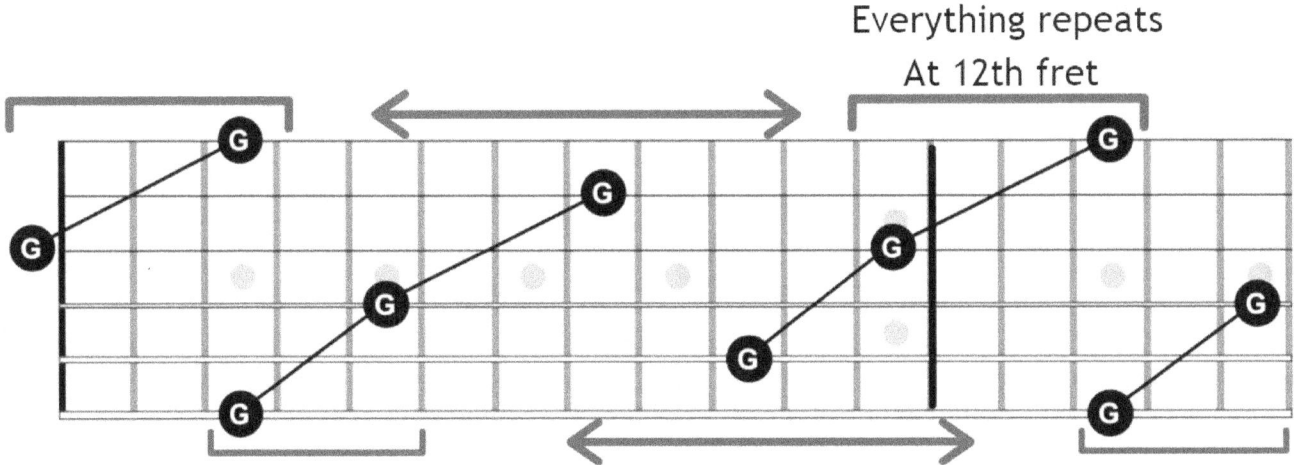

Remember, the guitar is a three octave instrument on average. There are a lot of redundant notes on the guitar. Usually 5 frets higher on the previous string will give you the same note again. (It's 4 frets when going from the B to the G string.)

Minor Pentatonic across 3 Octaves

Build up a B minor pentatonic scale starting from low E string first. Play each B with your first finger. The idea is that each octave plays and feels the same.

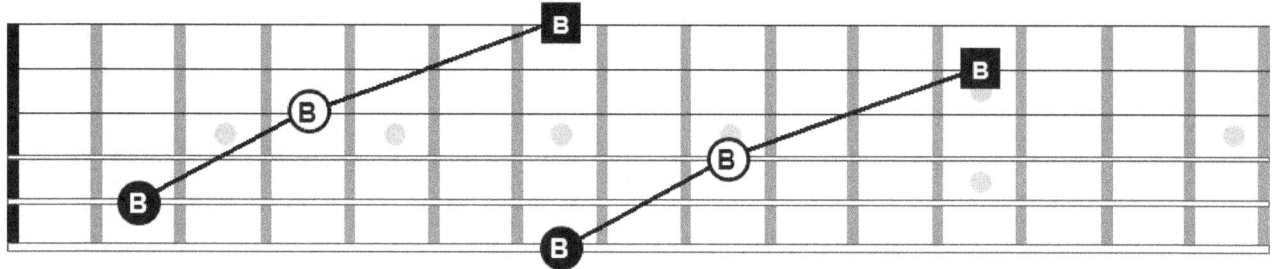

Staring on the low E string, add the second note of the Bm pentatonic scale. Use the same fingers for each octave (in this case, first and pinky). Pick up your whole hand at once when you change octaves.

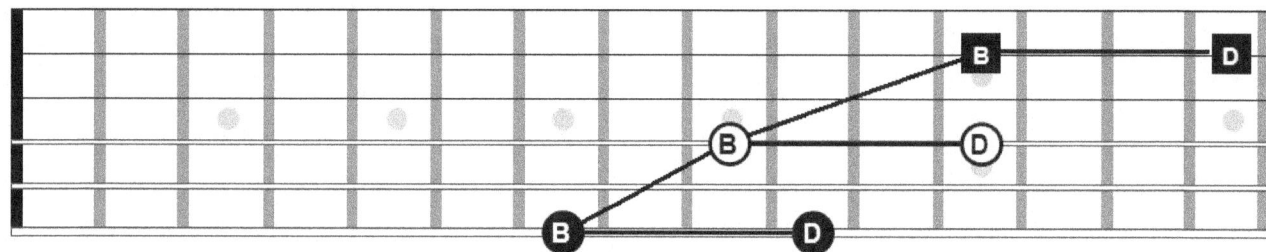

Add the next string (two more notes) from the B minor pentatonic scale. It should *feel* like pattern #1 is moving across 3 octaves. Use the same fingers for each octave. Pick up your whole hold hand for the new octave.

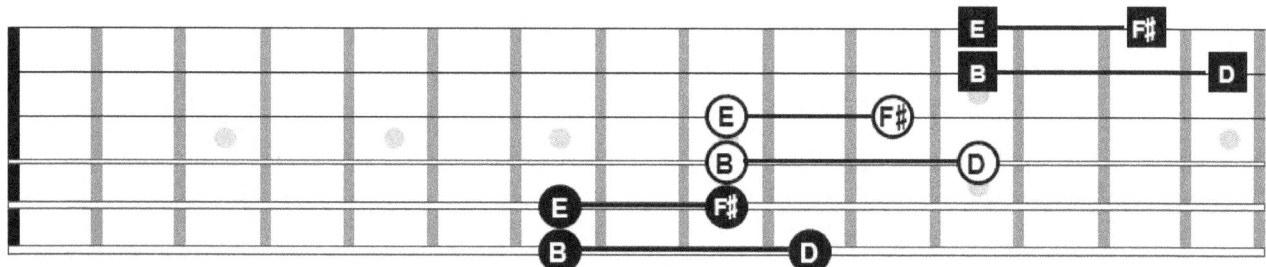

Finally, add the 5th note. It is a little tricky. Keep an eye on the B octaves, they are like fence posts. The 5th note of one octave is a whole-step behind the next root in the next octave.

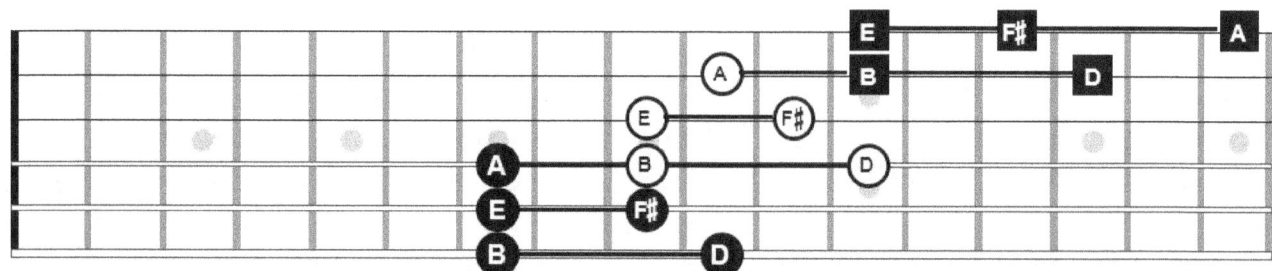

Additionally, it is easy to add the Blue Note. The Blue Note will follow the Short Octave to Long Octave (triangle note). It is much easier to navigate the Blue Note with Neck Anatomy than to solely remember where it is relative to each pattern.

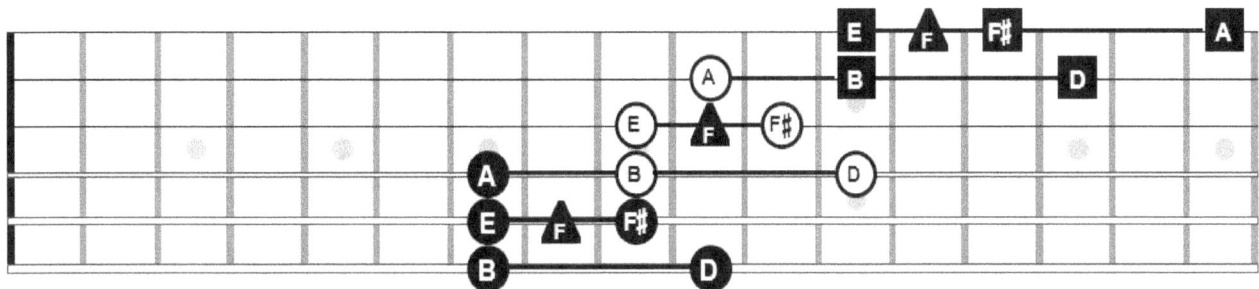

See how the Neck Anatomy view "sits on top" of the original scale patterns. The lowest octave is pattern #1, and the middle octave is the middle of pattern #2 (even though it feels like pattern #1). The third octave is the highest notes of pattern #3 (even though it feels like pattern #1), and finally the last A note and next octave of B (19th fret) can be thought of as pattern #4 going into #5.

It's important to learn to navigate the scale from the A string start. The B string adds its extra attention with a need to shift up when you cross onto it from the G string. You will also run out of fretboard real estate quicker this way. As you can see you only get a little more than two octaves worth of range when starting on the A string.

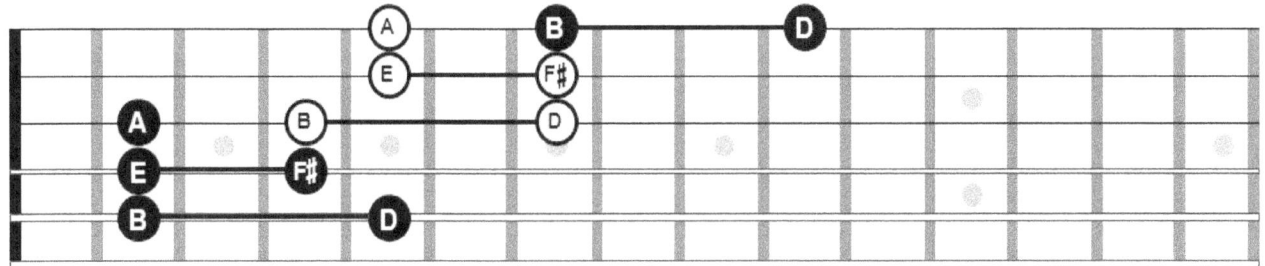

Major Pentatonic across 3 Octaves

It is even easier to do this for a Major pentatonic scale. If you think 1 2 3 from the root you can add two notes on the next string to make the full scale. The whole move can be played with your first and third fingers making it super playable. Many of my students over the years could play this move, knew it was "something pentatonic" but not much more. Once you see it, it is very easy to look at and play.

Here is a D note from the E string.

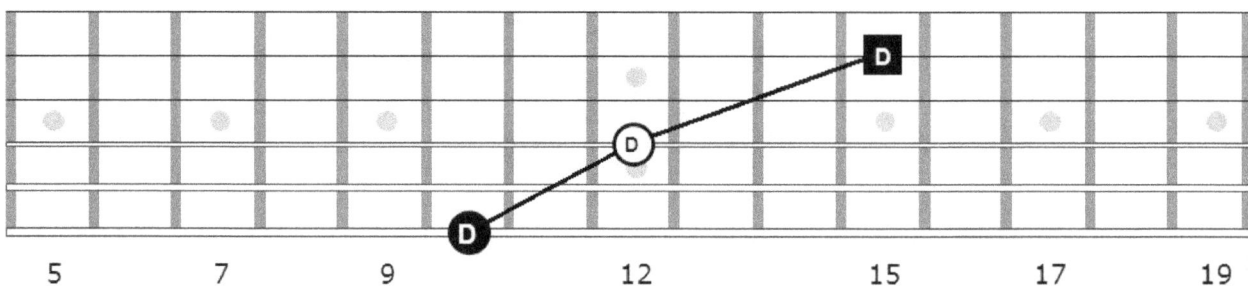

Next add the 2 and 3 of the scale creating a 1 2 3 (do re mi) from each root note. It's great to slide the E to the F# note with your third finger (ring finger).

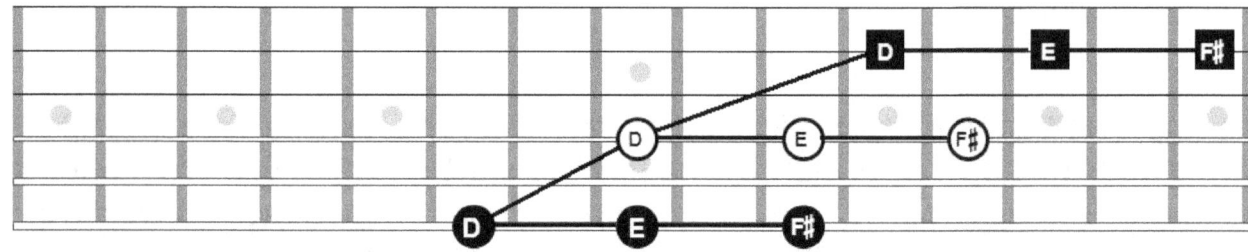

Lastly, add the two remaining notes on the next adjacent string. If you do slide the E to the F# note with your third finger you can easily play the A and B notes with same two fingers.

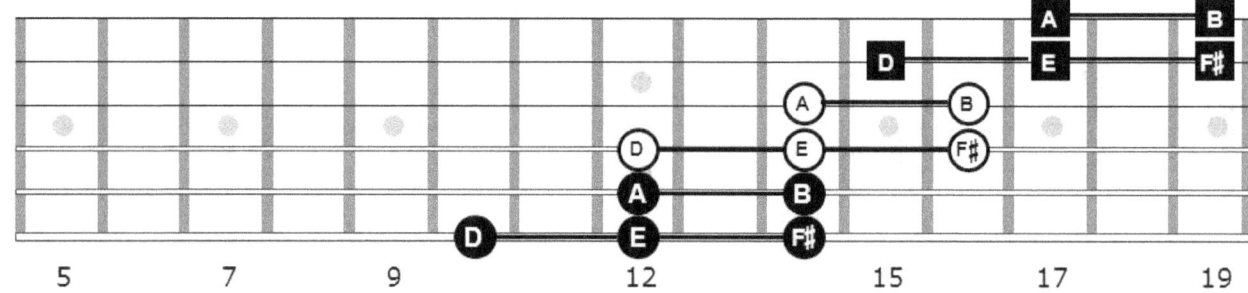

Always look at the octaves of the root, the D note. Pull back on your peripheral vision and keep an overview of each octave.

PRACTICE

Navigate 3 octaves of B, E, D, and G notes.

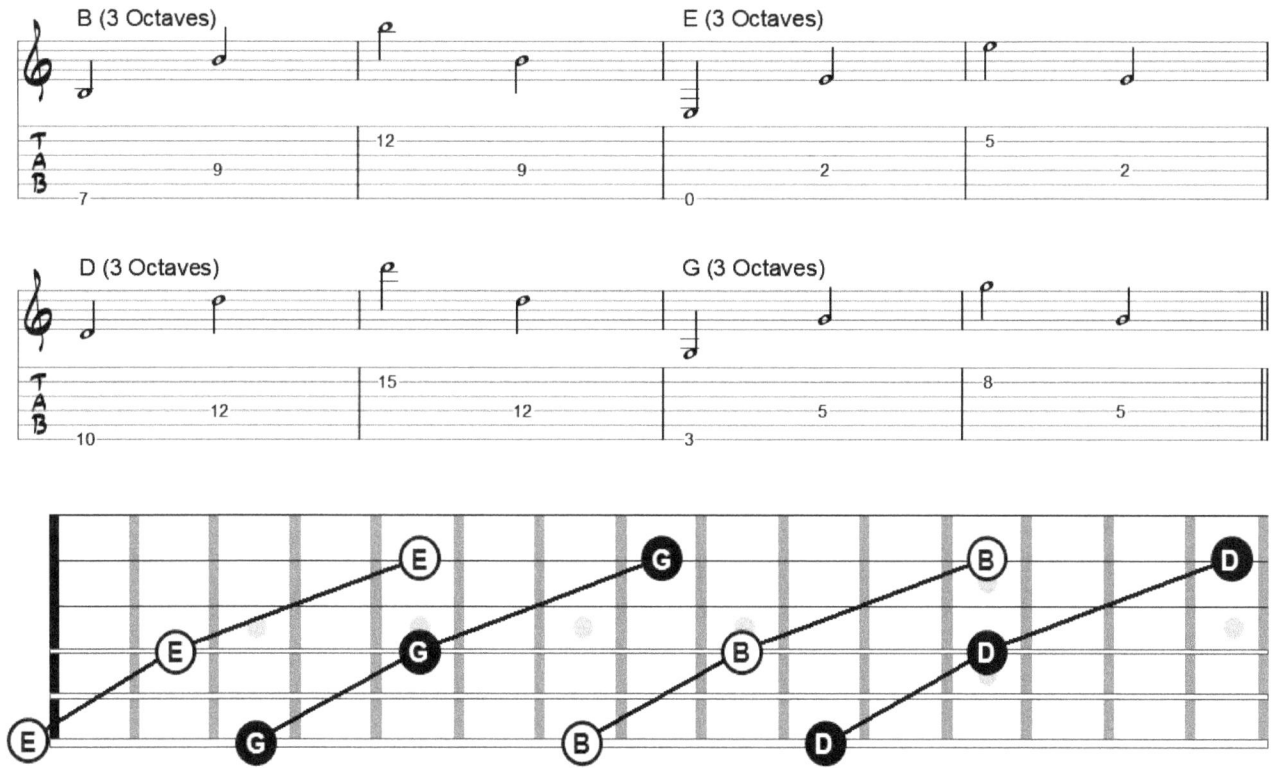

Add the second note. For minor pentatonic, it should feel like the "Rock and Roll Rule", using your first finger and pinky (3 frets). For Major pentatonic, it is just a whole-step (2 frets).

Here is B minor and its relative D Major.

Once you have more than a few notes you will have to start thinking a little different about how you might move your hand. You should be open to picking up your hand and moving it into the next octave position to be ready for any of the notes in that octave.

Here is a B minor pentatonic scale, the first four notes. They play exactly the same way for all 3 octaves.

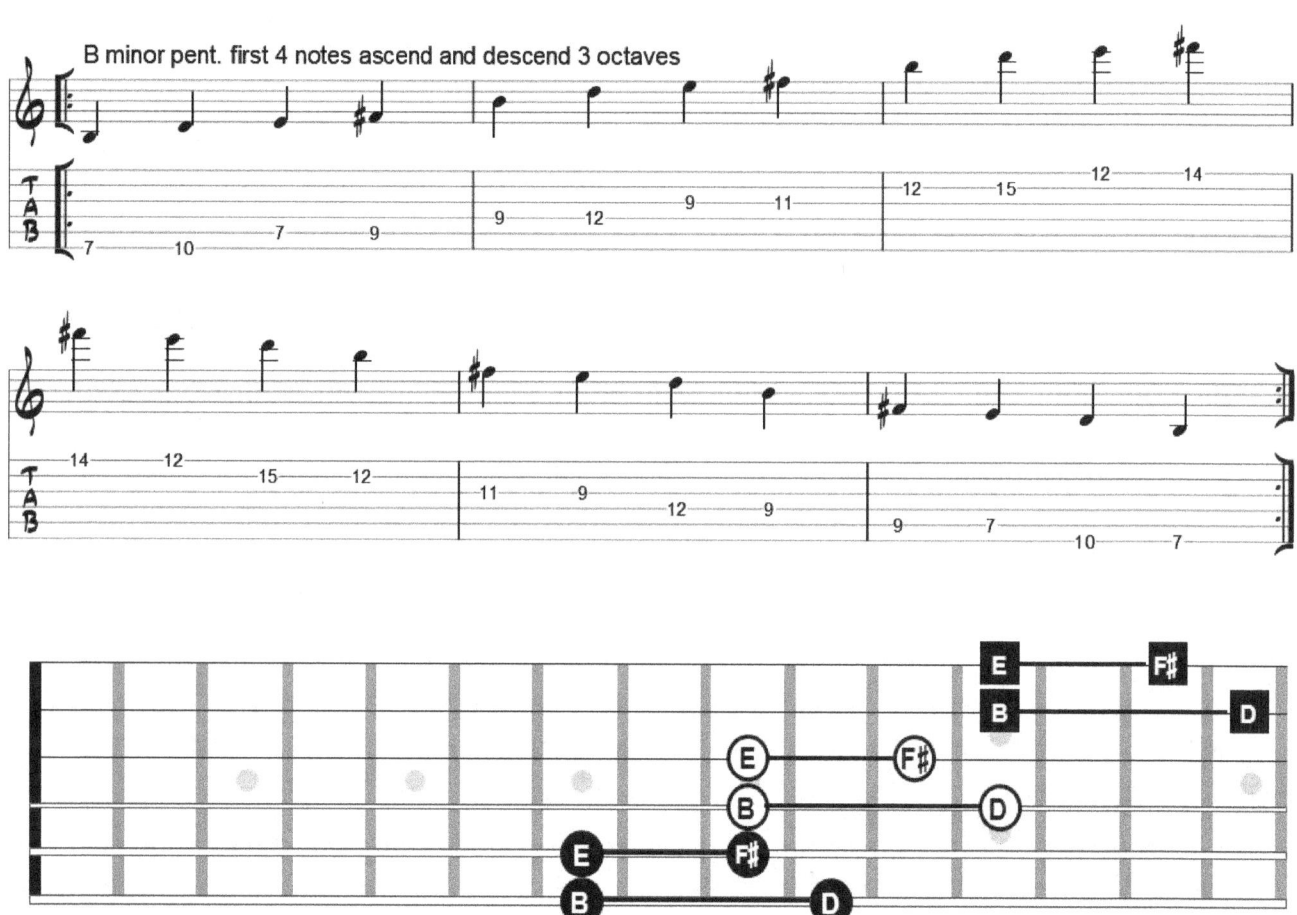

Keep your hand as a unit. Pick it up and when you put it down all the fingers are already in place to play the four notes. It is important to keep this happening when you add the fifth note of the scale.

Finally add the 5th note to the scale. Keep the hand in position to play the first four notes (B, D, E, F#) then add the fifth note (A). Once you do, then shift your whole hand into the area for the new octave. This will happen differently in the middle and top octave. In the middle octave you have to compensate for the B string (this is the Long octave shape). In the top octave we run out of room on the high E string.

Always watch the 3 root notes of B and eventually the last one on the 19th fret of the high E string.

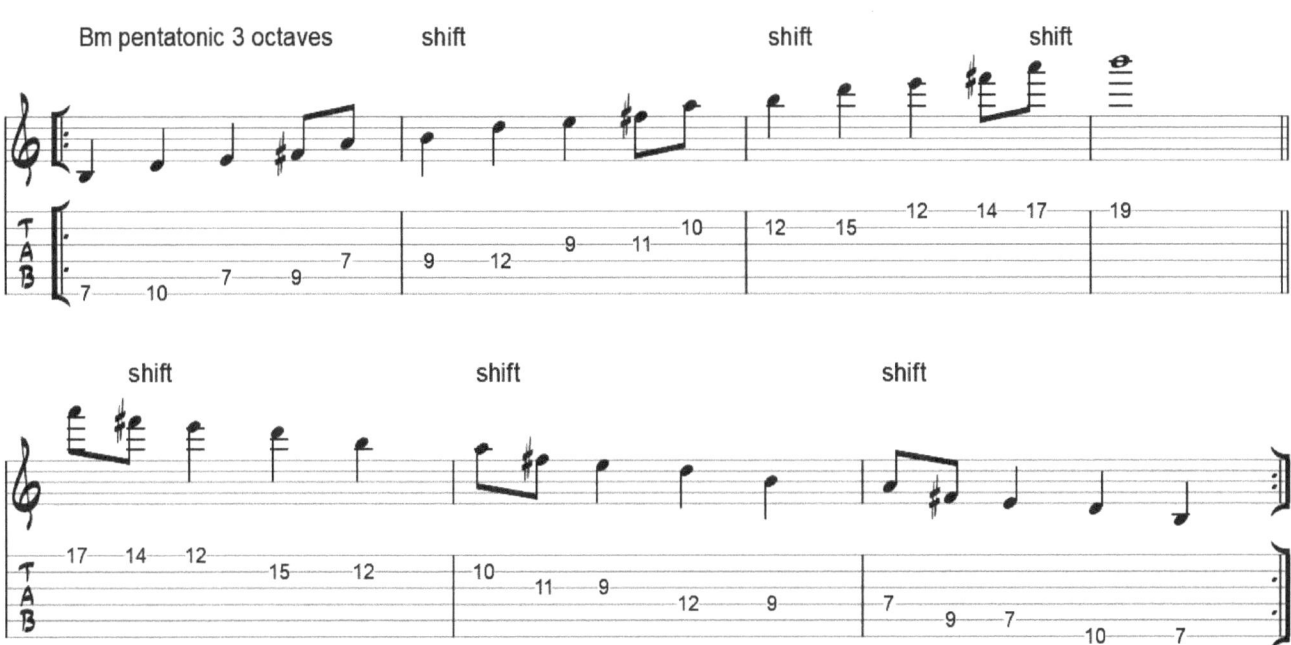

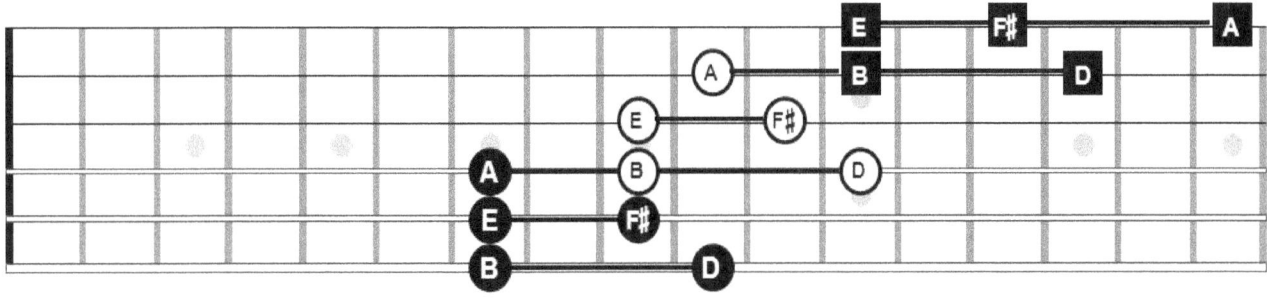

Here is a backing track to work this idea over. It is based on a B minor chord (B minor 7). If we solo with the global approach we would use B minor pentatonic the whole time. We can now navigate that scale for 3 octaves with Neck Anatomy. This is still true with the traditional 5 pentatonic shapes. You could also take a more advanced approach and play the changes, having access to 3 octaves for all the scales.

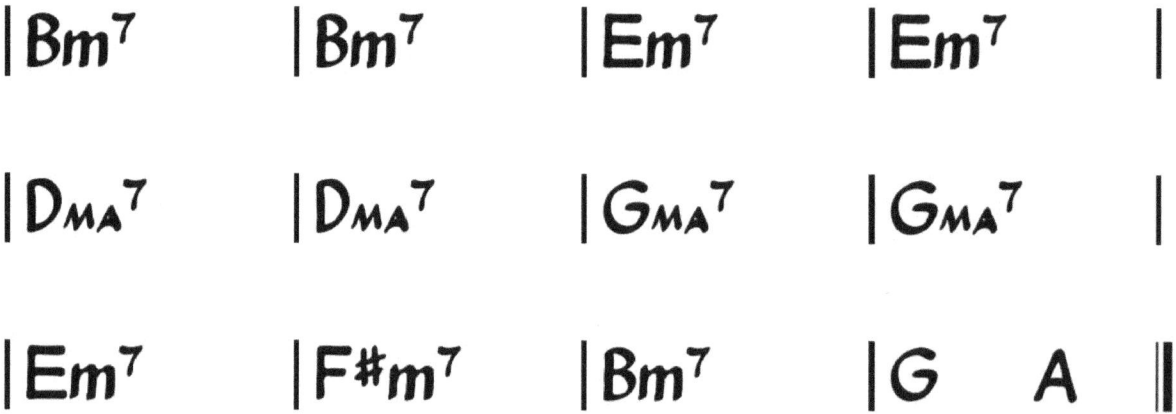

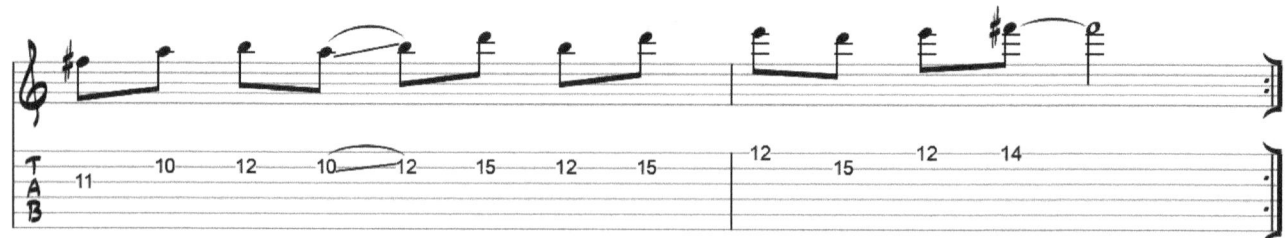

SUMMARY

We are musicians. We are guitar players.
We learn the language of music, Melody, Harmony, and Rhythm.
We learn the craft of playing the guitar as an instrument.
Always make your music decisions first and then go to your instrument/guitar.

MUSICIAN

- There are only 12 notes. (ABCDEFG are the Natural notes and there are 5 accidentals.)
- EF and BC are a ½ step apart (smallest distance).
- There are only 12 Major chords, 12 minor chords, 12 Major pentatonics, 12 minor pentatonics each based on one of the 12 notes.
- There are two inherent sounds of a Pentatonic scale, Major and minor (to match its respective chord).
- The **Blues Scale** is playing a minor pentatonic over a Major chord.
- There is a **relative minor to every Major** (1½ steps below the Major root). This means two-for-one.
- For soloing, match a scale to its chord.
- Playing **Globally** equals 1 scale for all the chords.
- **Playing the changes** equals a scale per chord. This "talks" directly to each chord, giving you its chord tones and color tones.
- **Sequences** are a powerful musical sound. They are really natural to listen to and great for composing and improvising.
- **Accents** give dimension to rhythm. Accents allow multiple rhythms to exist simultaneously. There is so much potential expressiveness with accents.

GUITAR PLAYER

- The 12 notes are the first 12 frets on the guitar that we navigate on the lowest E string.
- We use the **"Rock and Roll Rule"** to put pattern #1 on the fretboard after making the music decision about what scale we need.
- There are 5 patterns to connect our 12 fret fretboard for all 12 keys.
- We learned how to use **BSSBS** to play a minor pentatonic scale and **SSBSB** to play a Major pentatonic scale on any one string.
- We learned how to use **OCTAVE SHAPES** as a playable sounds as well as using them to unlock the fretboard.
- Use pattern #1 to get started with **PLAYING THE CHANGES.**
- Use the **CAGED** system to connect chord shapes to scale shapes.
- Bends are the most advanced of our legato techniques. We can see the power of **pre-bends** as they are the only way to allow the notes to bend "down."
- Knowing how hard and soft to pluck is essential to properly playing with dynamics. **Accents** can happen in the pick hand (hard and soft picking) as well as in the fretboard hand (when you play notes versus mutes).
- **Neck Anatomy** (how to see octaves) on the guitar is the single greatest revelation I've had about the guitar. It puts the simplicity of music in view and gets rid of the confusing three dimensional aspect of our fretboard.

CHAPTER 8

TUNE IN

"I am a musician and a guitar player. Music is my language and my guitar is my voice. Music is Melody, Harmony and Rhythm. I develop my language skills and my instrument skills. They are two separate worlds working together to complete the circle of music."

Rhythm is the number one factor to sounding great as a musician.

WARM UP

Muted String Ladder (MSL) using One Pick Per String (OPPS) for 4 strings

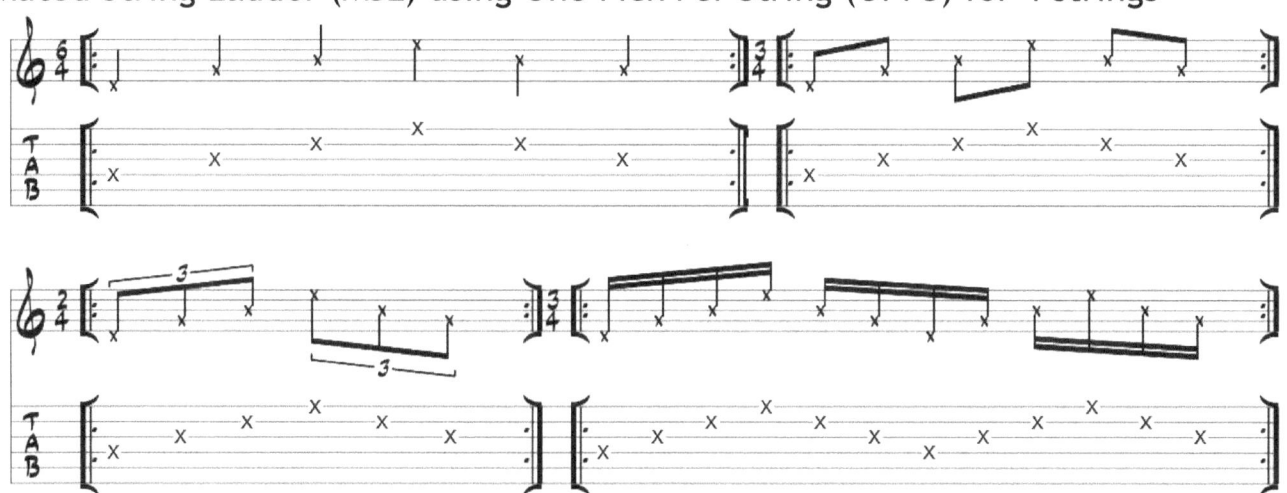

You will notice that the time signature changes often. This is simply because of the number of strings versus the rhythm. The time signatures show you how many beats it takes for the ladder to start over again. You can keep these ideas all in 4/4, it would take longer to come back to beat 1 but that doesn't mean that you can't play some of it.

SHELLS

1 2 4 *Stretch* is a shell shape that uses two whole-steps. Using 1 3 4 along with 1 2 4 enables you to play almost any scale beyond the pentatonic.

Use your Index (first) finger, your Middle finger, and Pinky to play the 1 2 4 *Stretch*. Keep your fretboard thumb behind the neck and behind the first two fingers. This allows your hand to open and accommodate the larger reach.

1 2 4 Stretch as eighth-notes

1 2 4 Stretch as triplets

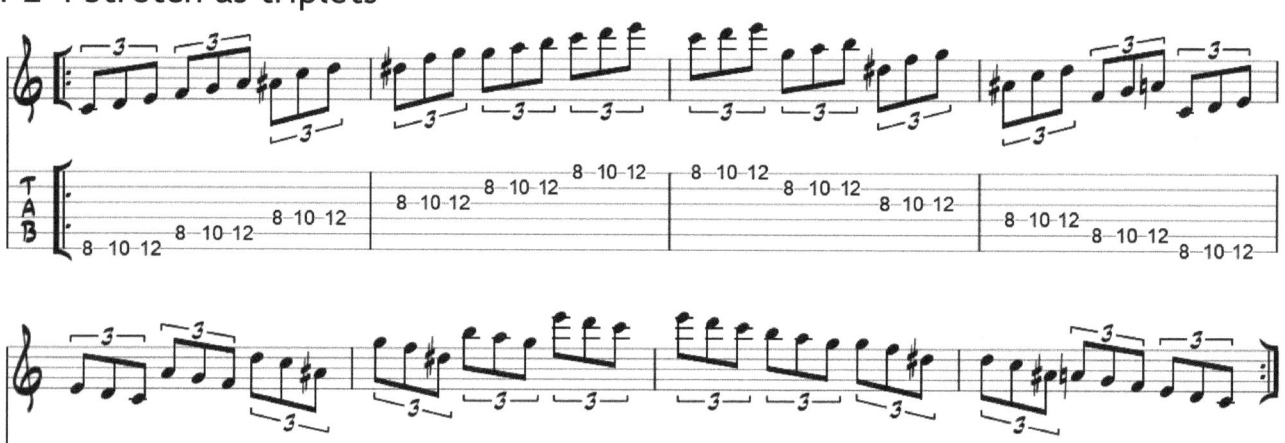

CHANGING GEARS

Here is a list of potential fingerings for gears 1-8. These are common musical groupings. You can also reverse the 1 3 4 fingerings (think SHELL). You can do this with 1 2 4, and the 1 2 4 *stretch*.

GEAR	FINGERS
Quarter-note (1)	1
Eighth-notes (2)	1 3
Triplets (3)	1 3 4
Sixteenth-notes (4)	1 3 4 3
Quintuplets (5)	1 3 4 3 4
Sextuplets (6)	1 3 4 1 3 4
Septuplets (7)	1 3 4 3 1 3 4
Thirty Second Notes (8)	1 3 4 3 1 3 4 3

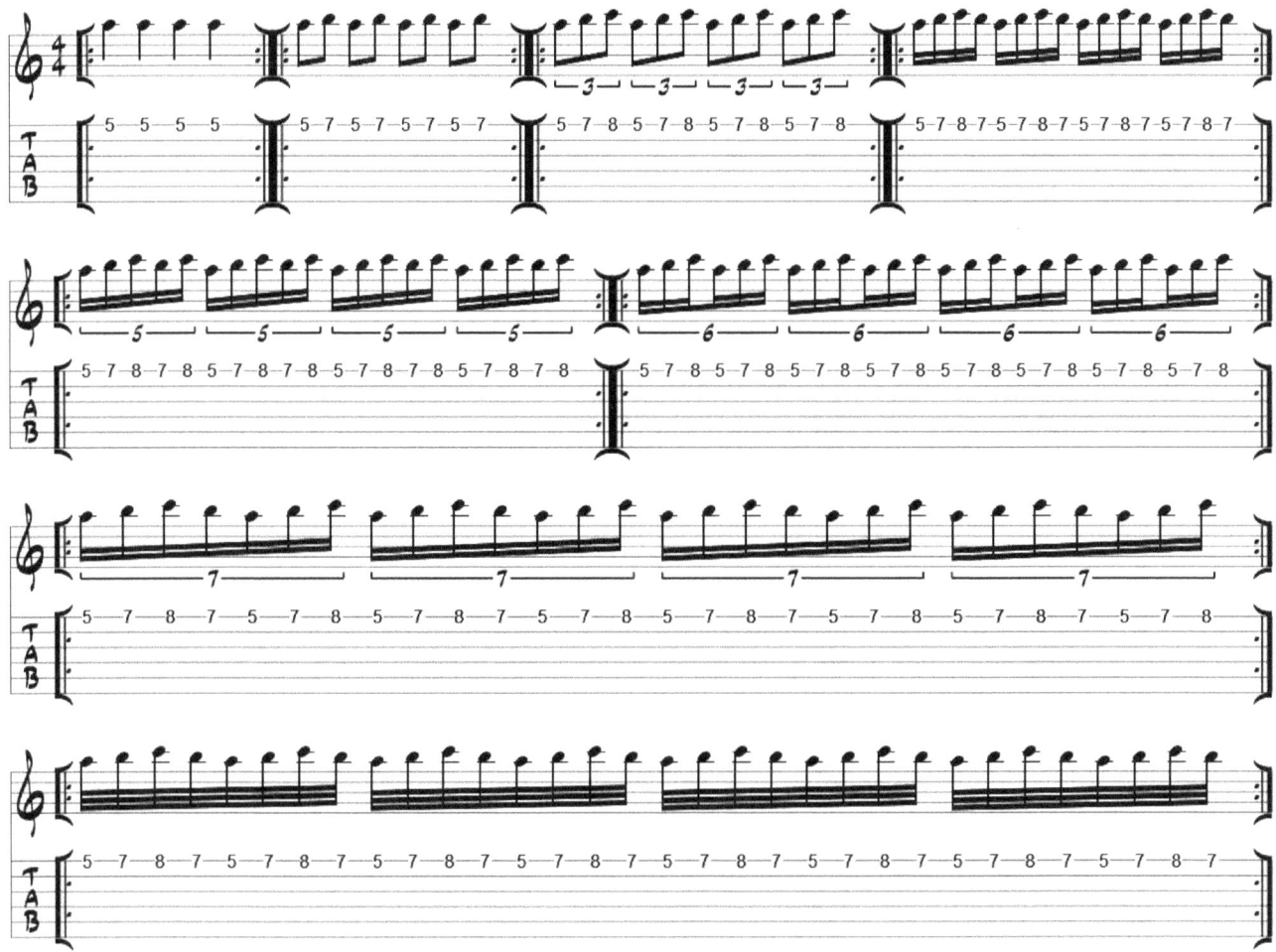

EXERCISE

Pick a tempo and a gear. Play each pattern low to high and back (or the reverse), or play them as "Round the block." This is D Major, B minor and B blues pentatonic. You can start in either direction.

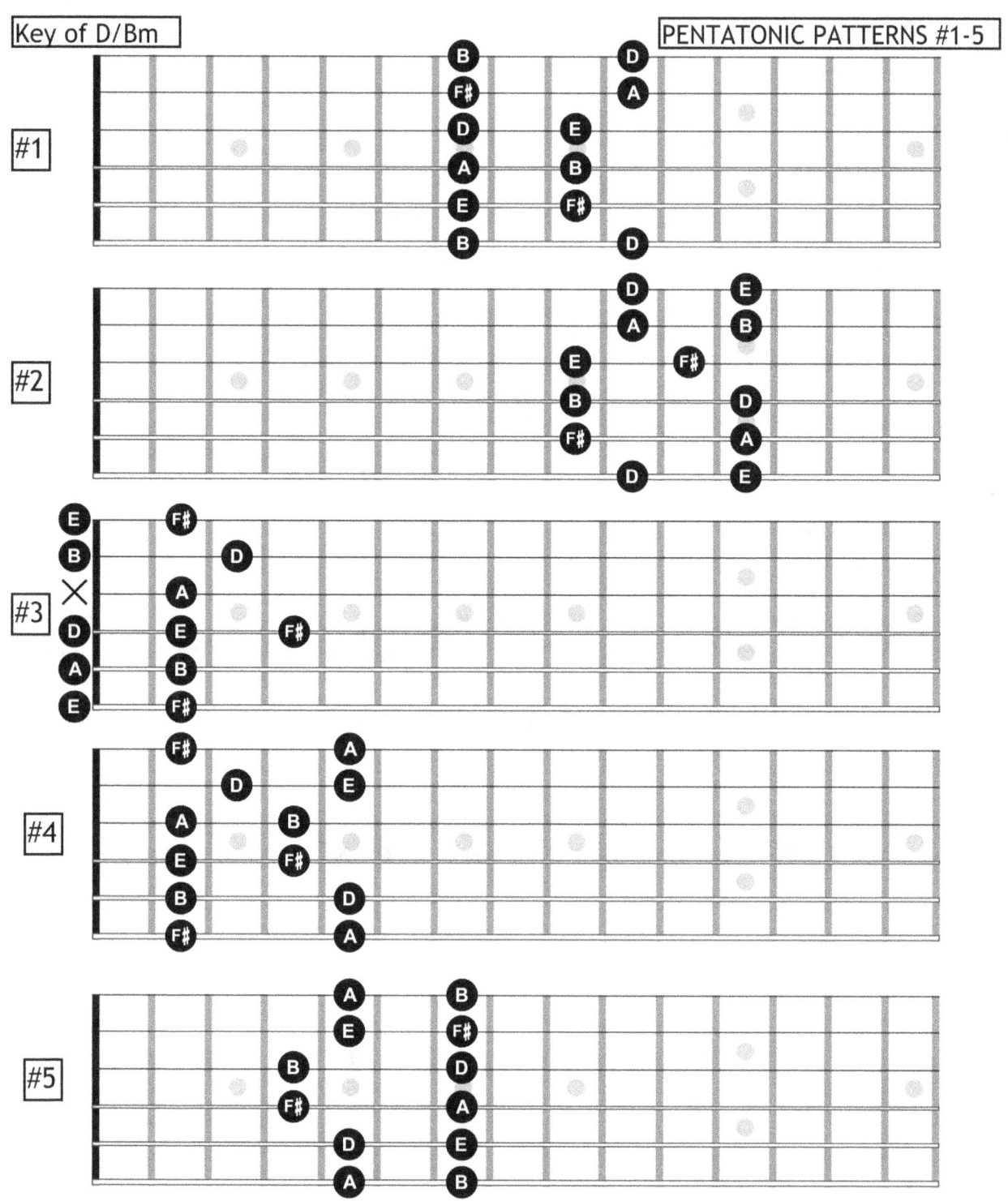

REVIEW

Using Neck Anatomy is one of the most effective ways to see scales, notes, and arpeggios move in three octaves. Once you adjust movement for the B string and the limits of the instrument, you can see how the guitar can play three octaves in almost the same way following short to long octaves.

Use a short octave to long octave to build a 3 octave B minor pentatonic scale. Here are the first four notes of the B minor pentatonic scale. They play exactly the same way for all 3 octaves. Lift your hand for each octave so when you place your hand down you will be ready to go for all four notes.

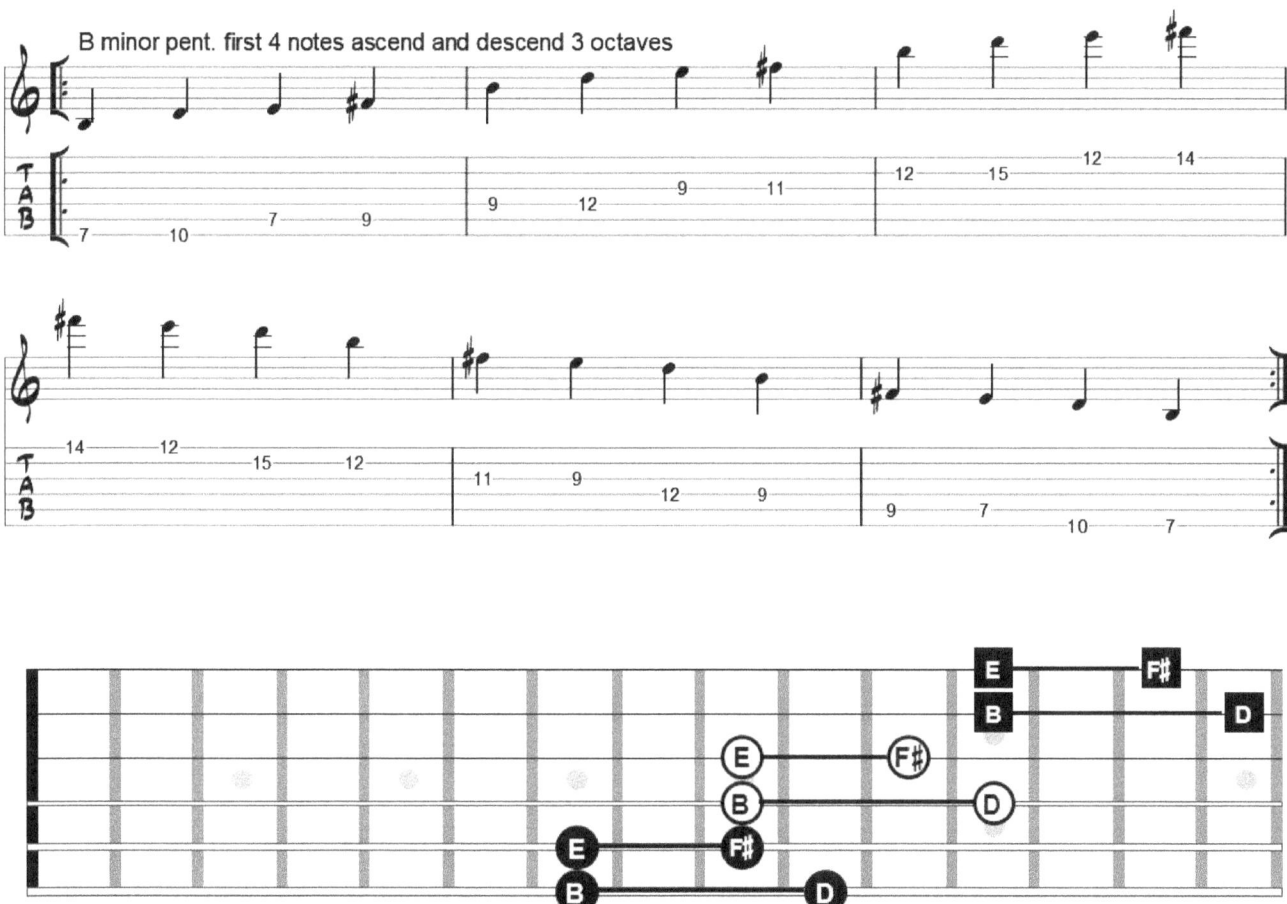

Now add the fifth note of the minor pentatonic. It is always a whole-step behind the next octave root note. If you are looking at your root notes with Short to Long octave, then you can see the last note behind it by 2 frets.

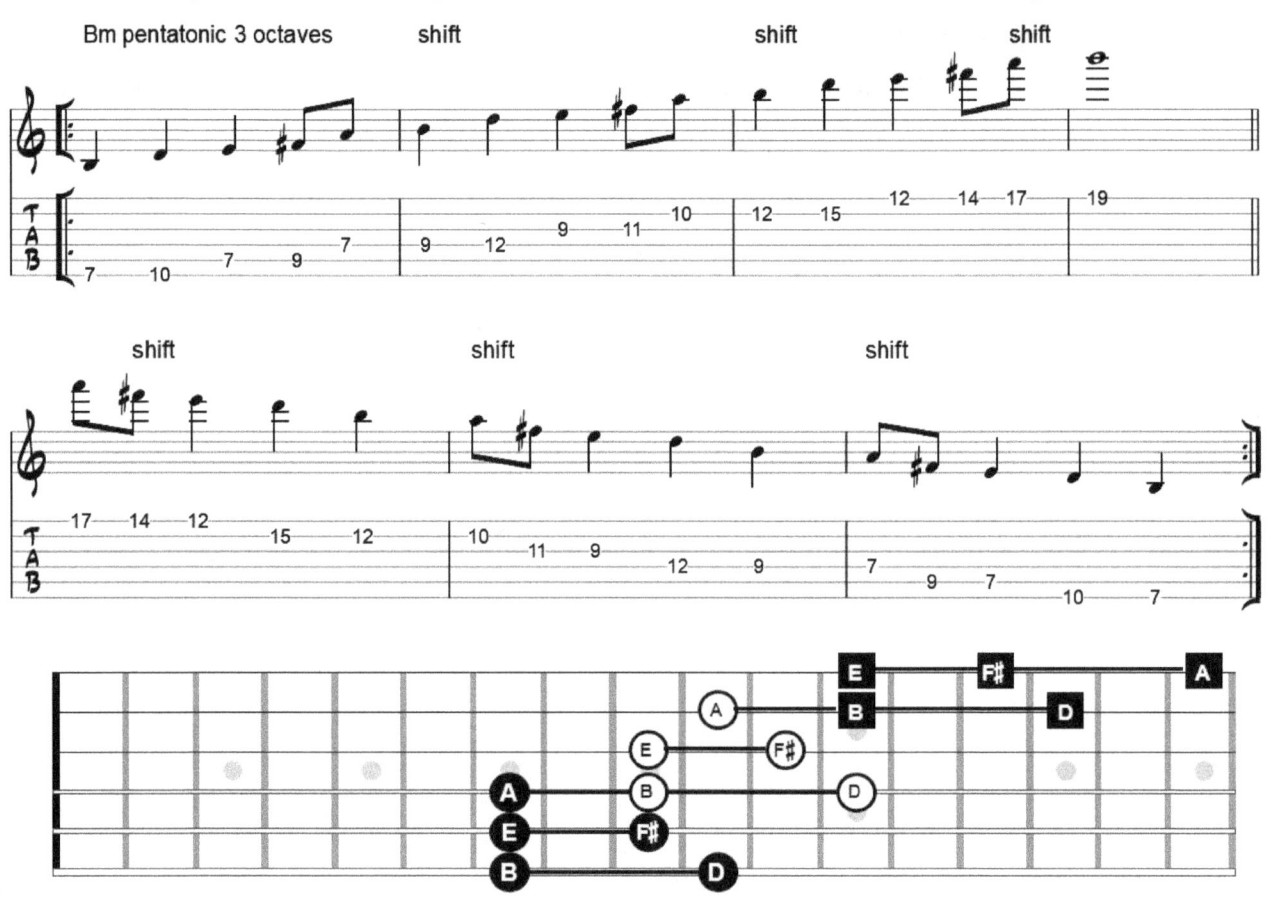

The MAJOR pentatonic is even easier. Here is D Major pentatonic

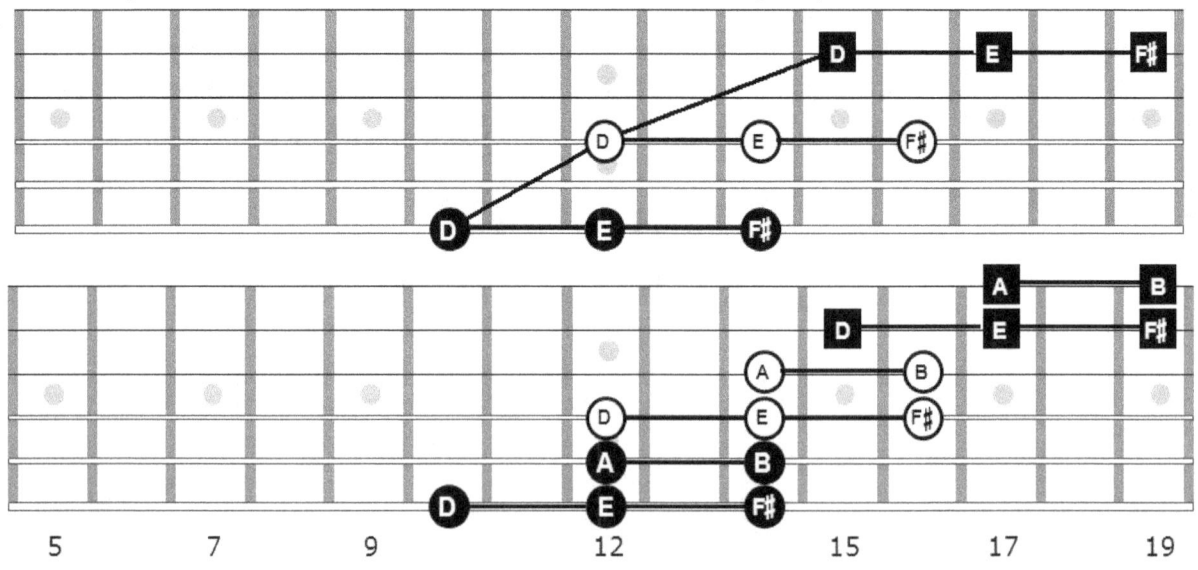

THE BLUES CROSS

Over the years as I figured out solos, licks and other ideas I started to see moves popping up over and over again. It was Eric Clapton who I first noticed using this movement that I call the "Blues Cross." It is a very easy little grip to play, and a movable pentatonic scale pattern. It plays very nicely with Neck Anatomy. It's also easy to see the Blue Note (BN).

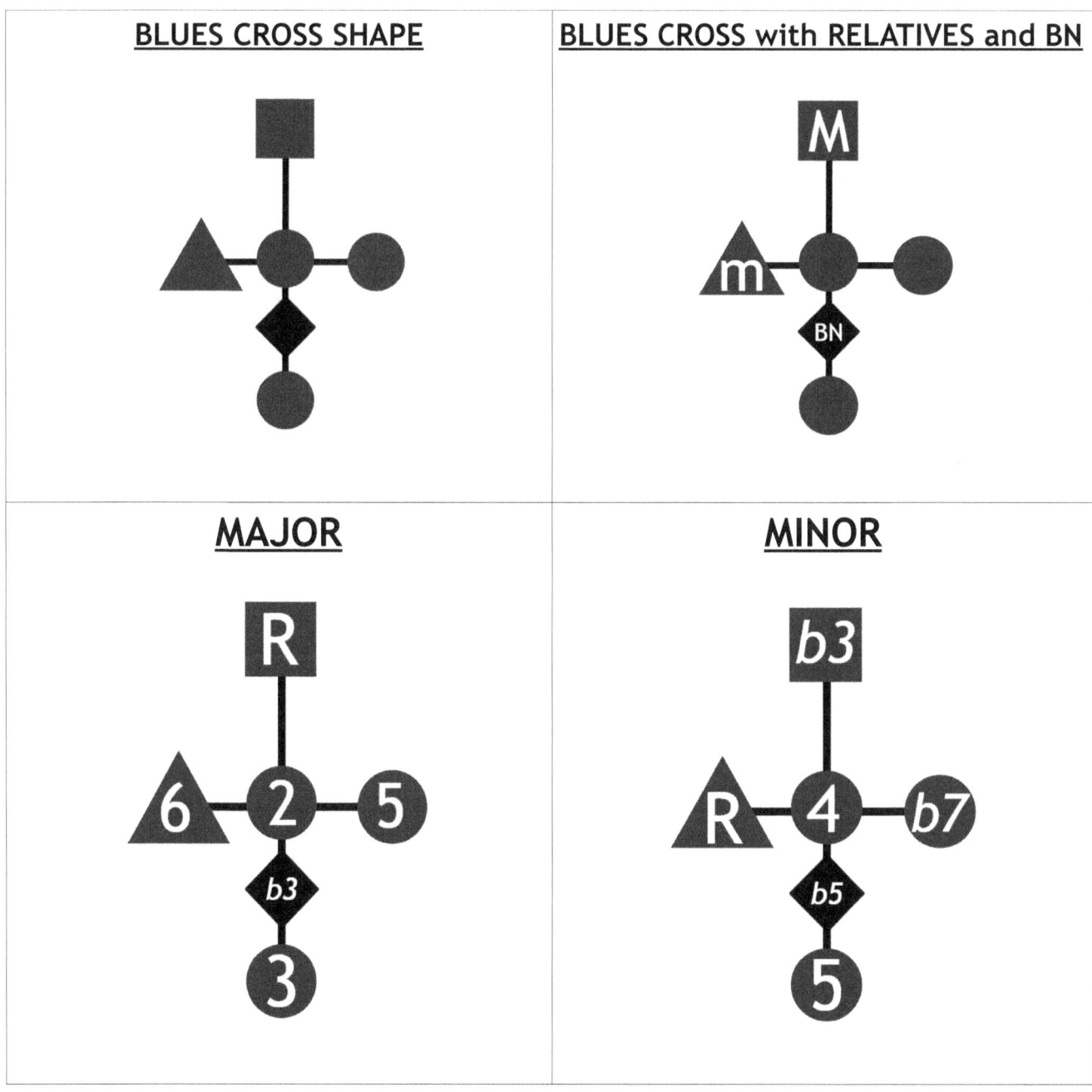

Here is our B minor pentatonic (D Major pentatonic) using the Blues Cross shape. You can navigate the octaves for B using Neck Anatomy. You can then move the Blues Cross for three octaves as long as you adjust for the B string. If you look closely you can see how the Blues Cross is really part of Pattern #1 and #5 when you start on the low E string. It's part of Pattern #1 and #2 in the middle octave, and pattern #2 (King Box) and pattern #3 in the highest octave.

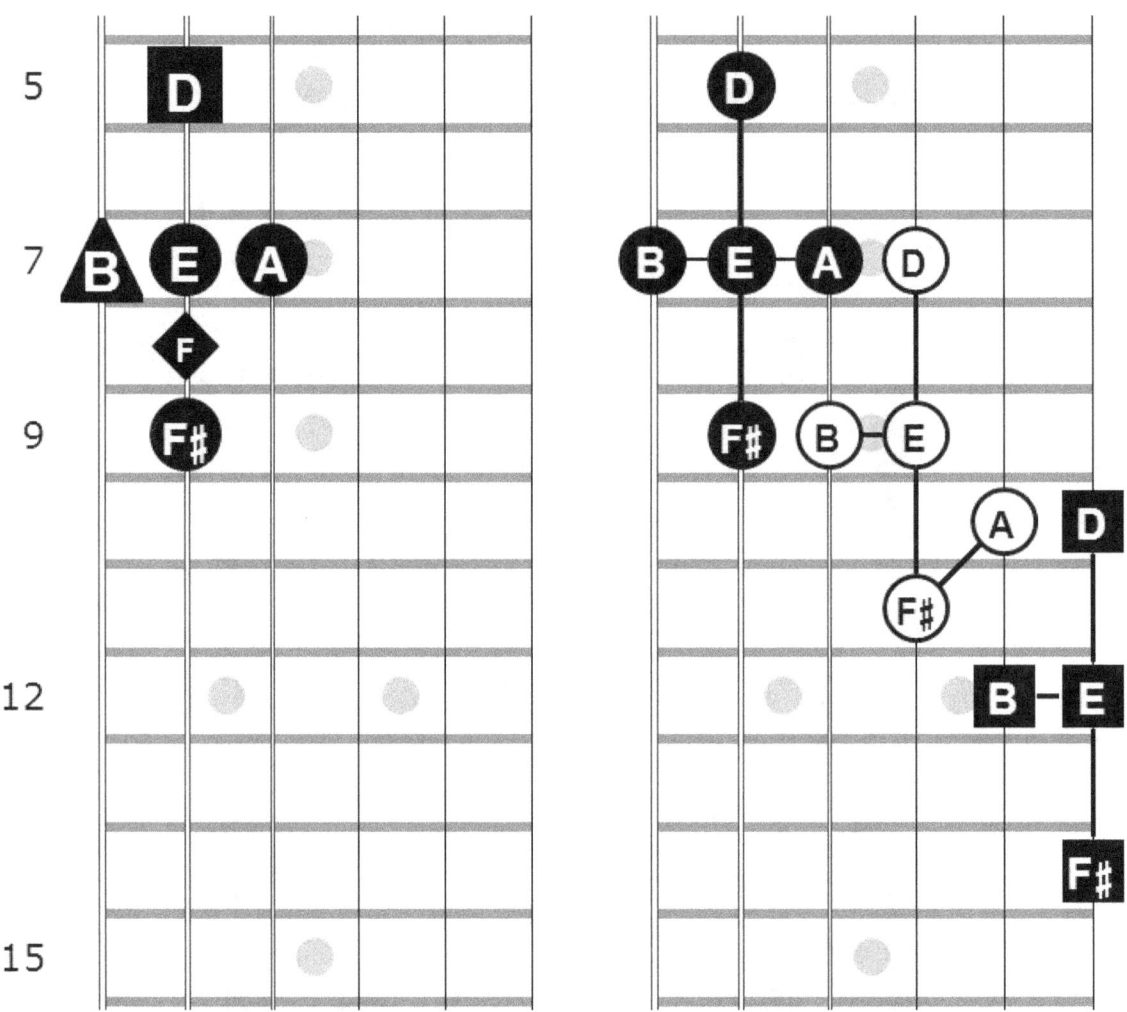

NOTE: In this illustration, the Blues Cross is notated in an upright position versus the horizontal diagrams. I believe it is easier to visualize it this way. As you grow as a guitar player you will be able to very easily adjust to the two different looks of upright versus horizontal.

PRACTICE

Let's practice each octave of a B minor pentatonic using the Blues Cross. Here is the first octave. I notated a slide in this to help facilitate the movement, but it also sounds fantastic. You don't have to always do the slide. When the Blues Cross is acting like a minor scale you will almost always start with your 3rd (ring) finger. This way you can play everything with your first (index) and 3rd (ring) fingers.

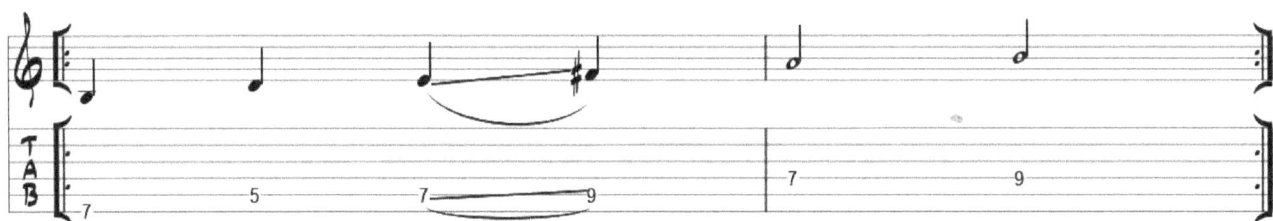

Here is the second (middle) octave of the Blues Cross for B minor pentatonic. You will immediately notice the shift (by 1 fret) on the B string. This move should feel extremely familiar. I call it the 1-2 Slide Lick.

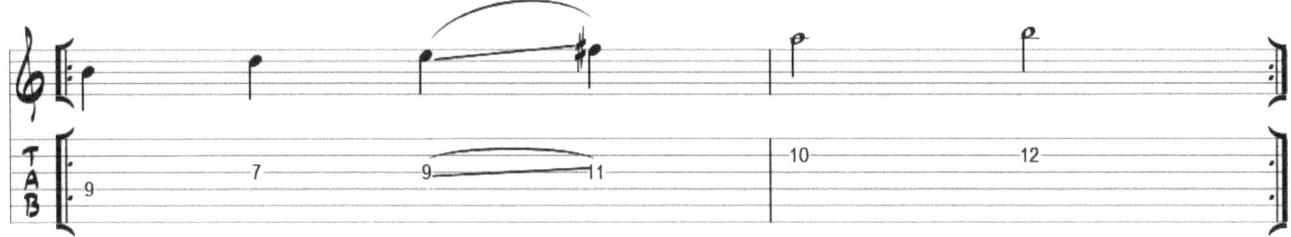

Once we add the third octave we hit a limit with our strings. We can only get the first four notes (just like using Neck Anatomy in the original shapes). As usual you can visualize the last note of the scale as a whole-step (2 frets) below the next root.

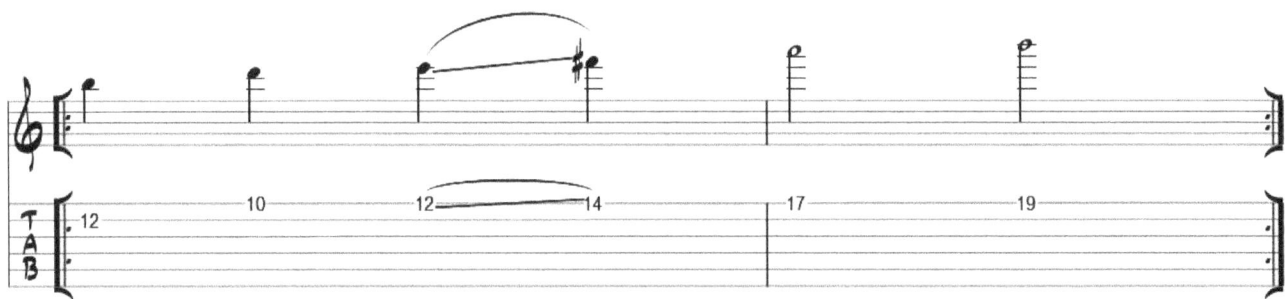

Finally we can do all three octaves with the Blues Cross following our Neck Anatomy Octaves.

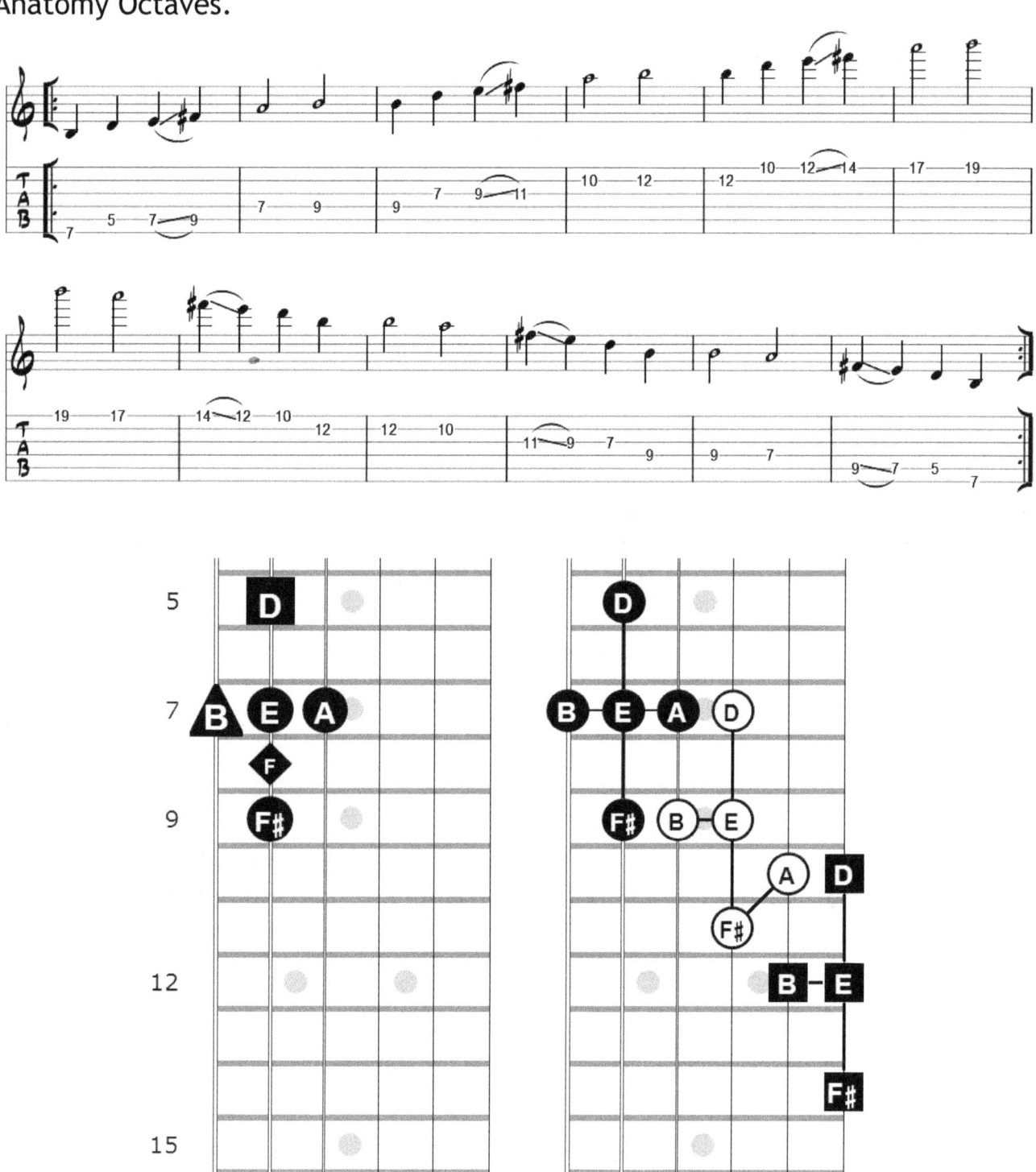

SUMMARY

We are musicians. We are guitar players.
We learn the language of music, Melody, Harmony, and Rhythm.
We learn the craft of playing the guitar as an instrument.
Always make your music decisions first and then go to your instrument/guitar.

MUSICIAN

- There are **only 12 notes.** (ABCDEFG are the Natural notes and there are 5 accidentals.)
- EF and BC are ½ step apart (smallest distance).
- There are only 12 Major chords, 12 minor chords, 12 Major pentatonics, 12 minor pentatonics each based on one of the 12 notes.
- There are two inherent sounds of a Pentatonic scale, Major and minor (to match its respective chord).
- There is a **relative minor to every Major** (1½ steps below the Major root). This means two-for-one.
- **The Blues Scale** is playing a minor pentatonic over a Major chord.
- For soloing, match a scale to its chord.
- **Playing Globally** equals 1 scale for all the chords.
- **Playing the changes** equals a scale per chord. This directly "talks" to each chord, giving you its chord tones and color tones.
- **Sequences** are a powerful musical sound. They are really natural to listen to and great for composing and improvising.
- **Accents** give dimension to rhythm. Accents allow multiple rhythms to exist simultaneously. There is so much potential expressiveness with accents.

GUITAR PLAYER

- The 12 notes are the first 12 frets on the guitar that we navigate on the lowest E string.
- We use the "**Rock and Roll Rule**" to put pattern #1 on the fretboard after making the music decision about what scale we need.
- There are **5 patterns** to connect our 12 fret fretboard for all 12 keys.
- We learned how to use **BSSBS** to play a minor pentatonic scale and **SSBSB** to play a Major pentatonic scale on any one string.
- We learned how to use **OCTAVE SHAPES** as a playable sounds as well as using them to unlock the fretboard.
- Use pattern #1 to get started with **PLAYING THE CHANGES.**
- Use the **CAGED** system to connect chord shapes to scale shapes.
- Bends are the most advanced of our legato techniques. We can see the power of **pre-bends** as they are the only way to allow the notes to bend "down."
- Knowing how hard and soft to pluck is essential to properly playing with dynamics. **Accents** can happen in the pick hand (hard and soft picking) as well as in the fretboard hand (when you play notes vs mutes).
- **Neck Anatomy** (how to see octaves) on the guitar is the single greatest revelation I've had about the guitar. It puts the simplicity of music in view and gets rid of the confusing three dimensional aspect of our fretboard.
- The **Blues Cross** is another easy and portable way to move a pentatonic scale around the whole fretboard without the need of the original patterns. (Knowing both is that much better!) It is also very convenient as you can play the patterns with your first and ring fingers making it super comfortable.

CHAPTER 9

TUNE IN

"I am a musician and a guitar player. Music is my language and my guitar is my voice. Music is Melody, Harmony and Rhythm. I develop my language skills and my instrument skills. They are two separate worlds working together to complete the circle of music."

Rhythm is the number one factor to sounding great as a musician.

WARM UP

Muted String Ladder (MSL) One Pick Per String (OPPS) 5 strings

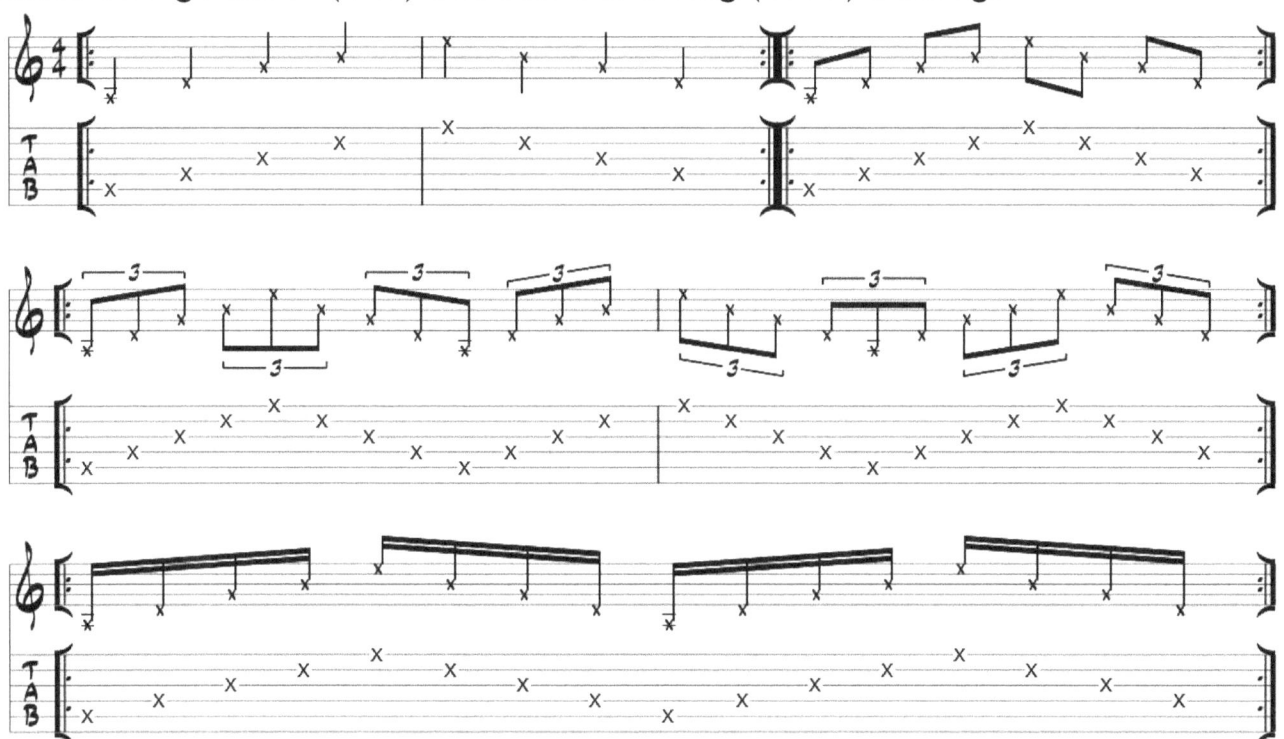

SHELLS
1 2 4 *Stretch* as triplets

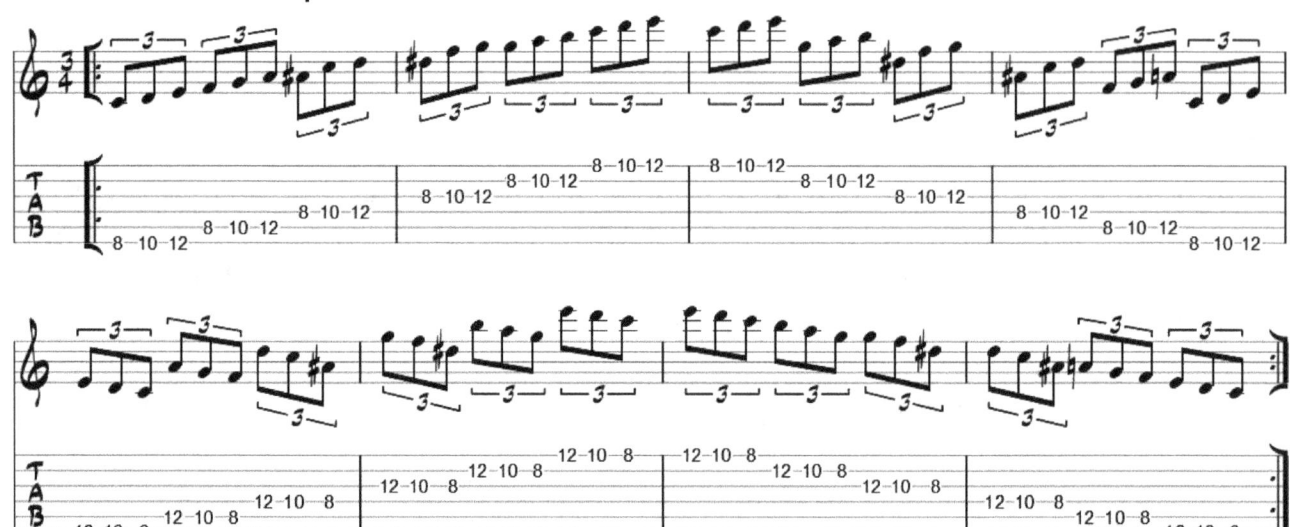

CHANGING GEARS
Ladders 1-6 with quarter-notes and then eighth-notes

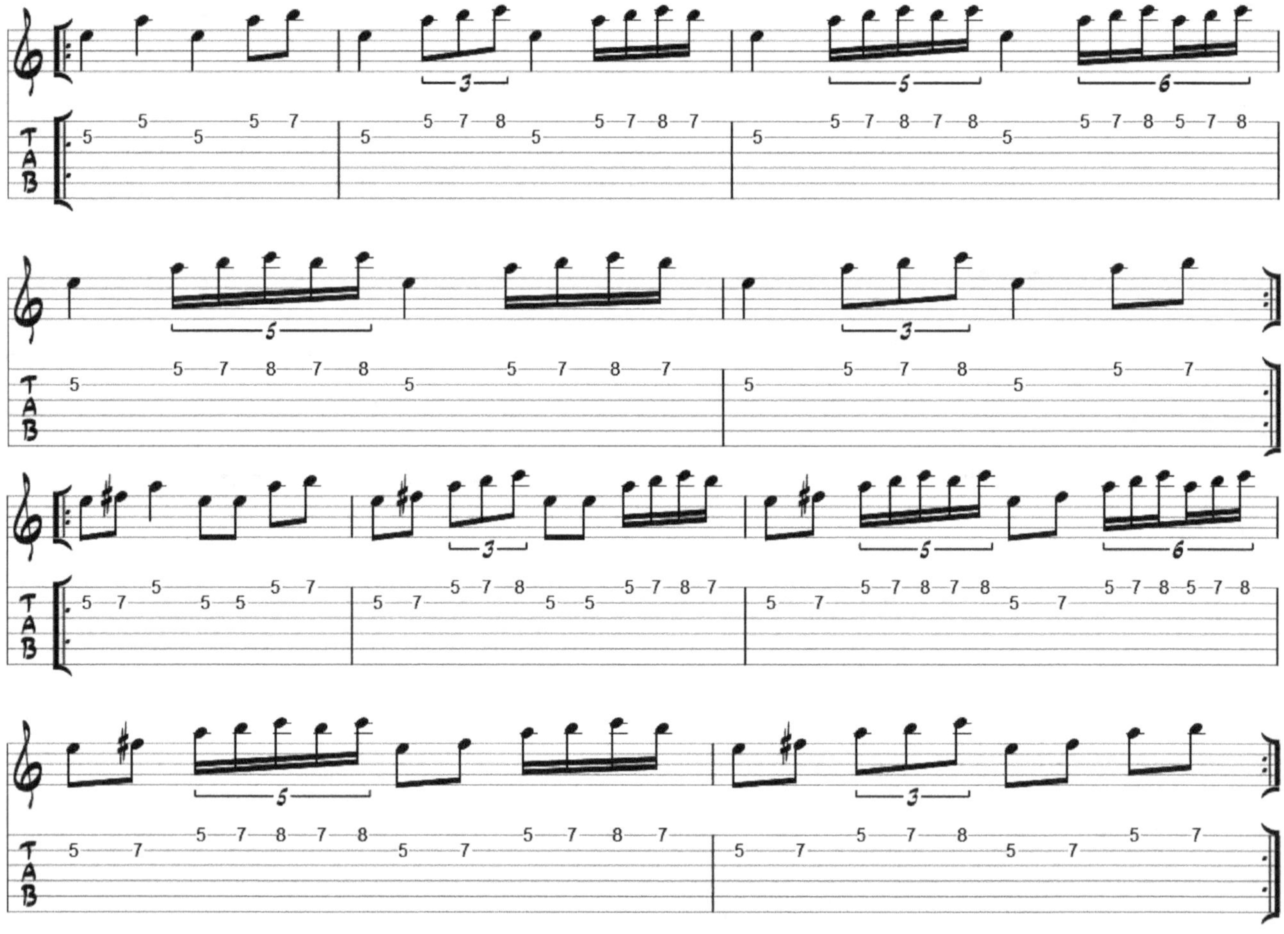

EXERCISE

Pick a tempo and a gear. Play each pattern low to high and back (or the reverse), or play them as "Round the block." This is A Major, F# minor, and F# blues pentatonic. You can start in either direction.

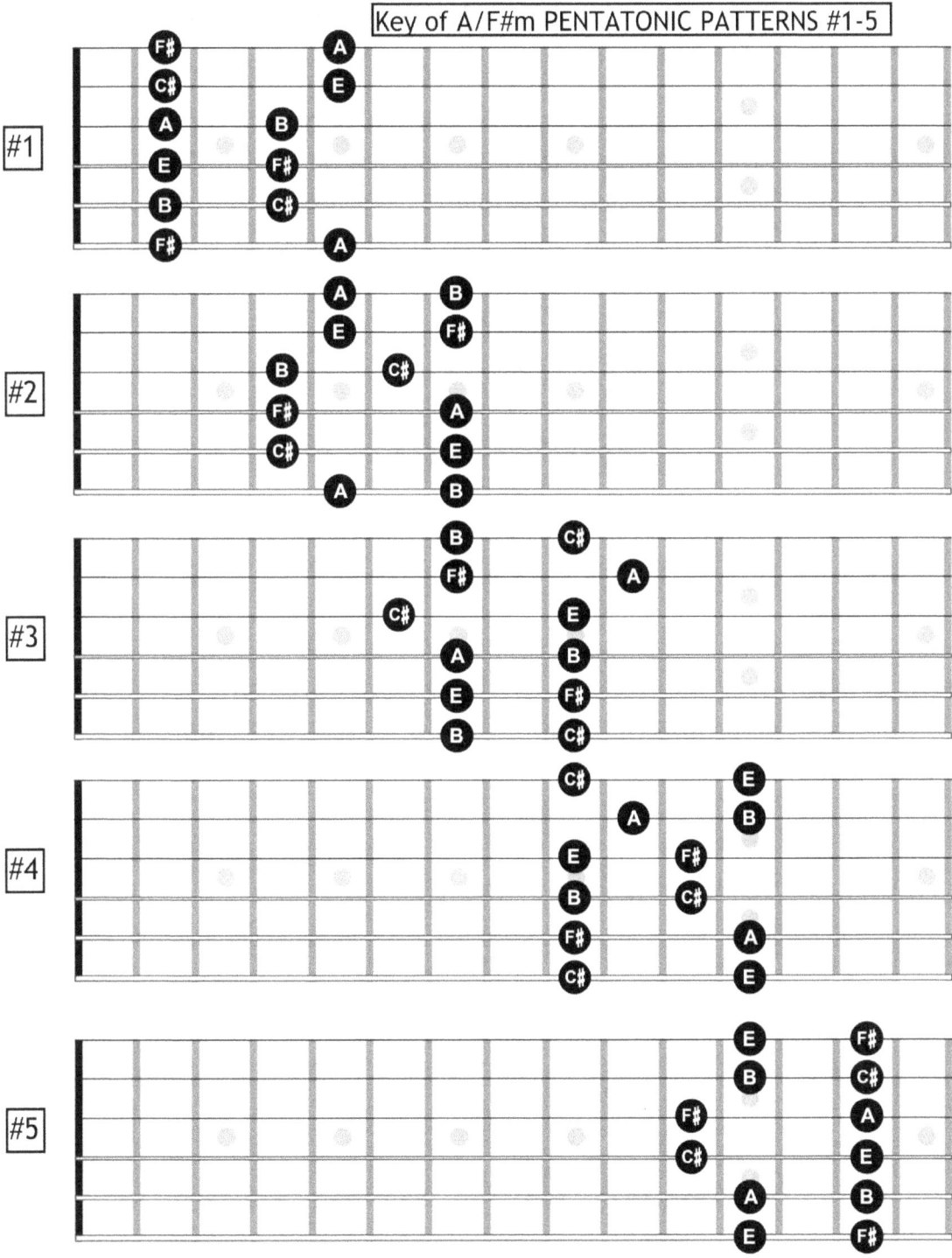

Key of A/F#m PENTATONIC PATTERNS #1-5

REVIEW

The Blues Cross is a simple little shape (of a cross) that represents the 5 notes of a pentatonic scale. You can move this shape through its octaves with Neck Anatomy and get a 3 octave movable pentatonic shape that can usually be played with just the index and ring fingers. You just have to adjust your movements for the B string.

The Blues Cross is a guitar player's device. It's still a pentatonic scale, and doesn't "sound" like anything more than a pentatonic scale. It still has the relative Major and relative minor relationship. The benefit of the Blues Cross is the simple ability to move it and play it with your most confident fingers.

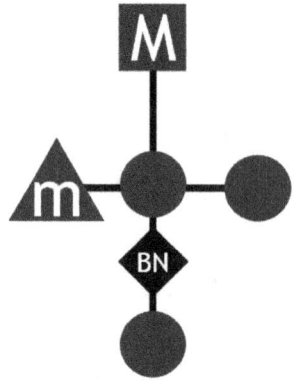

In the above diagram, the square is the relative Major and the Triangle is the relative minor. The small diamond is the Blue Note. Remember the Blue Note is literally the same note in a pentatonic scale but acts totally different depending on if it is Major (*b*3) or minor (*b*5).

Here is the B minor-D Major pentatonic scale. Each Blues Cross has a different note head shape for visual reference only.

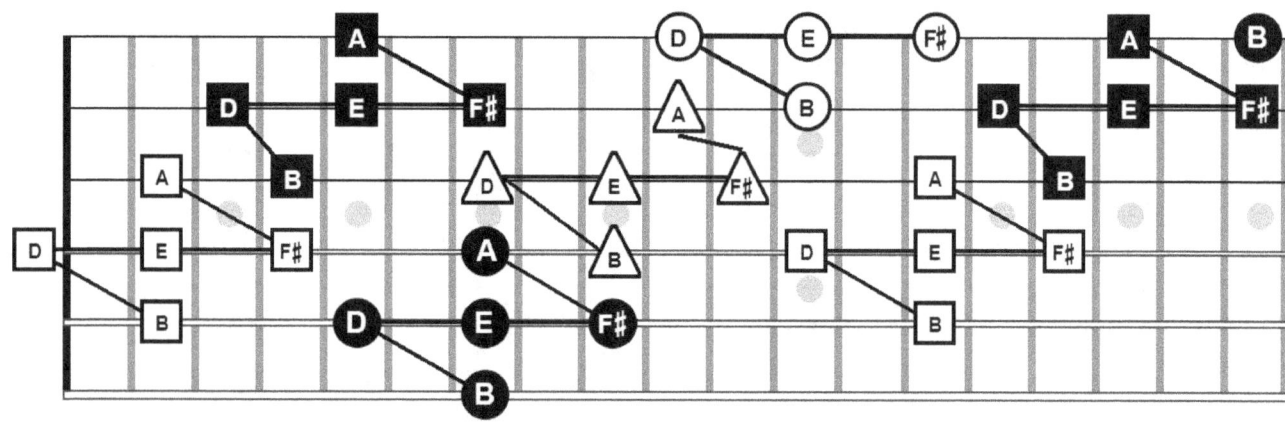

ROCK and ROLL RULE by PATTERN

The Rock and Roll Rule is when the First finger is on the relative minor root note and the Pinky is on the relative Major root note. Pattern #1 has this on the two outer strings. We use this to navigate our scales. Each of the other patterns has these two notes together but on different strings (Rock and Roll rule on different strings). There are more instances of the two roots in the patterns as well, but seeing them on one string can help us navigate. Again, this idea works nicely with Neck Anatomy.

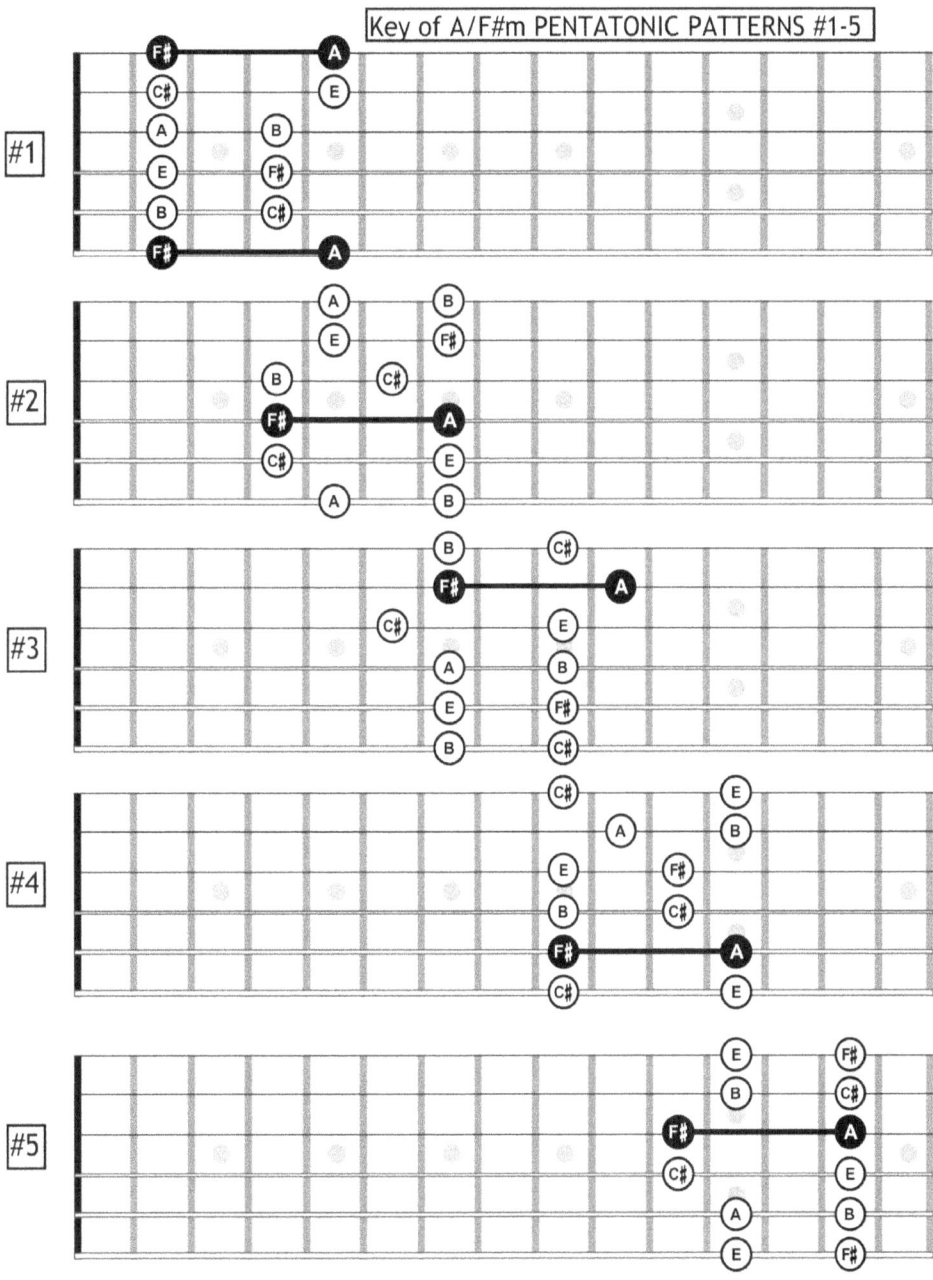

Key of A/F#m PENTATONIC PATTERNS #1-5

PLAY THE CHANGES with DIFFERENT PATTERNS

Learning to "Play the changes" brings new challenges and new rewards. The reward is a better sounding solo/melody that is connected to the sound of the song and locked in beautifully with the chords. The major challenge is keeping the chords going in your head as you solo, thinking about matching a scale for each chord, and then finding pattern #1 for that scale and navigating it on the fretboard in real time. Whew, that is a lot.

Once your brain gets used to this Alien level ability when you realize it is like when you learned bar chords. At first you were so excited you could play all (12) Major chords using one shape if you just move it up and down the fretboard! (This is just like pattern #1 of the pentatonics.)

When you tired of sliding the E form bar chord from G to C to G to D over and over again, you learned a new shape, the A form bar chord. Then you continued to learn the C and D shape bar chords. (This is the same experience as when you learned all 5 patterns of the pentatonic.)

Now when you play the changes, you are not limited to where pattern #1 is for the scale. You can start anywhere on the fretboard using any of the scale patterns for any scale. The idea is that you can play the changes and stay still if you use different patterns for each scale. Or, keep moving independently around the neck as the chords ascend or descend. Knowing the patterns for the chords allows you to freely move up and down the neck (or stay still) at any time for any creative reason you want or need.

Let's use this common I V vi IV progression in the key of A as an example.

As a musician we can see that A is the I chord, E is the V chord, F#m is the vi chord and D is the IV chord. The main chord is A, and the A Major pentatonic scale would work as the global scale.

$\frac{4}{4}$| A | E | F#m | D   ‖

CHORD (chord tones)	PENTATONIC SCALE
A (A C# E)	A Major-A B C# E F#
E (E G# B)	E Major-E F# G# B C#
F#m (F# A C#) *(relative of A)*	F# minor- F# A B C# E *(relative of A)*
D (D F# A)	D Major-D E F# A B

$\frac{4}{4}$ |A |E |F#m |D ||

Playing the changes as a musician, using pattern #1 as a guitar player, looks like below. Pattern #1 like a bar chord, Pinky on the root for A ,D, and E. The F#m is the relative* of A and they share the same scale, just a different root.

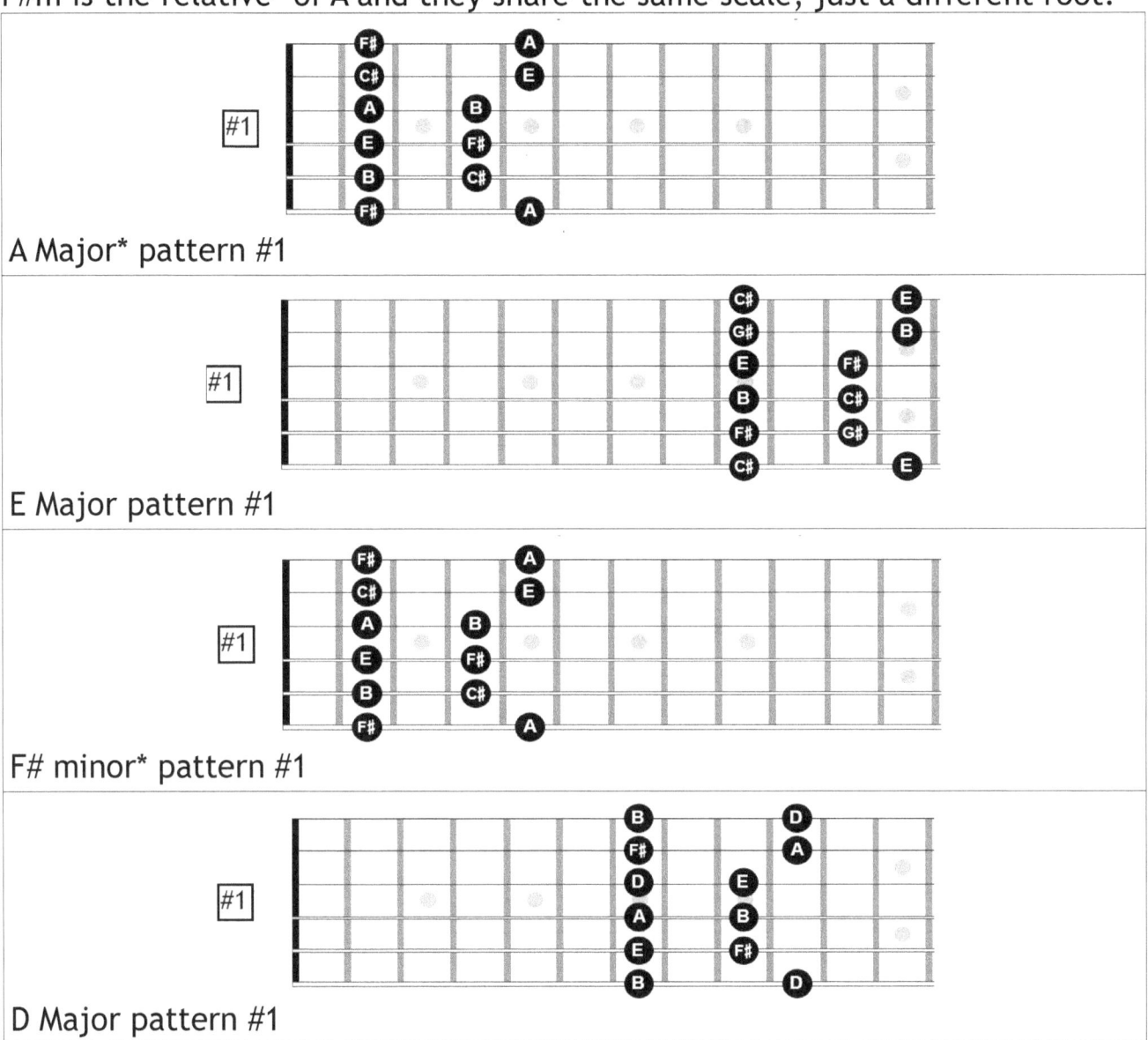

A Major* pattern #1

E Major pattern #1

F# minor* pattern #1

D Major pattern #1

As you can see and feel, there is a lot of movement necessary to maintain pattern #1 while playing these changes. Also, the key of E will always sound the highest and A/F#m will sound the lowest and that can feel limiting.

If you wish to stay in position you can use different patterns for a scale to help delegate where on the fretboard you want to be.

If you chose to stay within the first five frets of the guitar to play the changes we will need other patterns.

Use BSSBS to navigate the 5 patterns relative to pattern #1.

The A Major (and the relative F#m) pattern #1 is already in the first five frets so there is nothing new to do.

The E Major pentatonic pattern #1 is on the 9th-12th frets. In this case go backwards with BSSBS to find a different E Major pentatonic pattern. A small space (S) behind pattern #1 puts pattern #5 between the 7th and 9th frets. Go back a Big space (B) from there puts pattern #4 on the 4th-7th frets. Finally, go back a Small space (S) and that puts pattern #3 on the 2nd to 4th frets.

For the D Major pentatonic we take the same approach as we did for the E Major pentatonic. Pattern #1 is 7th to 10th frets. Pattern #5 is 5th to 7th frets. Pattern #4 is 2nd to 5th frets. Pattern #4 will be the pattern for D.

Here is an even easier way is to think like a musician. E is always a whole-step above D for anything in music, and vice versa. Visualize all of the patterns in E moving lower by 2 frets on the fretboard and you will find the patterns for D. For E Major, pattern #3 moves past the nut (not usable), but pattern #4 moves from the 4th-7th frets down to the 2nd-5th frets putting it in place.

Using these different patterns, you can now Play the Changes in this progression "in position" within the 1st to 5th frets.

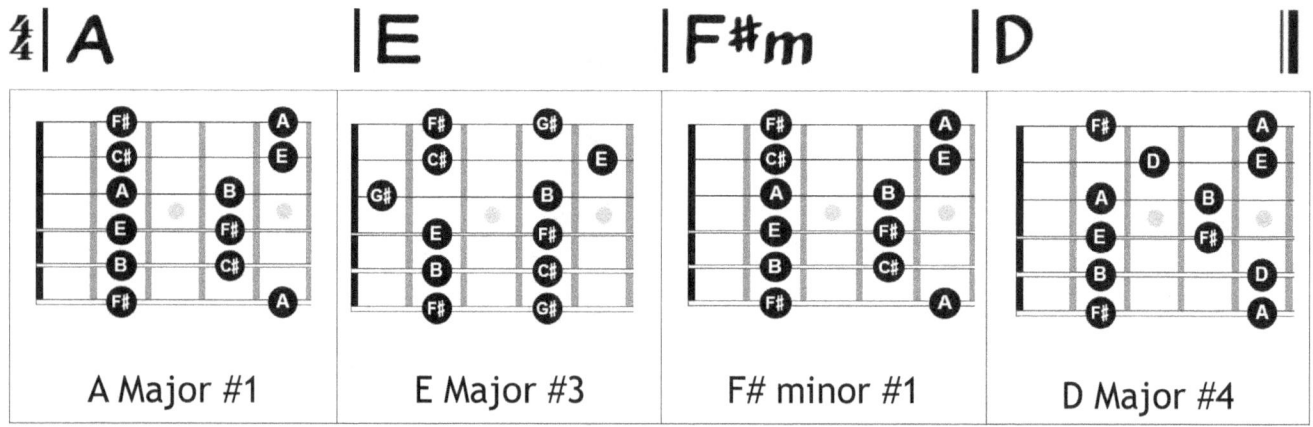

| A Major #1 | E Major #3 | F# minor #1 | D Major #4 |

PRACTICE

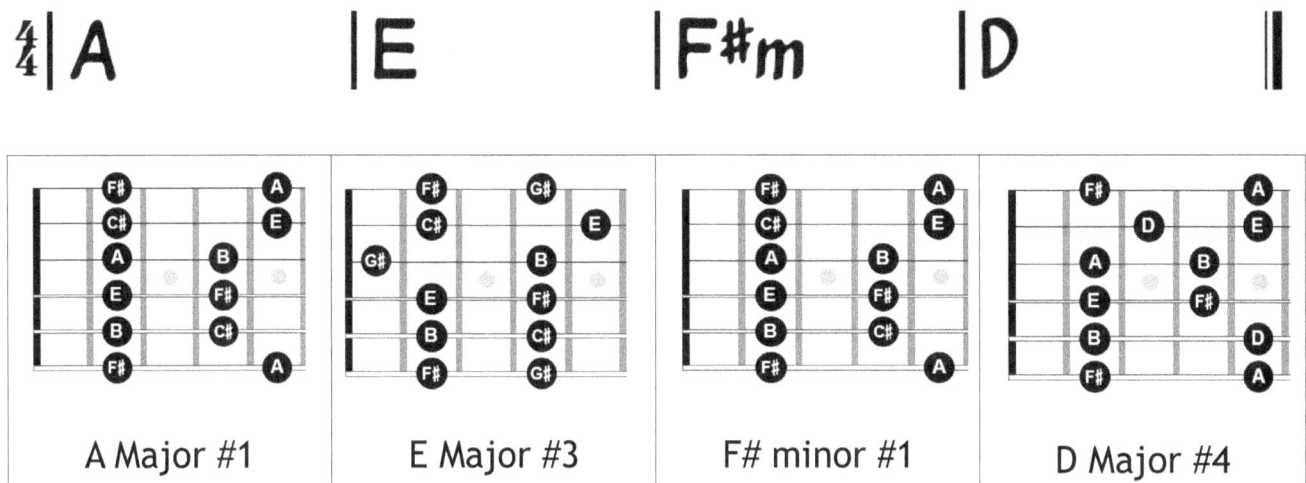

| A Major #1 | E Major #3 | F# minor #1 | D Major #4 |

Descend each pentatonic scale from the highest note in the pattern.

Descend one octave of the scale root to root.

Follow-along Backing Track
www.LeadGuitarWorkshop.com

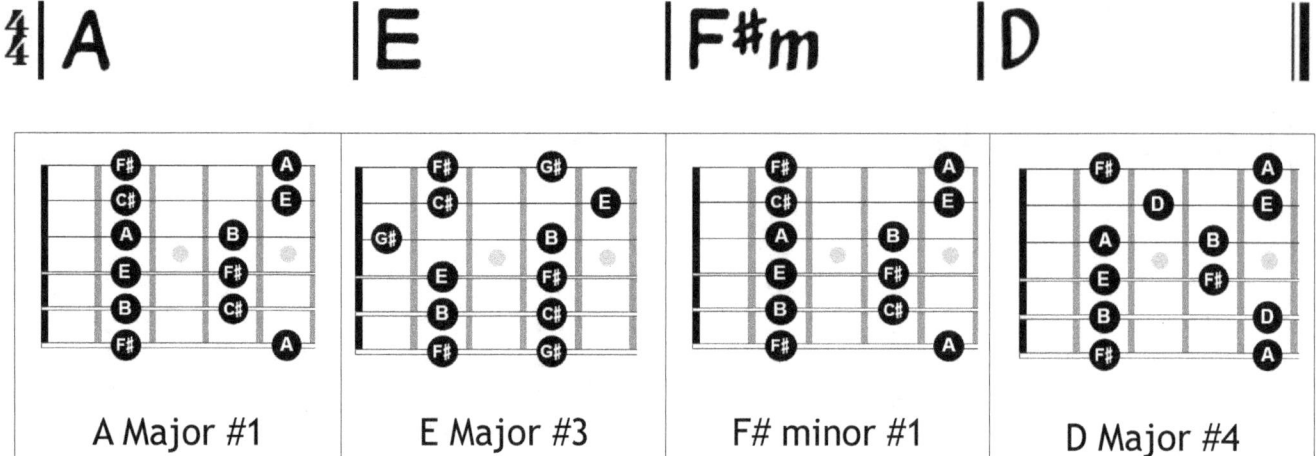

‖ A ‖ E ‖ F#m ‖ D ‖

A Major #1   E Major #3   F# minor #1   D Major #4

Play the top 4 notes of each pattern repeated as eighth-notes.

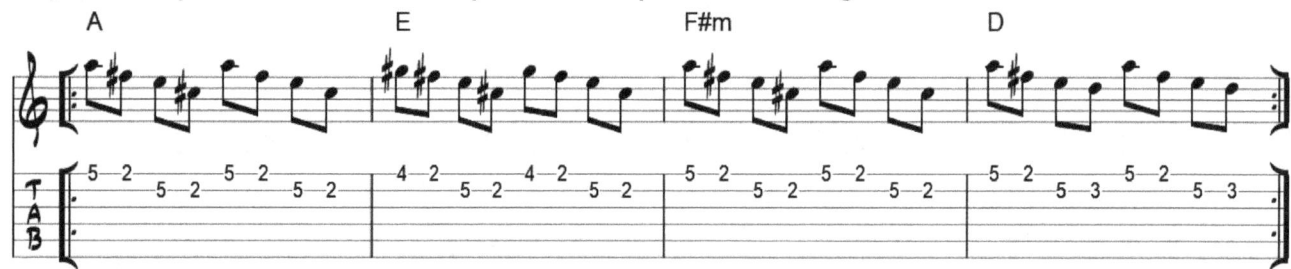

Use a 1 2 3 approach (the first 3 notes of the scale). This is a simple version. (The minor just uses the first two notes to establish that approach).

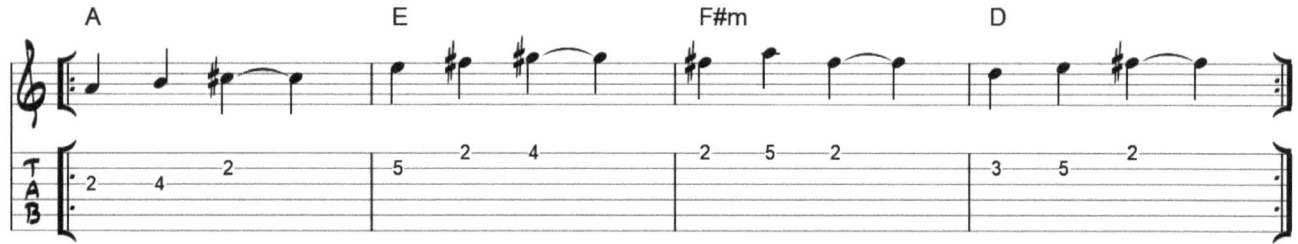

Use a 1 2 3 1 pattern for the major scales. Note that when you use 1 2 3 of the Major pentatonic (or the first 2 notes in a minor pentatonic) you use the 3rd of the scale/chord. The 3rd of a scale helps establish the chords quality as being Major or minor. (Minor pentatonic scale has a flat 3rd.)

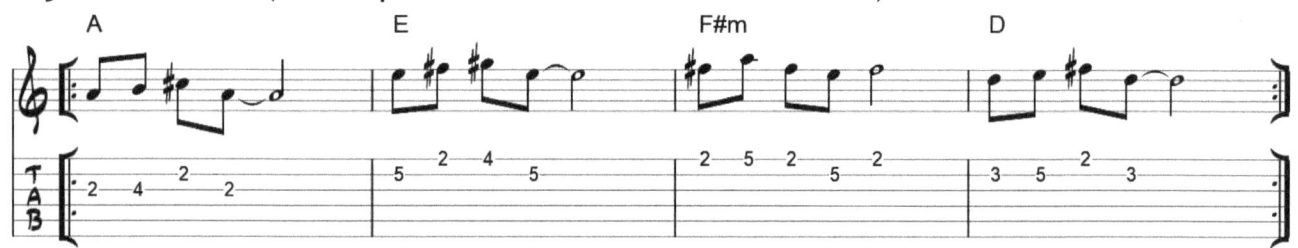

SUMMARY

We are musicians. We are guitar players.
We learn the language of music, Melody, Harmony, and Rhythm.
We learn the craft of playing the guitar as an instrument.
Always make your music decisions first and then go to your instrument/guitar.

MUSICIAN

- There are only 12 notes. (ABCDEFG are the Natural notes and there are 5 accidentals)
- EF and BC are a ½ step apart (smallest distance).
- There are only 12 Major chords, 12 minor chords, 12 Major pentatonics, 12 minor pentatonics each based on one of the 12 notes.
- There are two inherent sounds of a Pentatonic scale, Major and minor (to match its respective chord).
- There is a **relative minor to every Major** (1½ steps below the Major root). This means two-for-one.
- The **Blues Scale** is playing a minor pentatonic over a Major chord.
- For soloing, match a scale to its chord.
- Playing **Globally** equals 1 scale for all the chords.
- **Playing the changes** equals a scale per chord. This directly "talks" to each chord, getting you its chord tones and color tones.
- **Sequences** are a powerful musical sound. They are really natural to listen to and great for composing and improvising.
- **Accents** give dimension to rhythm. Accents allow multiple rhythms to exist simultaneously. There is so much potential expressiveness with accents.
- When you play the changes you are directly addressing each chord's own chord tones by using its own pentatonic.
- Any pentatonic scale contains the 3 notes of its chord and 2 color tones.

GUITAR PLAYER

- The 12 notes are the first 12 frets on the guitar that we navigate on the lowest E string.
- We use the **"Rock and Roll Rule"** to put pattern #1 on the fretboard after making the music decision about what scale we need.
- There are 5 patterns to connect our 12 fret fretboard for all 12 keys.
- We learned how to use **BSSBS** to play a minor pentatonic scale and **SSBSB** to play a Major pentatonic scale on any one string.
- We learned how to use **OCTAVE SHAPES** as a playable sounds as well as using them to unlock the fretboard.
- Use pattern #1 to get started with **PLAYING THE CHANGES.**
- Use the **CAGED** system to connect chord shapes to scale shapes.
- Bends are the most advanced of our legato techniques. We can see the power of **pre-bends** as they are the only way to allow the notes to bend "down."
- Knowing how hard and soft to pluck is essential to properly playing with dynamics. **Accents** can happen in the pick hand (hard and soft picking) as well as in the fretboard hand (when you play notes versus mutes).
- **Neck Anatomy** (how to see octaves) on the guitar is the single greatest revelation I've had about the guitar. It puts the simplicity of music in view and gets rid of the confusing three dimensional aspect of our fretboard.
- The **Blues Cross** is another easy and portable way to move a pentatonic scale around the whole fretboard without the need of the original patterns. (Knowing both is that much better!). It is also very convenient as you can play the patterns with your first and ring fingers making it super comfortable.
- The **5 Patterns** allow us to use our whole fretboard for any key! They help us smoothly play the changes and allow us to move independently of the motion of the chords.

CHAPTER 10

TUNE IN

"I am a musician and a guitar player. Music is my language and my guitar is my voice. Music is Melody, Harmony and Rhythm. I develop my language skills and my instrument skills. They are two separate worlds working together to complete the circle of music."

Rhythm is the number one factor to sounding great as a musician.

WARM UP

Muted String Ladder (MSL) One Pick Per String (OPPS) all 6 strings

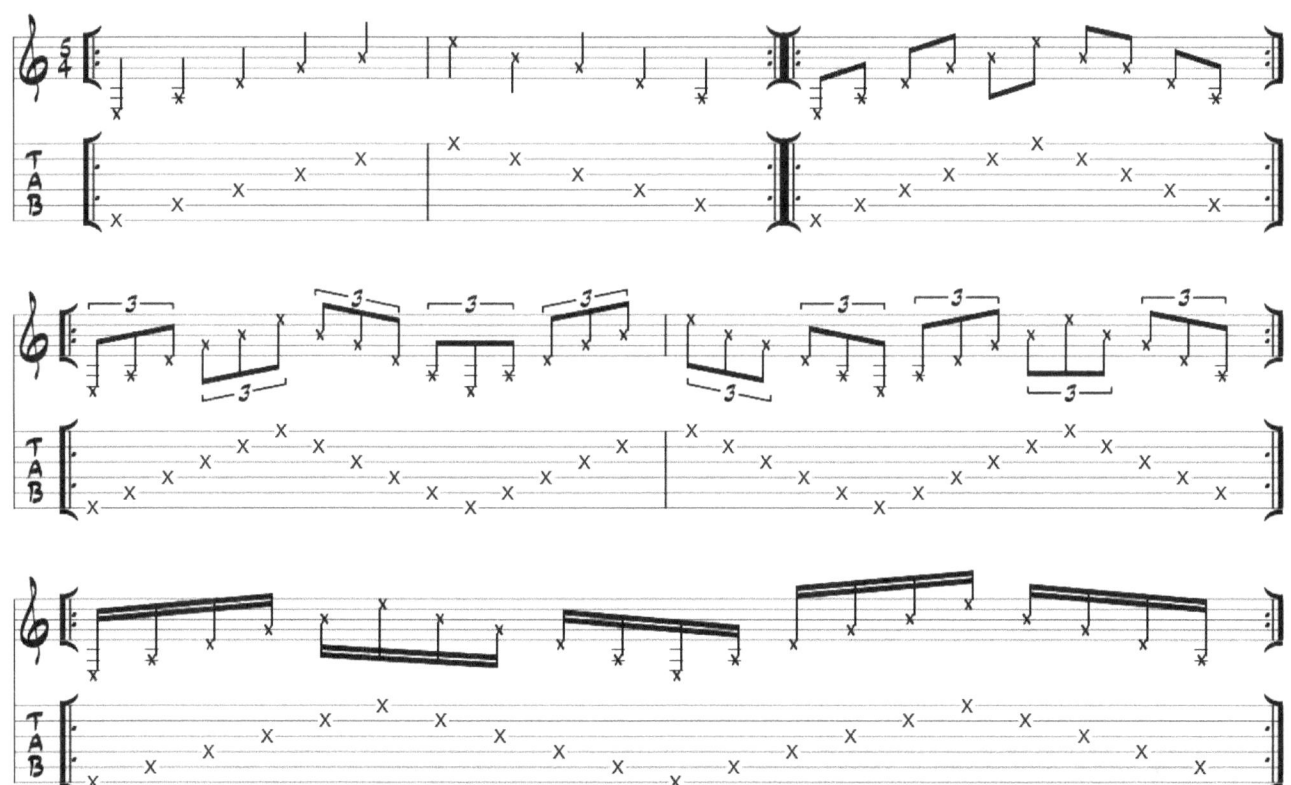

SHELLS

Of the shells, the 1 2 3 4 group is probably the least musical but most physical as it uses all four of your fretboard fingers. As a result you can use this shell to build endurance, strength, and picking accuracy.

GENERAL IDEAS

- Move up or down a fret each time you repeat.
- Start with open version 0 1 2 3
- Use ROTATIONS 2 3 4 1, 3 4 1 2, 4 1 2 3. Remember each one is it's own group, you play it back and forth, REVERSE the numbers and play it back and forth again achieving all combinations.
- Leapfrog the strings.
- Start on the 12th fret.
- Use a metronome.
- This shell exercise is 96 notes in 6 bars.
- Do the "Iron Hands." Set a metronome and start in the open position. Work your way up to the highest playable fret, and then work your way back down all the way to the open position. You can do the math.

1 2 3 4 as sixteenth-notes.

CHANGING GEARS

Ladder with gears 1-8 and quarter-note on the B string

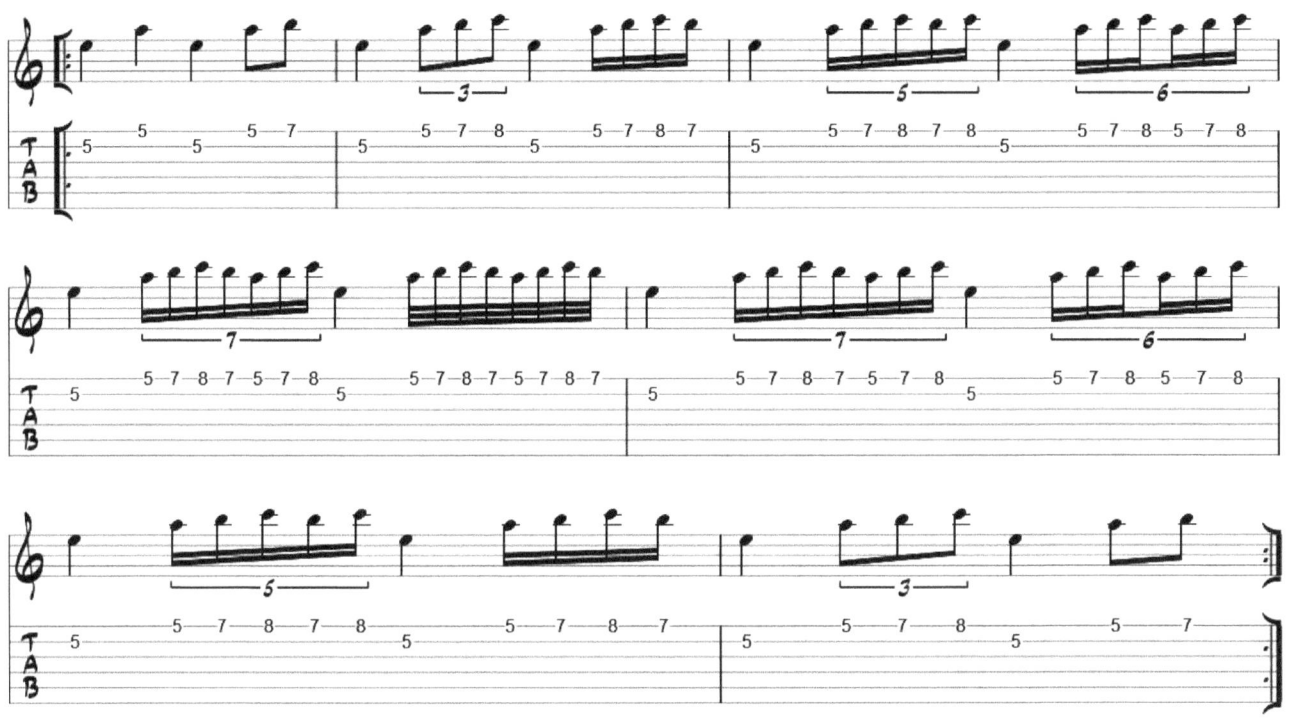

Ladder with gears 1-8 and eighth-notes on the B string

EXERCISE

Pick a tempo and a gear. Play each pattern low to high and back (or the reverse), or play them as "Round the Block." This is F Major, D minor, and D blues pentatonic. You can start in either direction.

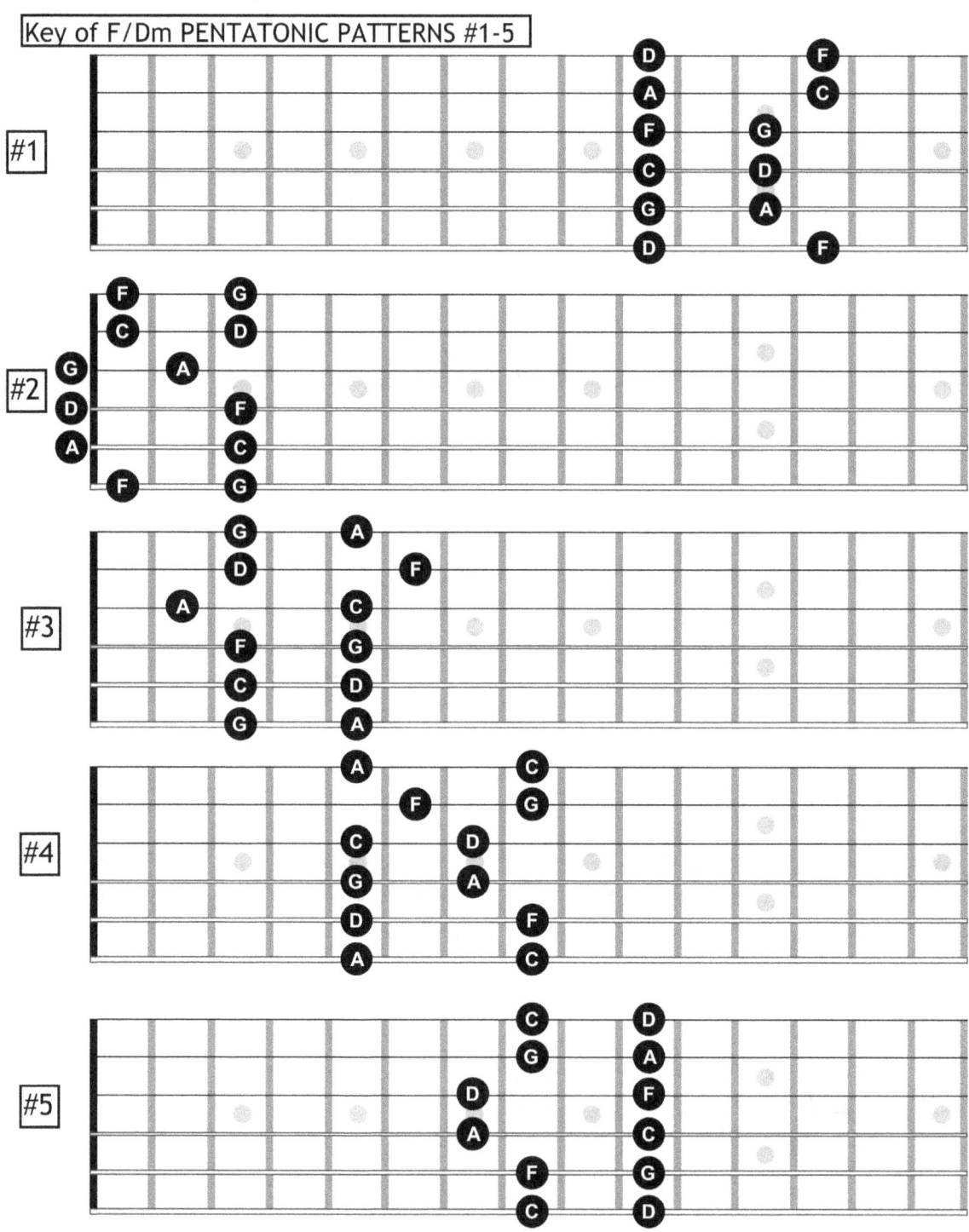

Key of F/Dm PENTATONIC PATTERNS #1-5

REVIEW

This course is an advanced look at pentatonics as musicians and especially as guitar players. In Level 3 continue the path started in level 1 and through level 2. We always have on our "lens" that we are musicians learning music and instrumentalists learning guitar. Music is always Melody, Harmony, and Rhythm.

TOPICS COVERED IN LEVEL 3

- **BSSBS (SSBSB)** This is the easy way to play a pentatonic scale on one string based on the spacing of the scale, B = Big = 3 frets and S = small = 2 frets. You can use this formula on every string and be able to use your whole instrument without the traditional 5 patterns. Ultimately as guitar players we use all available methods.

- **Octaves** Until this book we used the Short and Long octave shapes to build a 3 octave path called Neck Anatomy to help us see the notes on our fretboard. This time we used the octave shape as a musical device to simultaneously play octaves to give a warmer and bigger sound to melodies, riffs, and solos.

- **Playing Changes with same and different patterns** Playing the Changes is such a natural and wonderful way to play solos. As a guitar player we looked at two approaches. The slightly easier way is to think like a bar chord and just move pattern #1 up and down for every Major and minor pentatonic scale. Later in the book we looked at breaking away from that restraint and playing the changes with different pentatonic patterns freeing us up to move up and down independent of what key we were in.

- **CAGED** This system for guitar players is a great way to correlate the five basic chord shapes to the five pentatonic patterns. This works for Major and minor chords and scales. It is a tremendous way to connect your fretboard.

- **Sequences** These musical based ideas are essential for any musician. They are patterns applied to scales. They are great for your ear, your hands, and your dexterity, and are equally at home for practice and in real music.

- **Accents and Subgroups** The world of Dynamics is so important to how you sound as a musician and even as a human. Accents in particular create a whole new layer of rhythmic interest on top of the existing rhythm. Subgroups are when note groups correlate to the accents creating groups of notes that sound independent from the original rhythm.

- **Neck Anatomy scales** Continuing on with our octaves we always link them as Short octave to Long octave shape. Do that from your Low E string and then again from your A string. You will find all 6 of the same notes in the first 12 frets of your instrument. From there you can build scales. The goal is to have one scale shape that feels the same in other octaves and all over your instrument. Other instruments like Piano and wind instruments have this ability. This helps you focus on music by not constantly battling with how to find and feel out your notes.

- **Blues Cross** This guitar player technique another way to look at and play a pentatonic scale on the guitar. This particular method nicely lends itself to just using the first and third fingers to play a pentatonic scale for 3 octaves. It even adds a opportunity to play an awesome sounding slide.

The following Summary has been growing each chapter and from book #1. Always keep the perspective that we are learning on two levels, as a musician learning the language of music and as an instrumentalist learning the guitar. Each has their own questions and answers.

SUMMARY

We are musicians. We are guitar players.
We learn the language of music, Melody, Harmony, and Rhythm.
We learn the craft of playing the guitar as an instrument.
Always make your music decisions first and then go to your instrument/guitar.

MUSICIAN

- There are only 12 notes. (ABCDEFG are the Natural notes and there are 5 accidentals.)
- EF and BC are a ½ step apart (smallest distance).
- There are only 12 Major chords, 12 minor chords, 12 Major pentatonics, 12 minor pentatonics each based on one of the 12 notes.
- There are two inherent sounds of a Pentatonic scale, Major and minor (to match its respective chord).
- There is a **relative minor to every Major** (1½ steps below the Major root). This means two-for-one.
- The **Blues Scale** is playing a minor pentatonic over a Major chord.
- The **Blue Note** is an additional tone we add to further color the scale. It works in Major, minor, and blues.
- For soloing, match a scale to its chord.
- **Playing Globally** equals 1 scale for all the chords.
- **Playing the changes** equals a scale per chord. This directly "talks" to each chord, giving you its chord tones and color tones.
- **Sequences** are a powerful musical sound. They are really natural to listen to and great for composing and improvising.
- **Accents** give dimension to rhythm. Accents allow multiple rhythms to exist simultaneously. There is so much potential expressiveness with accents.
- When you **play the changes** you are directly addressing each chord's own chord tones by using its own pentatonic and specifically its chord tones.
- Any pentatonic scale contains the 3 notes of its chord and 2 color tones.
- When you add the two half-steps to the pentatonic scale you get the traditional seven note scales also know as the **Modes**.

GUITAR PLAYER

- The 12 notes are the first 12 frets on the guitar that we navigate on the lowest E string.
- We use the **"Rock and Roll Rule"** to put pattern #1 on the fretboard after making the music decision about what scale we need.
- There are **5 patterns** to connect our 12 fret fretboard for all 12 keys.
- We learned how to use **BSSBS** to play a minor pentatonic scale and **SSBSB** to play a Major pentatonic scale on any one string.
- We learned how to use **OCTAVE SHAPES** as a playable sounds as well as using them to unlock the fretboard.
- Use pattern #1 to get started with **PLAYING THE CHANGES.**
- Use the **CAGED** system to connect chord shapes to scale shapes.
- Bends are the most advanced of our legato techniques. We can see the power of **pre-bends** as they are the only way to allow the notes to bend "down."
- Knowing how hard and soft to pluck is essential to properly playing with dynamics. **Accents** can happen in the pick hand (hard and soft picking) as well as in the fretboard hand (when you play notes vs mutes).
- **Neck Anatomy** (how to see octaves) on the guitar is the single greatest revelation I've had about the guitar. It puts the simplicity of music in view and gets rid of the confusing three dimensional aspect of our fretboard.
- The **Blues Cross** is another easy and portable way to move a pentatonic scale around the whole fretboard without the need of the original patterns. (Knowing both is that much better!). It is also very convenient as you can play the patterns with your first and ring fingers making it super comfortable.
- The **5 Patterns** allow us to use our whole fretboard for any key! They help us smoothly play the changes and allow us to move independently of the motion of the chords.

ADDING MORE NOTES -The NINTH and FOURTH

I first noticed Carlos Santana adding a note in pattern #1 in the song "Europa." It was such a cool and dramatic sound, but I didn't know what it was because it wasn't in the pentatonic diagram (#1) that my teacher gave me. I also noticed Dickey Betts adding a note on the B string in pattern #1 in "Blue Sky." Again, it wasn't in my scale pattern, but I knew these new notes sounded awesome. In both situations I realized that the new note appeared within the big interval of the pentatonics. There are two places this interval exists. Therefore two notes could be added to a pentatonic scale.

When people think of scales they usually default to thinking *Do, re, me*. That is called *Solfege* and is a method for learning the 7 note Major scale (*Do, re, me, fa, sol, la, ti, Do*). Some folks mistakenly think there are 8 notes in a scale because of the word Octave. Octave refers to where the notes start over again, not end.

For years, I didn't understand that the pentatonic scale and the Major scale (and its relative minor scale) were related. Musically speaking the pentatonic scale is made up of whole-step intervals (2 frets) and minor third intervals (3 frets). We can see this clearly in the BSSBS concept. Within the Big interval, the minor third, there is room to add a half-step interval to add another note. This can happen in a couple of ways in two places in the scale. This will add two half-steps to the scale. The result will be the 7 note Major and relative minor scale.

Once you have a seven note scale with two half-steps many things change. New scale sounds and functions are created and these are referred to as the Modes. Without getting into the details of Modes you can start to capitalize on their colors by adding the notes in a couple of places to start. (There is an entire book from Lead Guitar Workshop dedicated to the modes, "Lead Guitar – Modes.")

The Major pentatonic scale is **R 2 3 5 6**. When we add the two half-steps the Major pentatonic scale turns into the Major scale (known as Ionian in the Modes) which is **R 2 3 4 5 6 7**. The half-step occurs between the **3 to 4**, and **7 to R (8)**.

The minor pentatonic is **R *b*3 4 5 *b*7**. When we add the same two half-steps they occur as the **2 (9th)** and the **b6**. The minor scale is **R 2 *b*3 4 5 *b*6 *b*7**. This will change in the Modes but we can isolate two great sounds.

Even though there is a place to add two notes to the scale there are potentially four places depending on where the half-steps are. Let's look at adding the 4th when we are in Major and the 9th when we are in minor. These are the two situations I see all the time.

THE FOURTH

When you add the fourth to the Major pentatonic you get a couple of really nice benefits. First you get the ROOT note of the IV chord in the key. Surprisingly enough, the Major pentatonic does not have that root note, which is one of its most important chords in the key after the I chord and the V chord. Having this root note really helps when you are playing the changes.

The other benefit to adding the fourth to the Major pentatonic is that you create a Melodic suspension in your sound. A melodic suspension is similar to the harmonic suspension (sus4 chords). They both use the fourth to add tension to the chord and now the scale. David Gilmour of Pink Floyd uses this sound all the time. It's one of my favorite sounds and really adds some nice dramatic singing soulfulness to it.

PATTERN #1 MAJOR Pentatonic with FOURTH

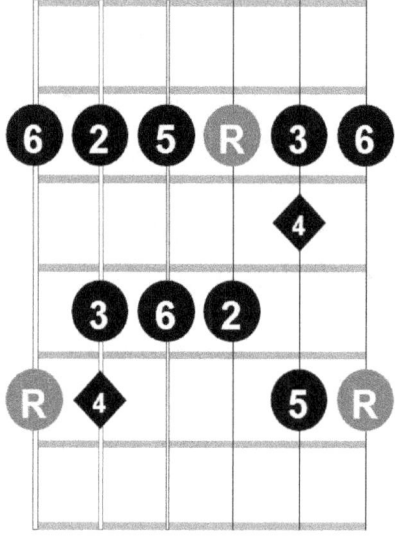

THE NINTH

When thinking minor pentatonic the ninth of the scale (which is the same as the second) is a super sweet and emotional note to add. Carlos Santana, David Gilmour, Hendrix, Jimmy Page, and Stevie Ray Vaughn all made extensive use of this sound as well as countless others. The same note occurs in all 3 octaves.

PATTERN #1 Minor Pentatonic with NINTH

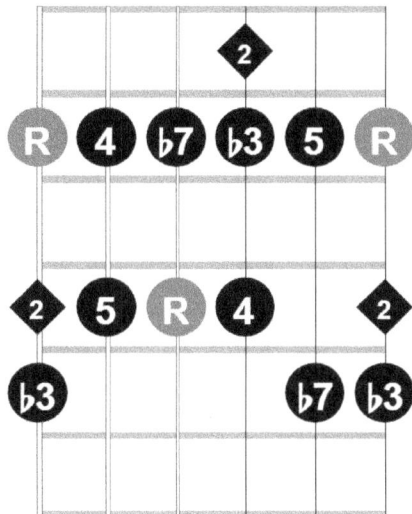

Pentatonic scales are very forgiving. They are easy to make sound good because they don't have a tricky half-step in the scale. Although those two half-steps add a lot of color, they add more chances for clunker notes, the ones that just sound out of place.

You can add both half-steps to the scale but you have to be aware of it, as it will often give you a result different than what you had hoped for. For this reason I recommend going with two of the most commonly used sounds.

Major pentatonic add the 4th
minor pentatonic add the 9th

PRACTICE

C Major pentatonic with the added 4th

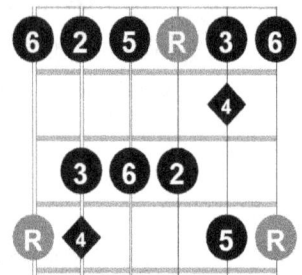

C Major pentatonic with added 4th Pattern #1

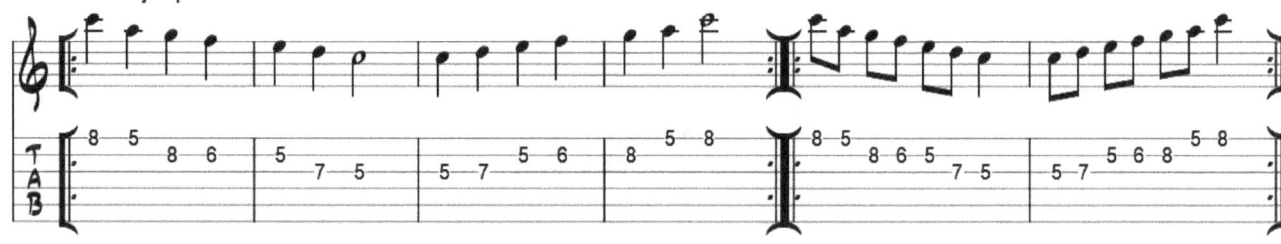

C Major pentatonic 12345 up and back

C Major Licks with added 4th

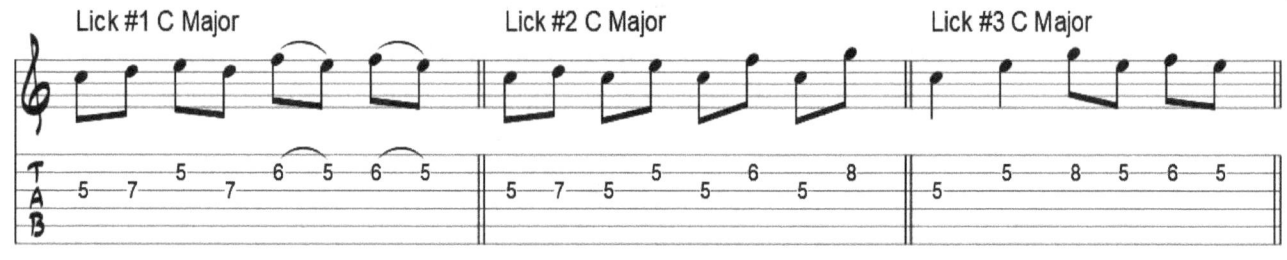

A minor pentatonic with the added 9ᵗʰ

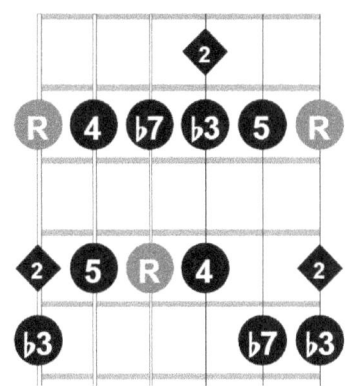

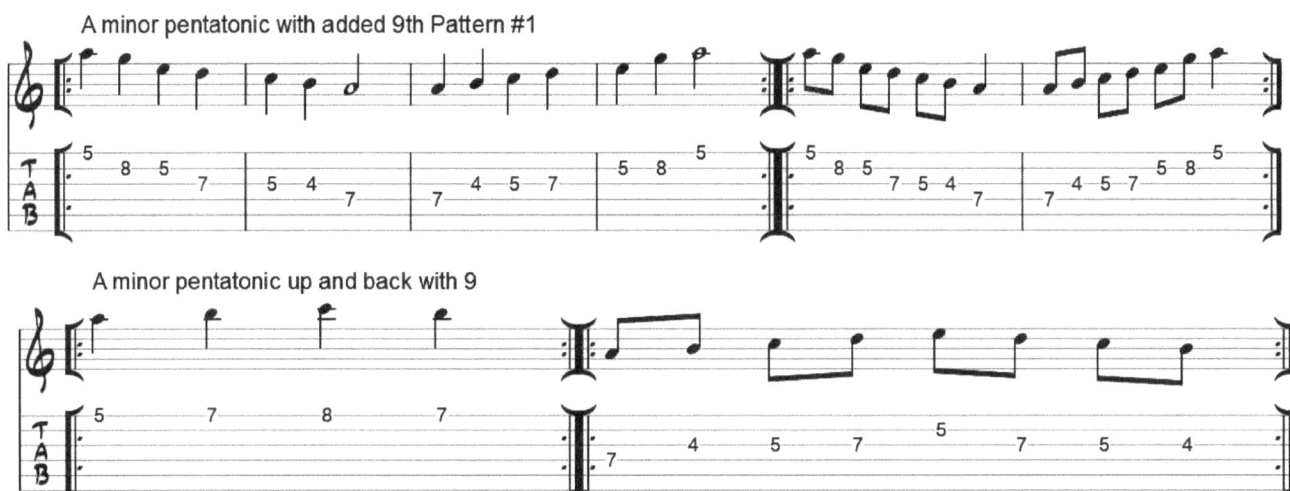

A minor pentatonic with added 9th Pattern #1

A minor pentatonic up and back with 9

A minor Licks with added 9ᵗʰ

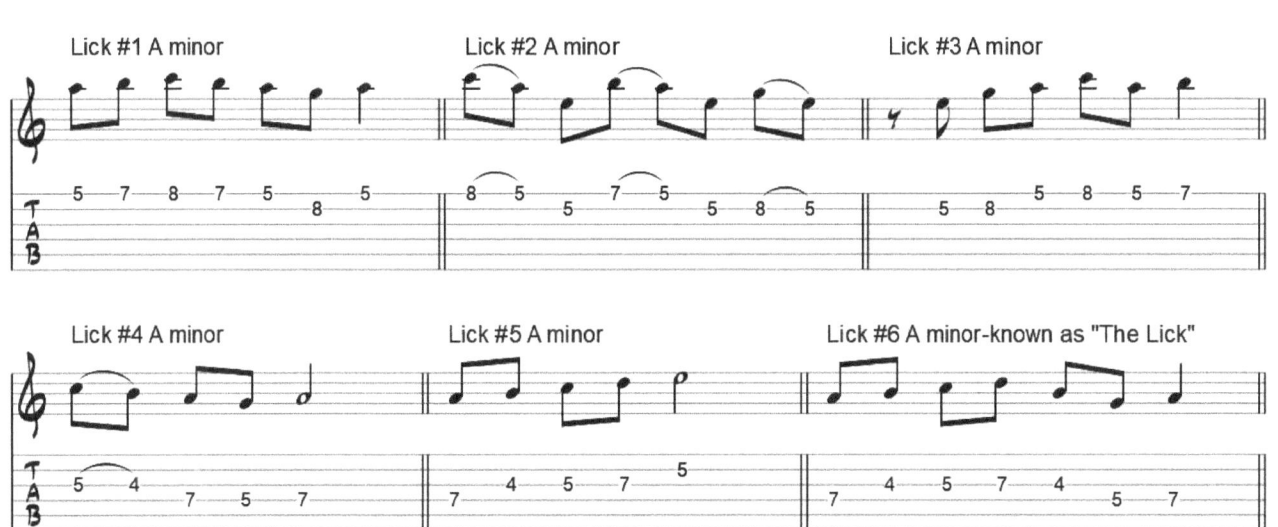

Lick #1 A minor

Lick #2 A minor

Lick #3 A minor

Lick #4 A minor

Lick #5 A minor

Lick #6 A minor-known as "The Lick"

BACKING TRACK

C Major chord progression and backing track with example solo using 4ths over the Major and 9ths over the minor chords.

PENTATONIC PATTERNS - ALL 12 KEYS

- Each of the 12 keys has its own following page. Pages are ordered in the circle of 5ths.

- Each key is written starting with Pattern #1 at the top.

- On each page the patterns are listed #1 down to pattern #5.

- At the bottom is a summation of the 5 patterns.

- Each key has the 5 notes of the scale in all of the diagrams. Get to know the notes in a key/scale.

- When jamming or practicing in a key look at the full pattern at the bottom of the page to really take advantage of the whole fretboard. Follow the notes.

- When looking at the full fretboard think Neck Anatomy to see all of the short to long octaves for all of the notes.

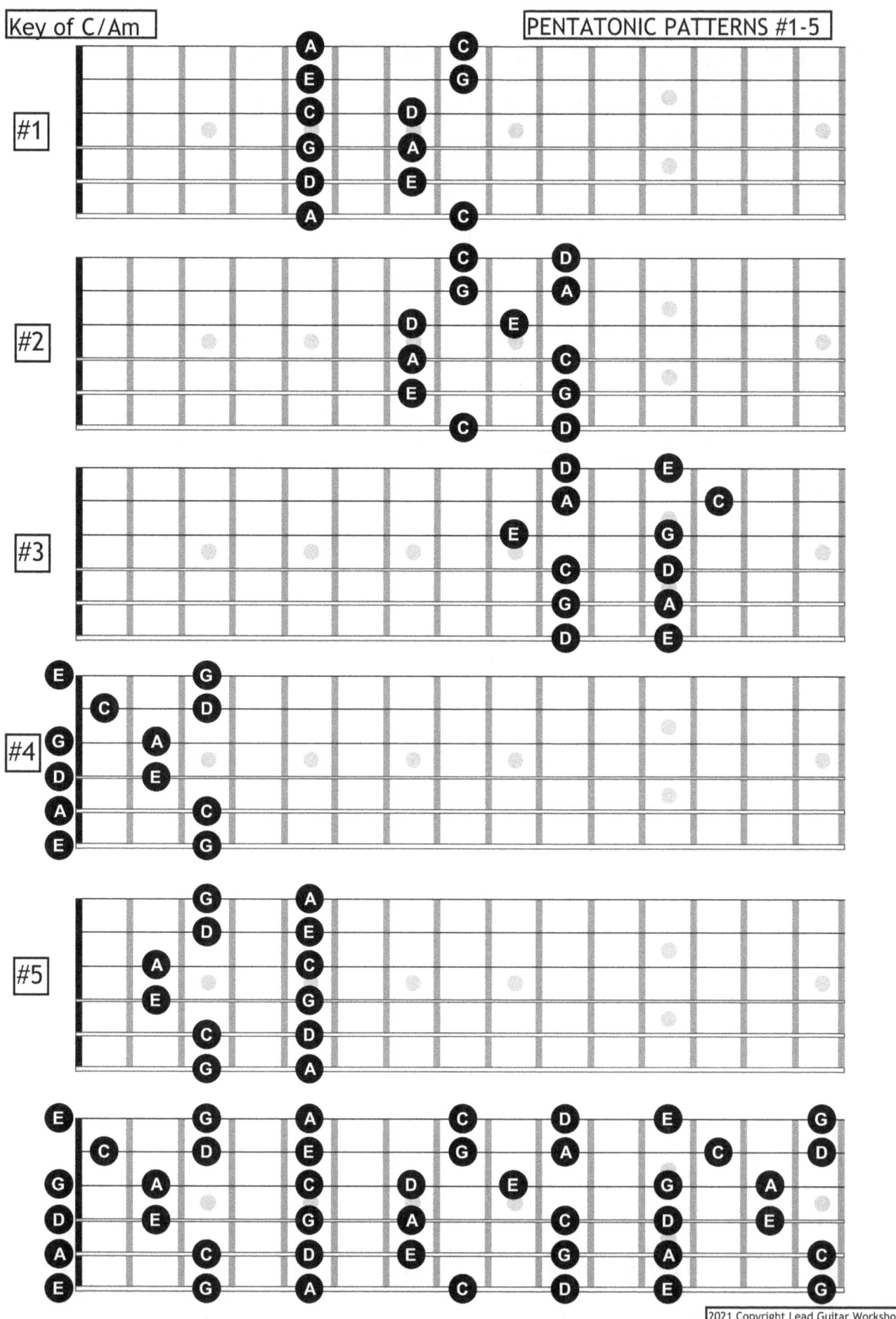

Key of C/Am

PENTATONIC PATTERNS #1-5

#1

#2

#3

#4

#5

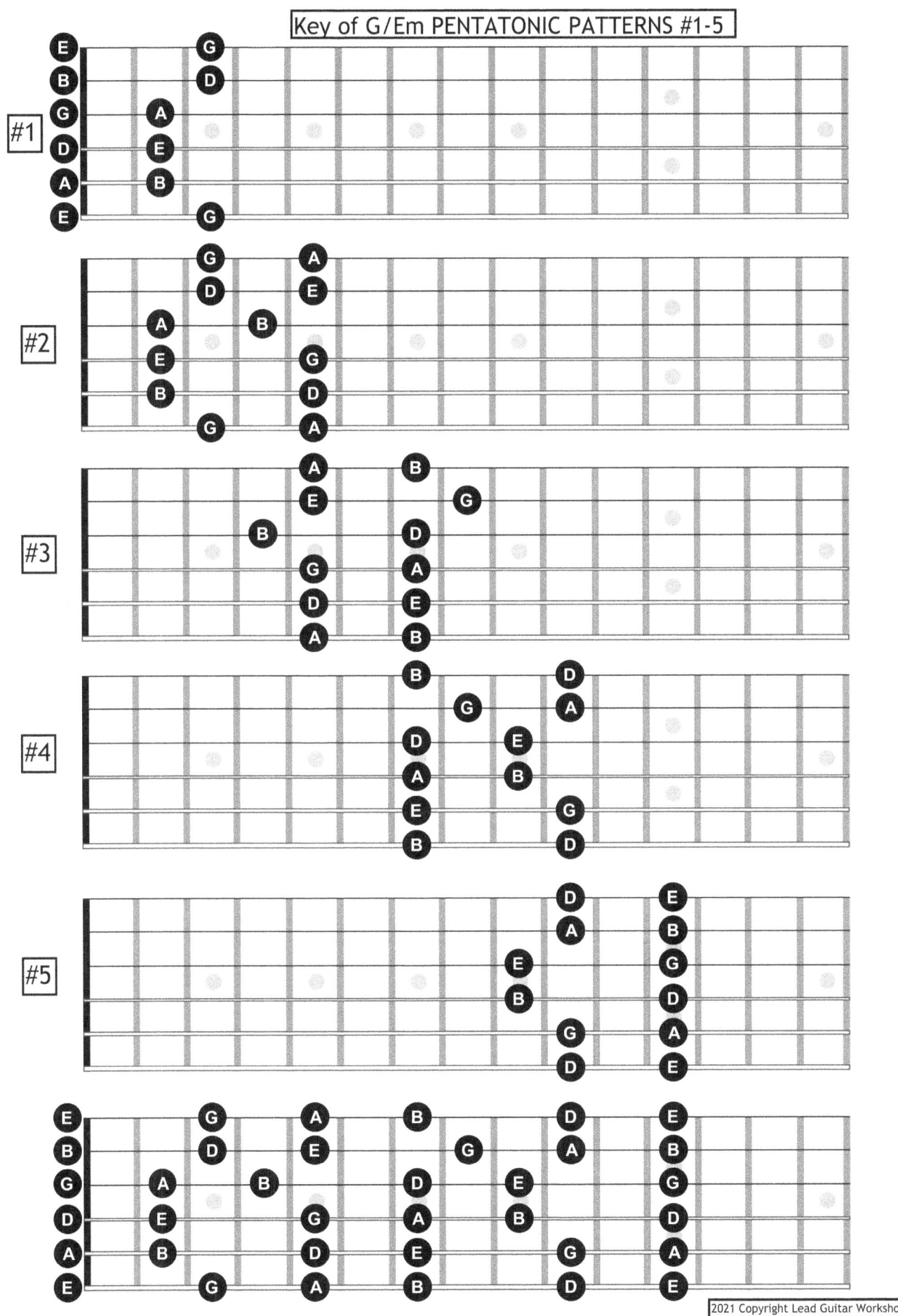

Key of G/Em PENTATONIC PATTERNS #1-5

2021 Copyright Lead Guitar Workshop

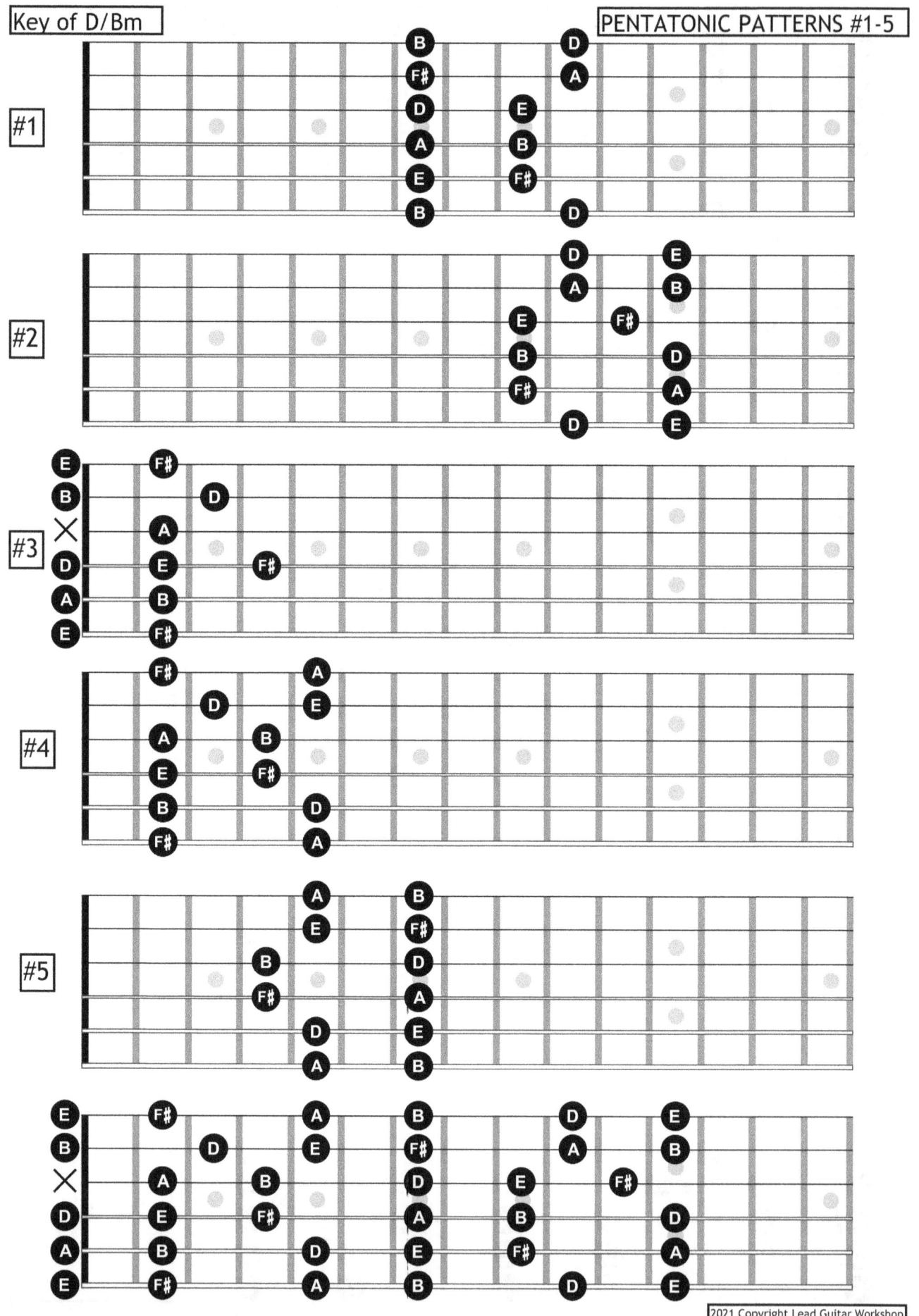

Key of D/Bm

PENTATONIC PATTERNS #1-5

#1

#2

#3

#4

#5

2021 Copyright Lead Guitar Workshop

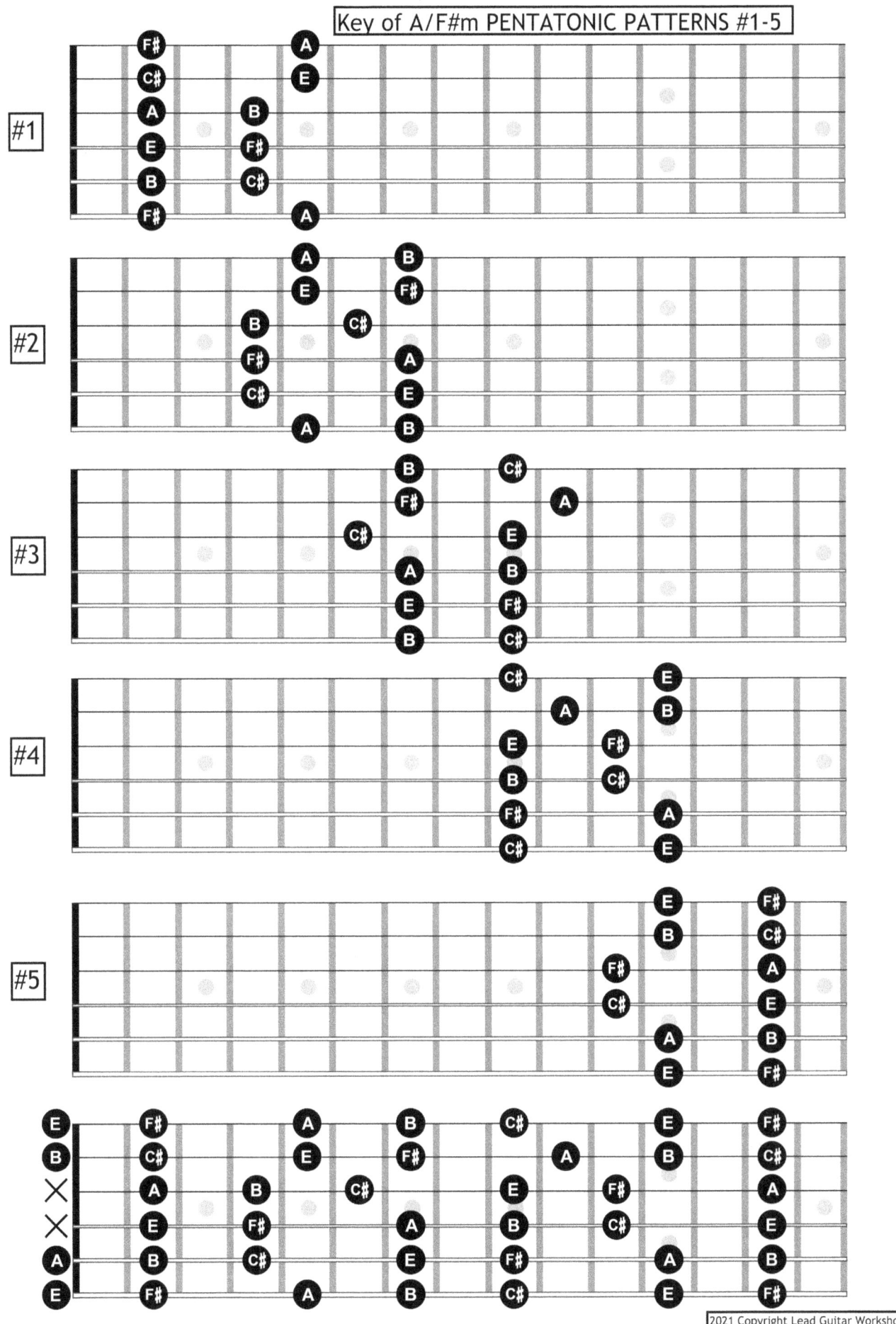

Key of A/F#m PENTATONIC PATTERNS #1-5

#1
#2
#3
#4
#5

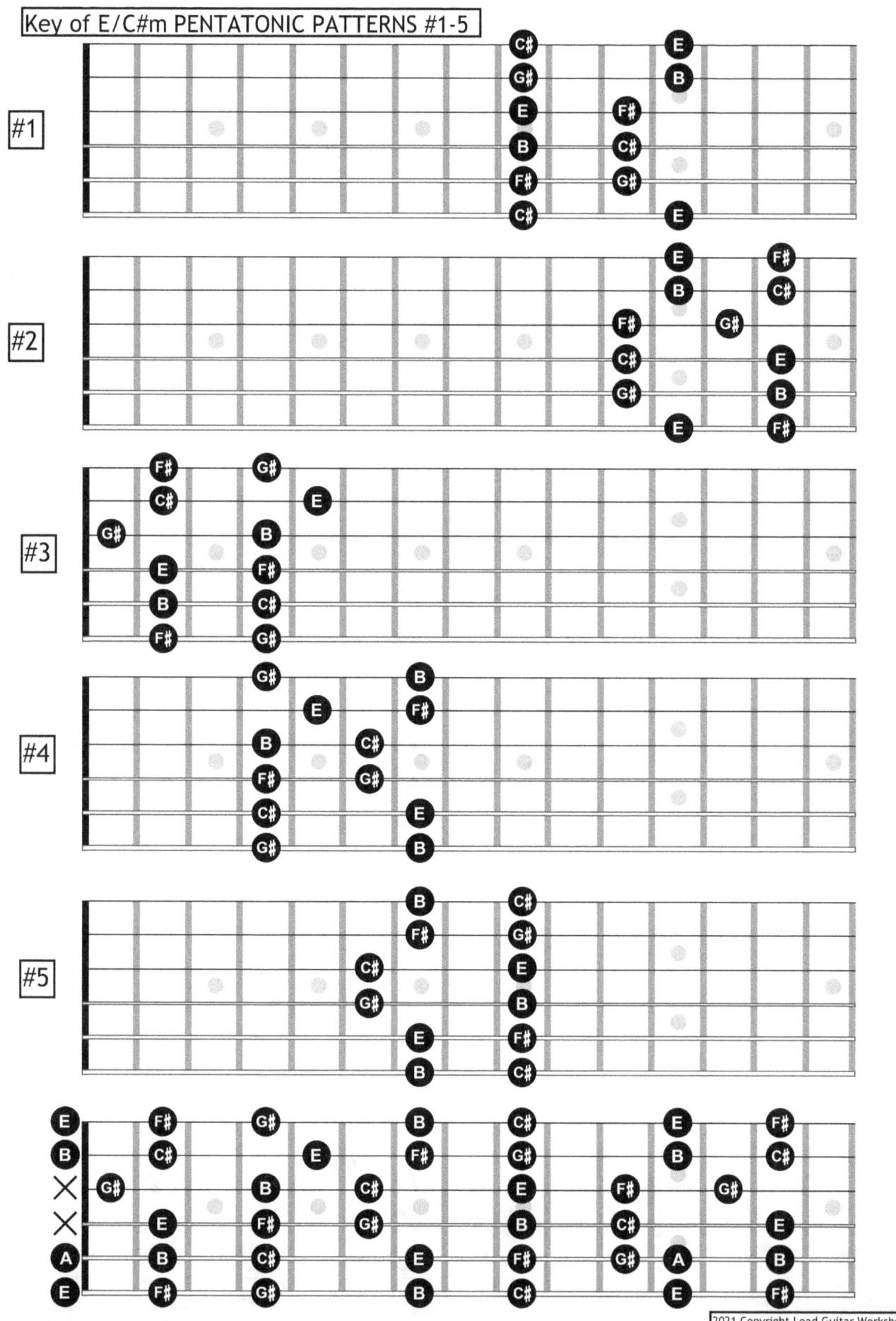

Key of E/C#m PENTATONIC PATTERNS #1-5

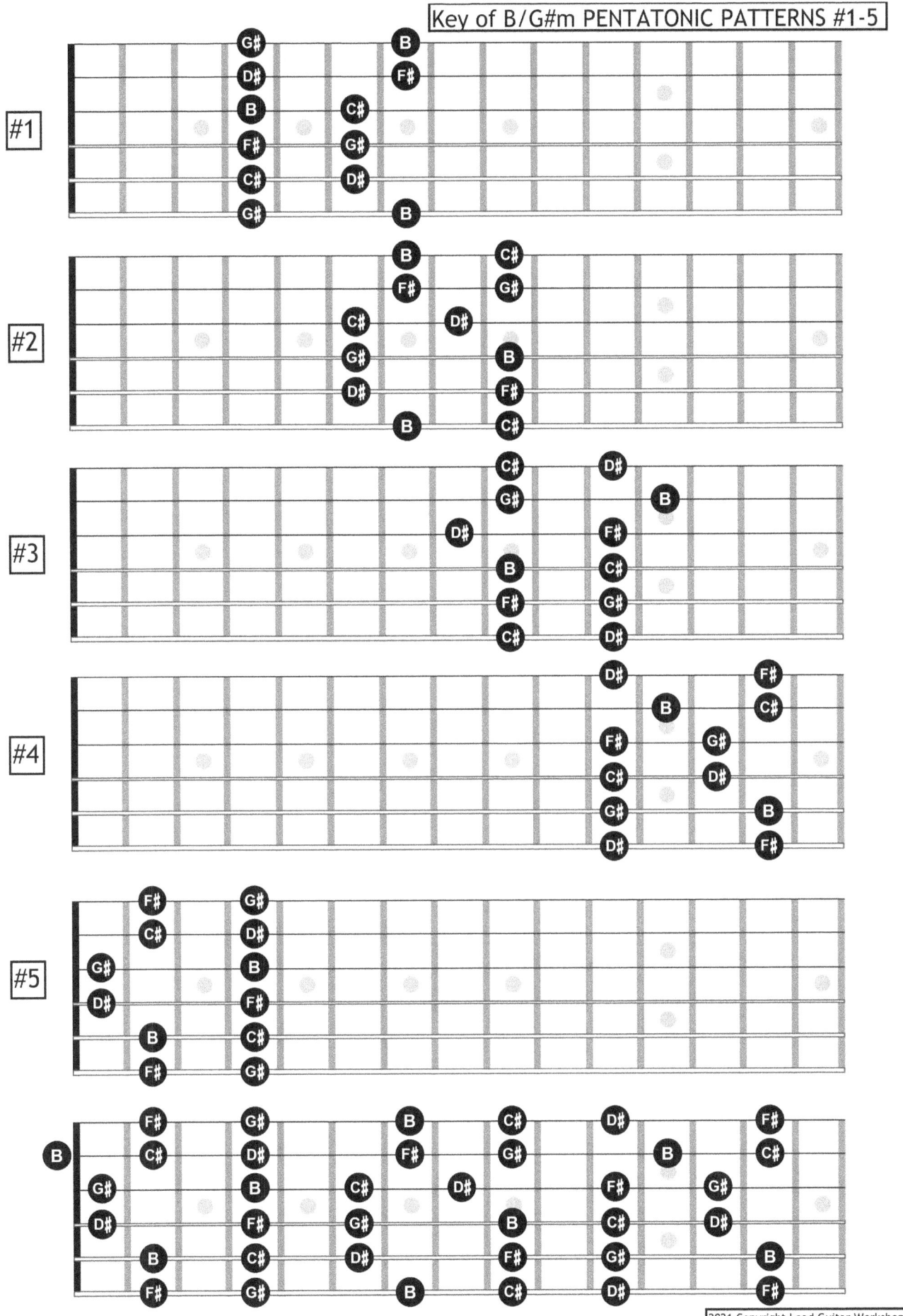

Key of B/G#m PENTATONIC PATTERNS #1-5

2021 Copyright Lead Guitar Workshop

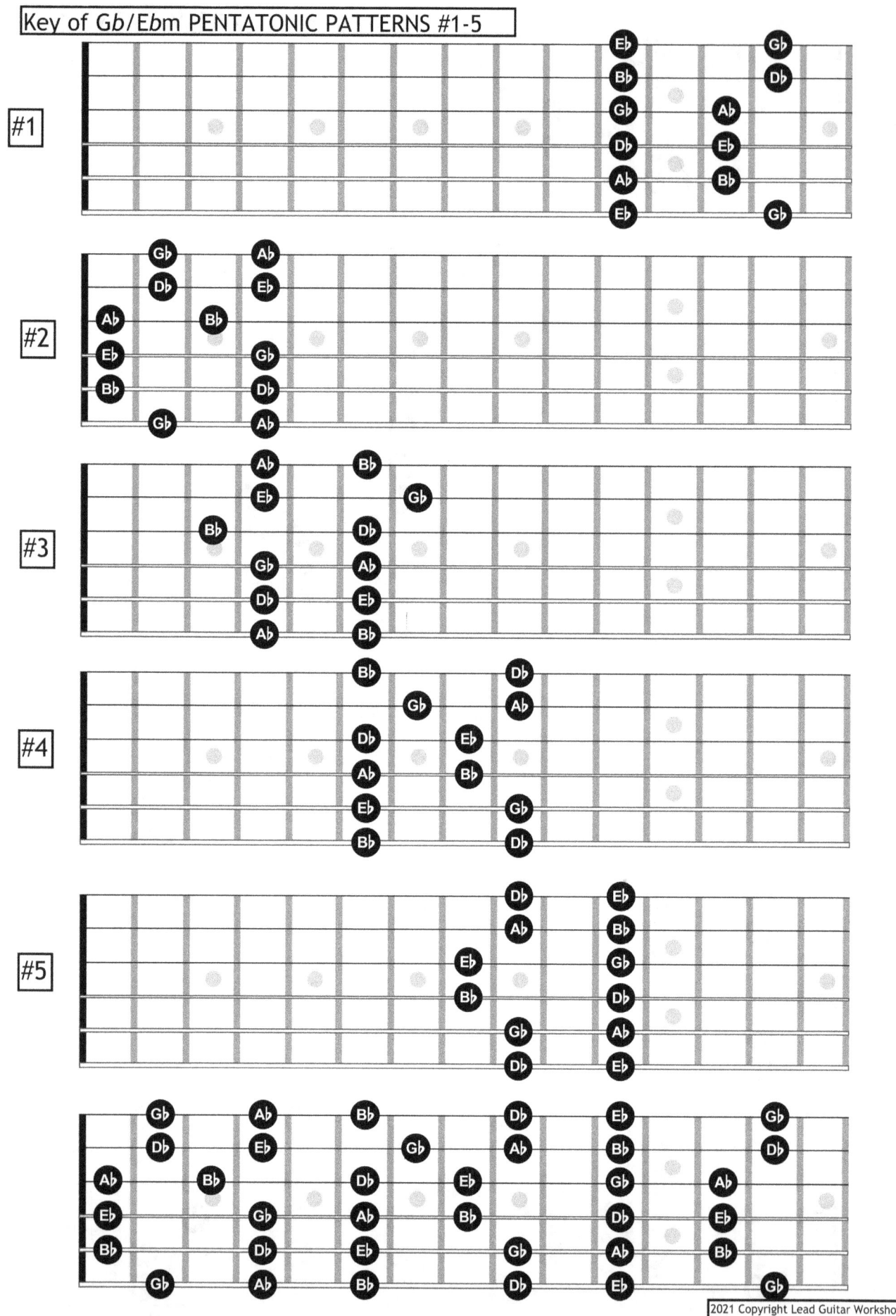

Key of Gb/Ebm PENTATONIC PATTERNS #1-5

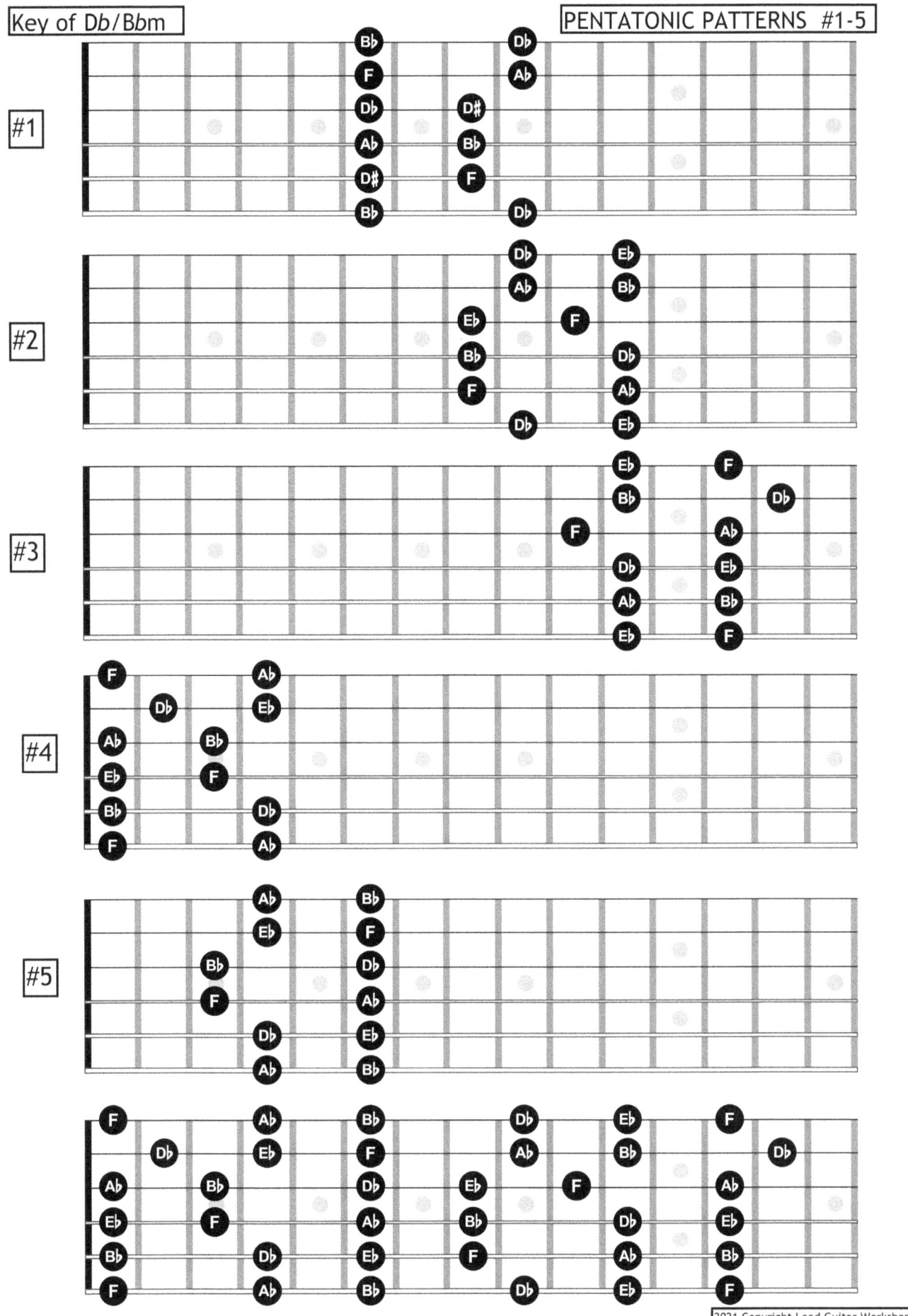

Key of D♭/B♭m

PENTATONIC PATTERNS #1-5

2021 Copyright Lead Guitar Workshop

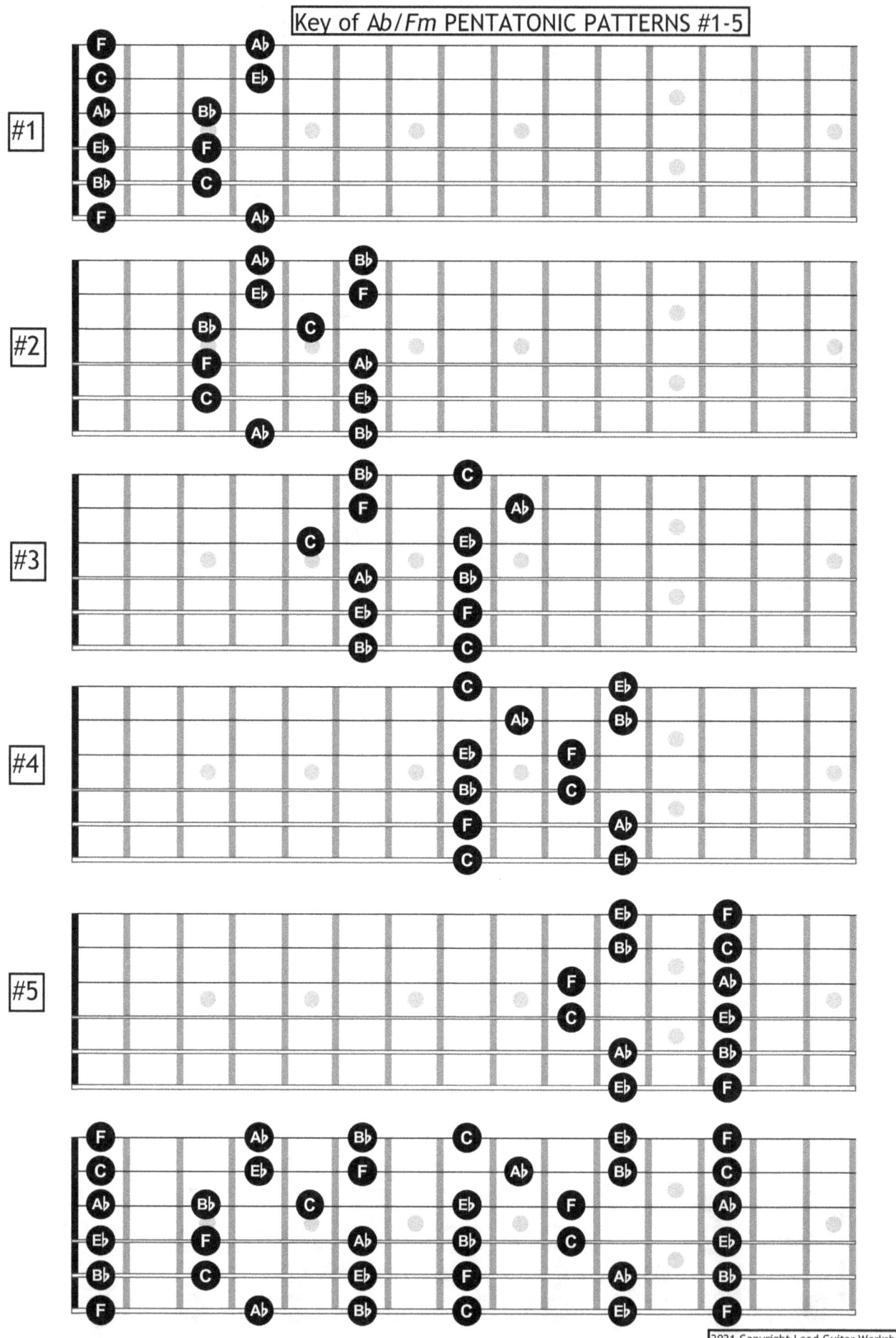

Key of A♭/Fm PENTATONIC PATTERNS #1-5

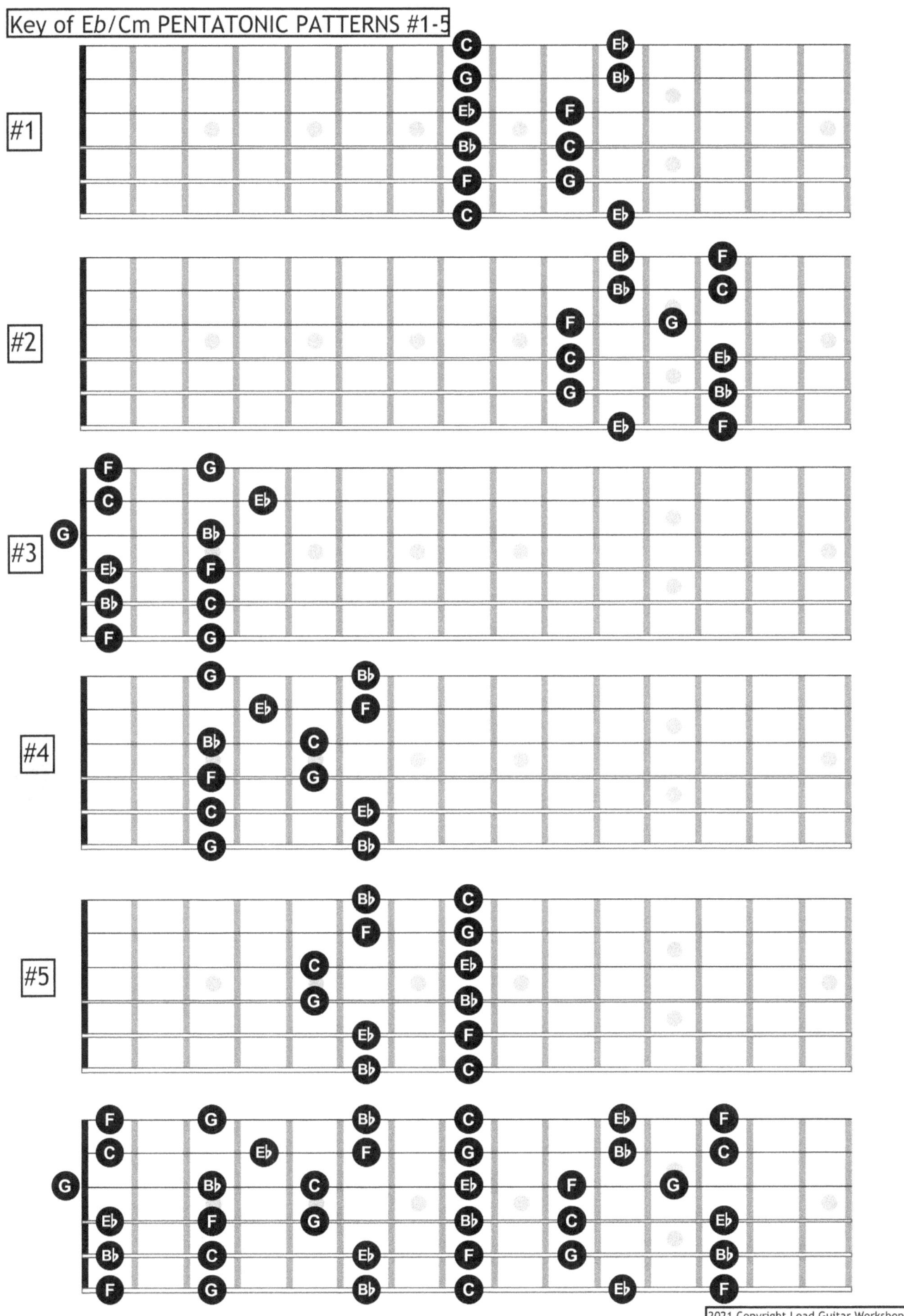

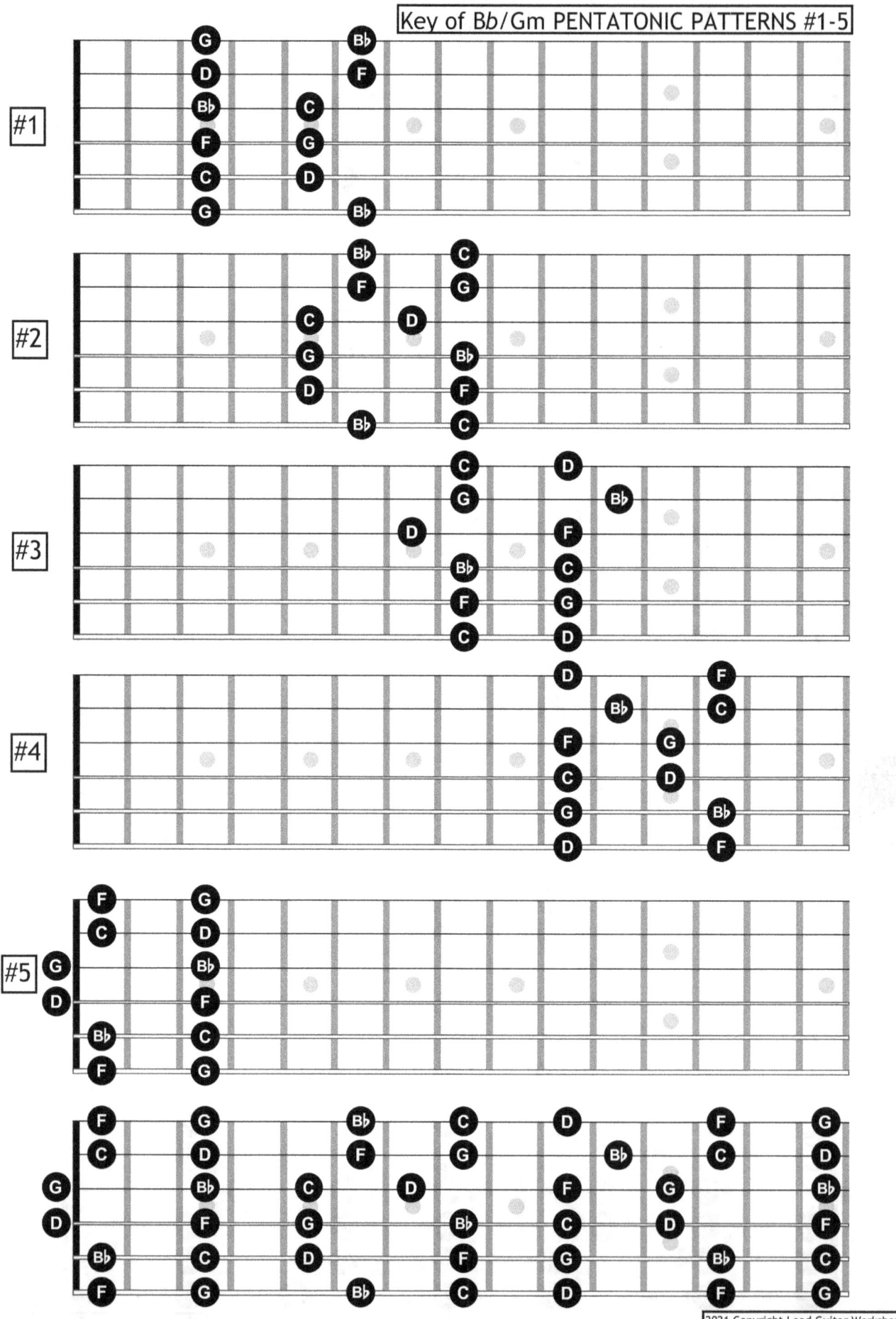

Key of B♭/Gm PENTATONIC PATTERNS #1-5

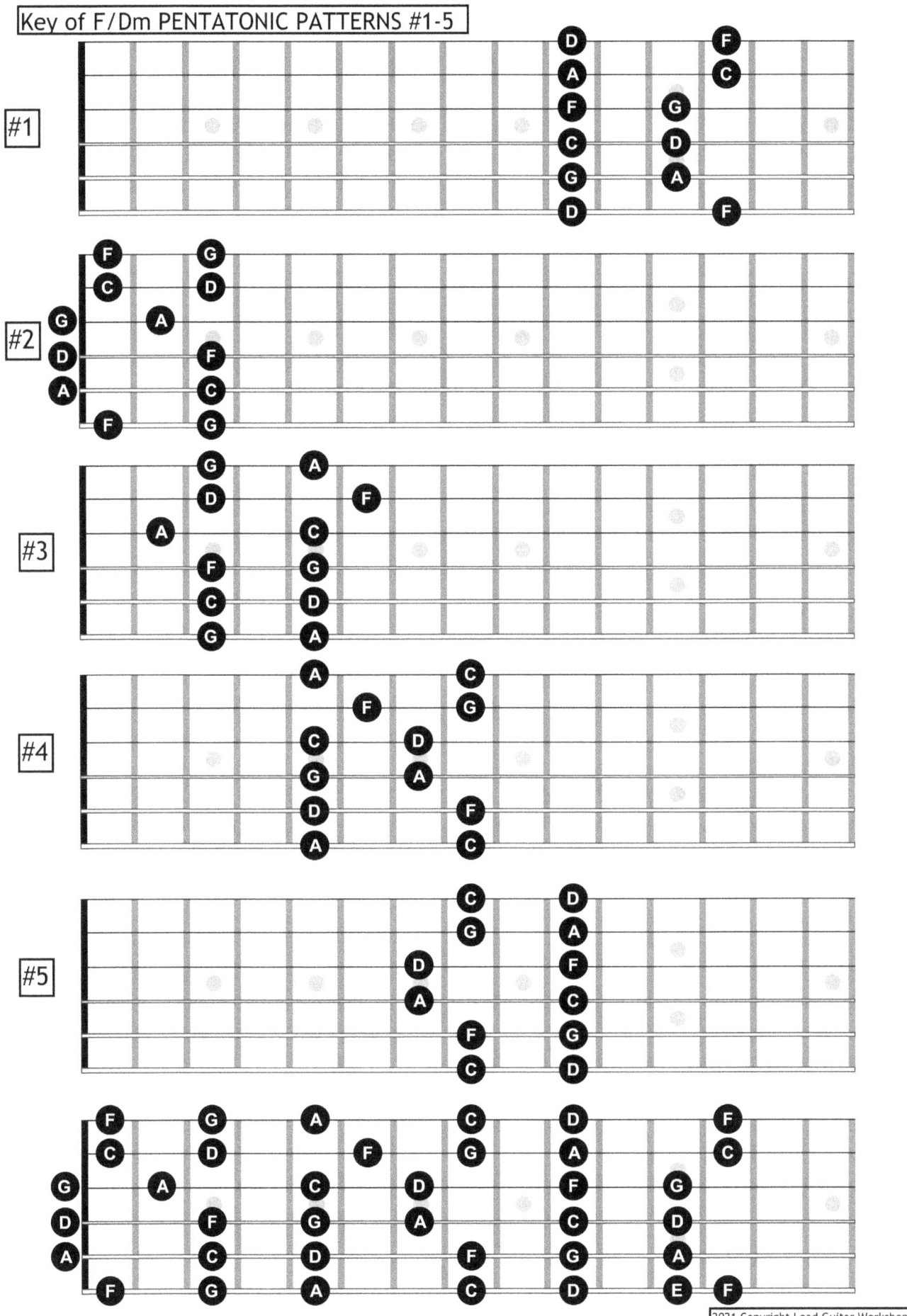

Key of F/Dm PENTATONIC PATTERNS #1-5

HOW TO PRACTICE

Tune in - 5%
Take a few minutes to clear your head. Turn off your devices and do what you need before you dig in and play. Remind yourself that you are a musician and a guitar player. Everything you play should be rhythmically based, always.

Warm up - 10%
Muted String Ladders, Shells, and Changing Gears are some of the best warm ups. They simply get your fingers, hands, and internal clock all synchronized. Muted String ladders focus on rhythm and pick control. Changing Gears really harnesses the ability to feel and play rhythms. The Shells are best of both worlds and are like "wax on, wax off." Practice real world moves and patterns.

Exercise - 15%
This is where you run scales and patterns. This is a great opportunity to play through the five patterns. Always play them in time and play them ascending and descending or as "Round the Block" zigzag the patterns.

Review - 15%
Just as important as learning something new, make sure you're understanding something you have recently learned. It's essential to build your growth by reviewing past topics and understanding them deeper.

New Topic - 15%
Learn something new. However easy or small, it is growth. Every little bit moves you towards your goal of sounding great as a musician. Maybe it's learning the names of the notes in a scale, or a lick, a chord, anything that helps you sound better. You can learn as a musician, as a guitar player, and as a rhythmist.

"Practice" - 40%
The best way to practice is not to practice, but to play! It's true. Every one of our heroes played music more than anything else. Practicing refers to some future date that you are preparing for. Playing is now. Play in time, carry the song, the beat, the groove, all of it. Self-Generating is the best way to play and get your practicing in. If you are practicing a turnaround in a blues, then you play the 12 bar blues and at the end you play the turnaround. If you miss it, keep playing and get it the next time around. This is what you would do onstage. Keep playing and you will get better, as you would if you "practiced."

THOUGHTS

The learning path in music is circular. You will learn something and come back around to it and get to know it better. Every time you do this you will gain more confidence and experience. There is only so much actual information you will need to learn. It is all about how to use and manipulate that material that makes the magic of music start. Learning music is not a linear path but a circular one.

Music is Melody (notes), Harmony (chords), and Rhythm.
Rhythm is the number one factor to sounding great.

Where attention goes, energy flows. So much of being a better musician is all about your mind set and what you focus your time and energy on.

"The process of learning consists not in what is brought to the learner, but what is drawn out of him." (Plato)

"The Student as a boxer, not a fencer. The Fencer's weapon is picked up and put down again. The Boxer's is part of him, all he has to do is clench his fist." (Marcus Aurelius-Meditations)

"The Student as a musician, not a guitarist. The guitarist's instrument is picked up and put down. The musician's is part of him. All he has to do is tap, clap, and sing." (Suke Cerulo)

You can play music without melody (just chords) and you can play music without chords (just melody, like your voice), but you can *never* play music without rhythm, it's impossible. As soon as you tap your foot or pluck a note, rhythm happens.

The language of music hasn't really changed in hundreds of years. It is much older than the guitar. Once you know the language, that's it. Now you can learn as many instruments as you want. You just have to adapt to the physical part of the instrument.

The instrument is silent without you. You are music!

GLOSSARY

Audiation Inner Hearing but also the musical knowledge behind it, to hear the knowledge.

Arpeggio The notes of a chord played in succession rather than simultaneously.

BPM Beats-per-minute. How music tempo/beat/quarter-note is measured.

Chord Usually three or more notes played simultaneously.

Chord Inversion The notes of a chord rotating in order (example R35, 35R, 5R3).

Chord Scale The scale matched to a particular chord, using its chord tones and appropriate notes in between to best fit for playing the changes.

Chord Tone A single note, as part of a chord.

Degree, Scale The number in the scale at which a note lives. There are seven notes in the diatonic scale. They are numbered 1-7 for their degrees.

Diatonic meaning "of the key". Notes and chords only in that key.

Diatonic Harmony The seven chords that naturally occur in all keys and its resulting formula.   (I ii iii IV V vi viidim)

Fingerpicking/Fingerstyle Fingerpicking is using fingers only to pluck the strings on guitar. Fingerstyle might include thumb and/or fingerpicks.

Gear (LGW) Slang for describing the different rhythms. First gear is quarter-notes, second gear is eighth-notes; third gear is triplets; fourth gear is sixteenth-notes, and so on.

Half-step The smallest interval in music. It is one fret on a guitar, and a single piano key to the next (for example white to black)

Harmonic Rhythm The rhythmic pacing of chord changes; how often the chords change (for example every two beats versus every four beats).

Harmony Chords or notes being played simultaneously to produce a sonorous sound. Chord progressions and the underlying chord motion.

HO PO Short for Hammer-ons and Pull-offs

Hybrid Picking When you combine the use of a pick and the remaining three fingers to get a combination of flat pick and fingerstyle.

Inner Hearing Hearing music in your inner ear by memory even if you don't know it musically. (Happy Birthday, Hot Cross buns, and others)

Key One of 12 families built around the 7 note Major scale. Contains 7 chords, one for each of its own notes built by the Rule of Thirds.

Legato When a musician connects the notes of a phrase in a smooth and consistent sound without any silence in between the notes.

Lick A slang term used to describe a group of notes, usually used in a lead solo. These can be recognized by style, genre, person, and more.

LGW Lead Guitar Workshop

Melody One note-at-a-time succession of notes in a pleasing fashion. The signature of a song and the part that is copyright protected.

Mode A function of a scale/key. When a Key or scale is based on any one of its chords/notes. This changes the half-steps in relation to where they live in the scale, producing varying sounds of Major and minor chord progressions and scales.

Monophonic Producing one note-at-a-time only.

Muted String Ladder (MSL)(LGW) A picking hand exercise to improve rhythm and confidence in Down, Up, and Alternate picking across the strings

Musical Truth (LGW) A term to describe some of the fundamental rules in music that every musician follows regardless of instrument.

<u>Neck Anatomy</u> (LGW) Using octaves in a short to long connection to help navigate the fretboard and move around like other instruments do and not be tied to changing patterns. There are 2 pairs of "short to long" octaves (E and A string).

<u>Pentatonic</u> Meaning "five notes of the home." These are ancient five note scales believed to have originated in Asia. There are two main types, Major and minor, and they are in all types of music all around the planet.

<u>Playing the changes</u> A slang term a musician uses when they change their note choices/scales/arpeggios to match each individual chord instead of a "Global" sound of playing one scale for all the chords.

<u>Polyphonic</u> The ability to play multiple notes simultaneously. Pianos and guitars are polyphonic, the human voice is not.

<u>Riff</u> A slang term for rhythm guitar part made up of notes instead of chords. Think "Heartbreaker" by Led Zeppelin, "Crazy Train" by Ozzy.

<u>Rhythm</u> The pulse in music. The basis for everything music. The measured beat and its subdivisions.

<u>Root</u> The "main" note in a Key/chord/scale/arpeggio. The one everything else revolves around. The sound that comes home resolves to the Root.

<u>Root Position</u> When a scale pattern, arpeggio, or chord shape has its ROOT as the lowest note.

<u>Rule of Thirds</u> Stacking every other note in a scale to create a chord. Three notes for a triad and four notes for a seventh chord.

<u>Self-Gen</u> (LGW) Using your inner ear and inner clock to start and play music yourself, in time, especially with consideration of switching between chords and soloing.

<u>Shell</u> (LGW) A hand dexterity exercise to help overcome any guitar playing issue. It involves a fingering, a performance method, and rhythm.

Staccato Each note is sharply detached or separated from the others.

Tied In music notation when an arch connects two or more rhythms to create a sustained sound. Especially useful to achieve lengths of time not possible with traditional rhythms (for example a note that last 1 ½ quarter notes.)

Tonic The "main" note/chord. Often the key but not always. It is the note/chord that everything else resolves to.

Tresillo A Latin based rhythmic figure where 8 eighth-notes are grouped in 3 3 2 notes to total 8.

Triad A three note chord. Usually achieved by stacking every other note in a scale for a total of three notes.

Voice Leading A term used for connecting the chord tones of one chord to another with the notes moving the least amount necessary to make the chord change. This makes a really smooth sound.

Whole-step The second smallest interval in music. It is two half-steps in distance. Most scales consist of half-steps and whole-steps.

ABOUT AUTHOR

Michael Cerulo (aka Suke) is a guitarist and multi-instrumentalist whose life long love and devotion to music has given him a very distinct and identifiable sound. Whether it's his fluid guitar melodies, the warm organic tone of his flute, or his own recordings where he plays and produces all of the music, Suke's individuality, creativity and talent are evident in all of his creations.

Born in a suburb of Boston, Suke was raised in a musical family. His grandfather (George Lane) was a composer, multi-instrumentalist and bandleader during the late 40's and early 50's. All four of George's siblings were musicians as well, often being employed in his big band. The youngest brother helped start **Berklee College of Music**. Suke began playing guitar and taking music lessons when he was twelve. Being persistent, with an unbending intent to learn and grow, he then enrolled in Berklee College of Music in Boston. After graduating in '94, while also working for MOTU music software, Suke became a full time touring musician. Suke composed, played guitar and flute with his band **Schleigho**.

Schleigho (pronounced shlay-ho) was formed at Berklee in 1993 and was touring around the country a year later. The band's style is a mix of jazz and funk, with each of its four members contributing equally to bring about an unprecedented wall of sound. Being predominately instrumental, the band's incredible talent and versatility allows them to go from opening for the Allman Brothers to playing high scale jazz venues while satisfying the most discriminating of tastes. The band released their first CD (*self-titled*) in 1995, *'Farewell to the Sun'* in 1997 and *'In the Interest of Time'* in 1998. In 2000 the band signed with **Flying Frog Records (owned and managed by members of the Allman Brothers)**. Under Flying Frog Records they released *'Continent'* in 2000, and *'Live at HoDown 2000'* the following year. Schleigho has met with great success over the years; from amassing a substantial and dedicated national following to *'Continent'* breaking into the top 20 on CMJ and college Jazz radio charts. Averaging over 200 shows annually across the country, they have shared the stage with **The Allman Brothers band, Derek Trucks, Bela Fleck, John Scofield, Karl Denson, Maceo Parker, G. Love and Special Sauce, Galactic, moe. and Soulive**, to name a few. Schleigho has performed at the JVC Jazz festival (NYC), the Gathering of the Vibes, the High Sierra Music Festival, and the Berkshire Music Festival, among others, and are veterans of the club/college circuit and large festival scene for over 20 years.

Suke also performed for years with the band **Conehead Buddha**, which is a song structured improvisational fusion of hip-hop, rock, and jazz, flirting with many styles from drum and bass to latin and reggae. It's a high energy show featuring Terence and Shannon Lynch.

Another avenue he has been steadily involved with is the production of music for multimedia. For the last twenty years Suke has been developing his production and engineering abilities in his own project studio to further enhance his musical visions. He created *Tone Over Tone* in which he composes, performs, engineers, mix's and masters recordings to be licensed for multimedia applications. This area of music production allows for infinite amounts of creation and timbre. Using conventional instruments, modern technology and a thorough musical background, Suke now creates breathtaking music that utilizes almost any instrument in creation with lush sound design.

His sound is refreshing and his performance is intense. You can always hear diverse musical influences throughout his compositions and soloing. Music from the likes of Jimi Hendrix and Van Halen to John Coltrane, Roland Kirk, and George Benson. From Jeff Beck and Ozzy to Herbie Hancock, Mingus and Miles. From Igor Stravinsky to Square Pusher and Amon Tobin.

Suke currently resides in New York City with his family and has been the *Director of Lead Guitar Program at New York City's "Best" Guitar School* since 2004. He has taught over 15,000 lessons and classes amassing a staggering amount of teaching experience. Suke is also responsible for the musical evaluations of incoming teachers and has often taught the other teachers at the school. The hundreds of students and thousands of hours teaching have help sculpt and mold the success of his teaching methods.

Whether it's playing in a group context, performing, teaching or creating and producing music, Suke always incorporates a fine balance of taste and technique with a result that's not soon forgotten. He always keeps his eye and ear to the future while respectfully paying homage to his influences and tradition.

www.SukeCerulo.com

www.LeadGuitarWorkshop.com